Korean American Families in Immigrant America

How Teens and Parents Navigate Race

Sumie Okazaki and Nancy Abelmann

NEW YORK UNIVERSITY PRESS

New York

NEW YORK UNIVERSITY PRESS
New York
www.nyupress.org

© 2018 by New York University
All rights reserved

References to Internet websites (URLs) were accurate at the time of writing. Neither the author nor New York University Press is responsible for URLs that may have expired or changed since the manuscript was prepared.

Library of Congress Cataloging-in-Publication Data
Names: Okazaki, Sumie, author. | Abelmann, Nancy, author.
Title: Korean American families in immigrant America : how teens and parents navigate race / Sumie Okazaki and Nancy Abelmann.
Description: New York : New York University Press, [2018] |
Includes bibliographical references and index.
Identifiers: LCCN 2017060985 | ISBN 9781479804207 (cl : alk. paper) |
ISBN 9781479836680 (pb : alk. paper)
Subjects: LCSH: Korean Americans—United States. | Korean Americans—
Family relationships—Case studies. | Teenagers—Family relationships—United States—
Case studies. | Children of immigrants—Family relationships—United States—
Case studies. | Korean Americans—Interviews. | United States—Race relations.
Classification: LCC E184.K6 O44 2018 | DDC 305.8957/073—dc23
LC record available at https://lccn.loc.gov/2017060985

New York University Press books are printed on acid-free paper, and their binding materials are chosen for strength and durability. We strive to use environmentally responsible suppliers and materials to the greatest extent possible in publishing our books.

Manufactured in the United States of America

10 9 8 7 6 5 4 3 2 1

Also available as an ebook

In Memory of Nancy Abelmann (1959–2016)

To Allen, Abby, and Lucy

KOREAN AMERICAN FAMILIES IN
IMMIGRANT AMERICA

CONTENTS

Introduction

Eight years after we had first met her and her family as part of an ethnographic study of Korean American families, we checked in with Jenny Park, a bright young Korean American woman in her early twenties and a key informant in our study.[1] We had met Jenny and her family when Jenny was just fourteen years old, and we kept in intermittent contact with her and her family in the ensuing years. We had known that after graduating from high school, Jenny had entered a prestigious conservatory for cello; and, as you will learn, we had thought that Jenny was on her way to becoming a professional musician, just as a well-honed family plan would have predicted. By that summer, however, Jenny had decided on a radical change in her career path. Having recently graduated from a renowned conservatory, she had garnered a coveted spot at a respected summer music festival and was truly enjoying it. But in our conversation, Jenny revealed that she had decided, come fall, that she would begin her exit from a musical career by moving back home and taking pre–veterinary science coursework at a local community college.

This was huge news. When we first began writing the chapter on Jenny and her family, it had been easy to settle on calling it "A Music Strategy" because that title so encapsulated her Korean-born mother's strategy for raising her American-born daughter—and for that matter the seeming consensus of the entire family when it came to Jenny's future. Yet, it was also true that even in our early encounters with Jenny, she had talked about someday wanting to become a veterinarian. Nancy was indeed a bit amazed during that check-in in 2012 when Jenny recalled a discussion with us from her teen years: "Do you remember what I told you back then? About my wanting to become a veterinarian?" When we learned of Jenny's big change of plans, we could not help but wonder what Jenny now thought about her considerable (albeit impressive) musical detour toward her dream career. We were also curious about how and when Jenny had told her mother about this big decision—and most of all about how her mother had reacted.

We will save those details for a later chapter, but here we want to draw attention to the fact that Jenny seemed remarkably at peace with having engaged in long and arduous musical training that had taken her off-course from pursuing a career she had envisioned. At different points over the years, Jenny told us that she realized that music was the only career that her pianist mother could have imagined for Jenny. Not only that, it was the only career for Jenny that her mother could have facilitated with her own skills and know-how. Indeed, Jenny had told us several times during her teen years that she had thought of her music training as nearly inevitable. Yet, perhaps because as an adult she could now walk away from a music career despite an enviable resume, knowing that she possessed the personal fortitude to undertake rigorous training, Jenny let us know that there was no reason to harbor resentment toward her mother, who had steered her down this path. Furthermore, it was clear that her musical skill would always be a valuable asset as a source of personal enjoyment as well as supplementary income. This sort of retrospective narrative echoed the findings of a previous 2003–2004 campus study that we had conducted with Korean American emerging adults who were students at the University of Illinois at Urbana-Champaign in east central Illinois: namely, that Korean American emerging adults often sympathized with, and forgave, immigrant parents who "could not help" but parent them in a certain way (such as working long hours and being absent from the children's daily lives, holding children to impossibly high standards, not behaving like their White friends' parents, and so on). At that time, we were impressed by the disjuncture between what seemed like difficult childhoods and the young adults' generous, forgiving reflections on family life and well-being. Indeed, that University of Illinois study spurred us to learn more about how Korean American teens and their parents navigate family life and visions of success in America.

* * *

This book is a result of a decade-long, mixed-method, longitudinal research collaboration between an anthropologist and a psychologist. In the early 2000s, we—Nancy Abelmann and Sumie Okazaki—embarked on two successive studies of Korean American immigrant families: first with the college students on the flagship campus of the University of Illinois, mentioned above, and then with high-school-age teens and their parents in the greater Chicago metropolitan area (dubbed "Chicagoland"). The "Chicagoland study" was born of our shared intrigue with the apparent resilience of Korean American emerging adults—many of whom we were teaching at the University of Illinois—and more generally, our curiosity about how immigrant Asian American families navigate the sometimes-tricky landscape of the late teen years and young adulthood.[2] Our research collaboration was seeded in the spring of 2000, and what started as a collegial conversation about our respective work grew over a decade and a half into research projects and co-authored works as well as a close friendship.

Each of us brought our disciplinary lens and methods to this project. Until our collaboration, Sumie, a research psychologist whose expertise is in Asian American mental health, had largely employed quantitative methods. Nancy, a cultural anthropologist who specialized in the Koreas and Asian America, had used ethnographic methods in all of her previous work. We began with a mixed-method study on campus that combined a survey and interviews with Korean American and White American college students, then expanded the study into a mixed-method study of Korean American teens and parents. The Chicagoland study, which forms the basis of this book, included collecting survey responses from 205 Korean American teens and 101 Korean immigrant parents, a pool from which we recruited families in which both teens and parents were interested in taking part in the family ethnography portion of the study. In the end, we worked with five Korean American families who engaged with us intensively in the mid-2000s when the focal teens in the families were high school students, and then we followed them into young adulthood over the subsequent years. The ultimate aim was to explore the question embedded in the title of the book: How do Korean American teens and parents navigate immigrant America?

The five family ethnographies, foregrounded against the larger sociocultural landscape of Korean American immigrant communities, were born out of archival research and the original data we collected through surveys and fieldwork. In 2003, we began doing the fieldwork to understand the "lay of the land" of the Korean American families in

Chicagoland, but the bulk of the Chicagoland study data were collected between 2004 and 2006, largely in the northern suburbs of Chicago. This period was then followed by years of annual or biannual contacts with various members of the five focal families, ending in 2014. To carry out the study, we recruited five graduate bilingual, bicultural researchers (Jin-Heon Jung, Grace Chung, Hyeyoung Kang, Euna Oh, and Chu Kim-Prieto) who came from various disciplines (anthropology, human development, counseling psychology, and social psychology) and a rotating cast of undergraduate assistants who worked with us for one or more semesters on various phases of the project. Because the graduate researchers played an integral role in our ethnographic data collection (with each student focused on one or two families), they are featured by name in the book, especially in the family ethnography chapters.

Our primary argument in the book is that Korean American parents and children work hard to accommodate to one another as they navigate immigrant America. Throughout the book, we use the phrase "making family work" to refer to the immigrant parents' and their children's psychological efforts to acknowledge each other's hardship and to satisfy both their personal and their families' aspirations to lead fulfilling American lives. While appreciating this intergenerational work, we write against both the psychological literature and public discourse on Asian American immigrant families, which have long fixated on intergenerational cultural conflict between "Asian" (to indicate old-fashioned, "traditional") parents and "American" (to indicate modern, individualistic) youth. In psychology, this dichotomous line of thinking is particularly well developed in discussions of the so-called acculturation gap: the idea that immigrant children acculturate to their new cultural environment more quickly than their parents and that these differences can result in family distress. In recent years, this contrast has been enlivened by robust discussions of Asian and American parenting. Indeed, with the popularization of the "Tiger Mother" and reports of "foreign" competition from China and India for Ivy League admissions, these culturally charged modes of parenting—with their implied effects on children's psychological health—have become part of the public discourse throughout the world. When we planned the Chicagoland study, we searched for scholarly portraits of Korean American teens and parents and were surprised to find that parents and teens were seldom featured together in one study. We surmise that the isolated generational sketches of parents and youth have contributed to the aforementioned tendency to imagine generations pitted against one another—generations that can all too easily be conflated as "Korean" and "American." We think this approach both names a false dichotomy and underestimates the considerable intimacy and collaboration between parents and teens to make their families work.

What, then, did our study find? In short, both our survey and ethnographic data revealed that acculturation differences between parents and teens—long assumed in the psychological literature to account for distress—did not necessarily make for family hardship. We found instead parents and teens struggling to figure out how best to navigate toward a healthy existence within American society, which they understood to be riddled with nativism and racism. This is not to say that the parents did not speak about cultural distinctions or that they were unconcerned about academic achievement. We certainly encountered many references to values and behaviors that were "Korean" and "American" in the course of our fieldwork. And surely, to abnegate the concept of "culture" entirely in a study such as ours would be foolhardy; that would be tantamount to asserting that what are among the most important concepts in people's lives (in addition to being the topic of a great volume of scholarly analysis) are wrong-headed or meaningless. Indeed, families often organize their thoughts and pattern their days in relation to ideas of "American" and "Korean" cultures.

However, our ethnographic approach allowed us to observe that the cultural and conceptual landscape was in fact in flux: teens and parents alike used the words "Korean" and "American" to point to, struggle with, and even mean different things. For example, as we will see, we show that even though a casual observation of Jenny's mother's rigorous cultivation of her daughter's classical musical career could appear stereotypically "Asian," music was also a way for the immigrant mother to give her daughter a healthy sense of self and to guide her well into a fulfilling career. This mother and daughter also shared an intimate, friendship-like relationship—partly based on their shared sensibility toward music—that they both agreed was quintessentially an "American" mother-daughter relationship. Classical music, while standing so easily for things Asian or cultural, coexisted with other meanings, which included the family's understanding of race and racism, gender, and identity; it is this sort of complexity and conceptual flexibility that we find throughout our data.

Moreover, while the Korean American families did grapple with concerns about academic and career achievement, what these parents anguished over most was how to fortify their children with protective psychological health and character traits that would allow them to succeed. And as teens grew into young adults and their career pathways began to emerge, they too were anguished over how to navigate their path toward adulthood, which, in many cases, was diverging from their parents' dreams and expectations. Ethnographic chapters on each family introduce the parenting strategies and adolescents' responses, which were at times defiantly resistant, sometimes accommodating, and at other times enormously appreciative. We examine the delicate negotiations between parents and teens in the intimacy of family life, as we follow them from homes to shopping malls, music recitals, churches, workplaces, and schools. The heart of the work rests on the hours and hours of conversations with various members of the five families who shared moments and stories—both mundane and profound—with us, and the countless hours that we worked together to make sense out of, and to do justice to, the intimate stories entrusted to us by the families.

Portraits of Immigrant Asian American Families

Our approach to understanding immigrant parents and teens in this book departs in two ways from the dominant discourse in the psychological and social science literature on Asian American families. First, we argue against the dominant discourse about immigrant Asian American family relationships as inevitably conflicted because of the acculturation gap between parents and children. Second, we argue against the portrayal of immigrant Asian American families (especially parents) as obsessed with narrow standards of academic and occupational success. Instead, we put forward a portrait of immigrant Korean American families who are fully cognizant of the challenges of living and thriving as visible racial minorities in the United States and who are first and foremost concerned about psychological well-being and a healthy sense of identity as Korean Americans.

Directly or obliquely, this literature has suggested that there are "Asian" and "American" parenting styles, and that parents—slower to acculturate to American mores—hold fast to Asian ways while their second-generation (or immigrant) children embrace the American ways. Further, it has often been assumed that these parenting styles entail particular cultural values: that Asian parenting (a.k.a. tiger parenting) is somehow culturally distinctive (e.g., with its emphasis on strict parental control, high expectations for children's academic achievement, etc.) from the American (or Western) parenting that their American-born children often clamor for (e.g., with its lenient, open, egalitarian, and whole-child focus). Imagined then are culture clashes that are founded in nonimmigrant understandings of the relationship between parents and teens. Indeed, the psychology of immigration has taken a considerable interest in acculturation generally and in the negative effects on mental health of an acculturation gap between parents and children more specifically. This acculturation gap–distress hypothesis—first proposed and tested by José Szapocznik with Cuban American families in Miami seeking help for their teens with substance abuse and acting-out problems (Szapocznik and Kurtines 1993)—has also been widely applied to understand the parent-child dynamics in Asian American immigrant families, with mixed results (Telzer 2011).[3] Family psychology literature suggests that families with a greater intergenerational gap (with parents holding fast to the old, and children reaching aggressively for the new) will have poorer outcomes. For immigrant families, then, the acculturation gap is the generation gap plus some. With children and parents on a different page, family life is imagined to be contentious at best and at worst dysfunctional, both individually and collectively.

Adding to the portrait of immigrant Asian American parent-teen relationships as fraught with conflict and distress is the "tiger mother" meme that entered into public discourse during the years of our study. We began this chapter with the story of Jenny's transition from adolescence to early adulthood because it highlights the complex emotional work that both her mother and she put into maintaining their intimate and loving relationship in the face of Jenny's decision to depart from the career path that the immigrant mother had so long dreamed of for her daughter. We are keenly aware that the story of a Korean immigrant mother pushing her second-generation daughter into a high-pressure classical musical career can seem so very stereotypical in relation to the widespread image of the Asian "tiger mother." In keeping with our critique of the gross categories of "Korean" and "American," we think it is telling that Mrs. Park's musical regimen for Jenny during her adolescence was not so easily registered—by either Mrs. Park or Jenny—as necessarily "Korean." This was the case even as Jenny herself had taken note all along of the contrast between her unique friendship with her mother and her mother's sometimes unforgiving musical management. As Jenny reflected on the long musical detour in her career trajectory toward the health profession, it was not that she had to absolve her mother of her "Korean" sins, but rather that she had to come to terms with how it was that her loving mother (whom she still called her "best friend") had chosen to parent in the way she had.

Jenny and her mother were one of the sixty-three child-parent pairs in our study to have both completed the survey. Like their parent-teen peers in the study, Jenny had emerged as more identified with American culture than her mother on a scale assessing acculturation to American culture, whereas both mother and daughter were similarly and moderately identified with Korean culture on a scale of enculturation to Korean culture. At a glance, this mother-daughter's so-called acculturation gap, namely, the difference between parent and child in the extent of American acculturation, was entirely typical. However, we will see considerable rumination by Jenny as well as both her mother and her father over what aspects of their lives are "American" or "Korean." And the reader will find in Jenny's family, as throughout this book, that the matter of what is culturally Korean or American was pretty confused. We argue that cultural and ethnic identities do not work like fixed points on a spectrum, as psychological scales of cultural identities often seem to suggest, but rather like fluid nodes in the ongoing negotiation that comprises immigrant family life. Indeed, we found that those family conversations about "Korean" and "American" matters were, most often, discussions about their awareness of race, racial stereotypes, and racism in the United States. And while Korean and American identification scores on a psychological scale might help to locate the teens and parents in relation to each other and in relation to their ethnic peers at a particular moment, the personal significance of those similarities and differences can only be decoded by peering into the lives and relationships of those individuals.

Drawing on focused ethnographic observations, we argue in this book that immigrant parents and teens are less interested in standing their ground about either Korean or American ways of being—or about the cultural differences implied in that distinction—than they are in surviving and thriving in the United States as Korean Americans. We found Korean immigrant parents strategizing, above all, as to how best to navigate a racialized America in which they realize that their children will always be racial minorities. Like many immigrant Korean American families, the parents were working in a variety of occupations, ranging from low-skilled service-sector employment (e.g., in dry cleaning, nail salons, delivery service) that often did not match their Korean credentials to highly skilled service-sector jobs (e.g., nursing, musician) and white collar (e.g., corporate, IT) work. Three out of the five families featured in the book were living in some of the least expensive housing within affluent suburbs, keenly aware of their relative class status within their surrounding communities. And we observed teens thinking hard about how to accommodate their parents' take on immigrant America while simultaneously forging their own pathway to adulthood, college, and career. None of this is to say that parents and teens did not use the words "Korean" and "American" to narrate their family's past, their daily lives, or their imagined future. However, we encourage scholars to listen very carefully to how complex and even slippery those notions of "culture" often are. Likewise, we do not intend to argue that acculturation or acculturation differences between parents and teens are irrelevant to understanding the family dynamics in immigrant Korean America, but we do mean to say that singular numerical indices that are used to approximate individuals' cultural affinities only tell a partial truth.

The Roadmap of the Book

In the next two chapters, we present the community context in which our family ethnographies took place. In chapter 1, we set the context for our study, including highlights from the study that we conducted on the campus of the University of Illinois that served as the impetus for the study of Korean American teens and parents in Chicagoland. We present the findings—as well as new questions sparked by the findings—of that campus study in light of the prevailing narrative about Korean American (and Asian American) families from previous scholarly works about the nature of intergenerational relationships in immigrant families. We also place the Chicagoland Korean American families featured in our study in the context of the local, national, and transnational conversations that were ongoing among, and about, Korean American and Korean families and teens at the time of our study.

In chapter 2, we set out what we think of as the lay of the land, describing our Chicagoland research process, which took us from survey data collection to family ethnography, starting from the Korean American churches where we recruited most of the teens and parents for the study, and we describe the ethnic geography of the Chicagoland Korean American community at the particular site we chose. We detail, through our ethnographic observations of the churches, neighborhoods, and institutions, the places that matter in the lives of the Korean Americans in our book. Altogether, we visited seven Korean churches (two Protestant, four Catholic, one nondenominational) as well as two Korean American community service agencies, a suburban high school with a large Korean American student population, and an apartment complex located in the same school district popular with many recently immigrated Korean families. We surveyed 205 Korean American teens and 101 parents, from whom we selected and followed five families for two years and beyond. We briefly discuss what the survey revealed about how the Chicagoland Korean American parents and teens viewed individual and family well-being. Among Korean American teens in our study, their perception of how well their family was functioning correlated highly with their individual psychological distress and wellness. However, although the survey responses did reveal glimpses of parent-child acculturation gaps and individual distress, the survey findings did not conform very well to the familiar story of a generational gap in acculturation between parents and teens as the primary driver of family or individual difficulties. Whereas the survey gives a broad-brushstroke picture of Korean American families with teens, it also left us with many intriguing questions. We end the chapter by describing how we selected the families for intensive and long-term follow-up.

Next, the book presents five chapters of family ethnography, with each chapter featuring a Korean American immigrant family who generously invited us into their lives, sometimes with pride but often with questions they also wanted to answer for themselves about what was going on in their families. The five families featured in this book reflect a diversity of family dynamics. In chapter 3, we introduce Ben and his family (the Kohs), a Catholic family who live in a modest single-family home. We met Ben as a quiet, athletic fourteen-year-old whose mother was concerned about his well-being, particularly about whether his personality would withstand the racism of high school and beyond. His parents also faced economic challenges as workers (and one-time owners) at dry cleaning shops and as semiskilled laborers (i.e., a bus driver); their concerns about Ben navigating American adulthood were rooted in their own experiences with racism over the course of their employment. In chapter 4, we feature Doug and Esther (the Chungs), who were a junior and a senior in a predominantly White suburban high school. Their father owned a video rental shop, and their mother was a highly skilled nurse. Their family, while much more established in the United States and apparently well integrated into the fabric of "American" life (which included the family's considerable effort to escape the ethnic enclave), nevertheless struggled over the children's choice of career and friendship networks.

In chapter 5, we reintroduce Jenny (the Parks), who at fourteen was already a distinguished cellist whose mother was a church pianist and whose father was, at the time, a UPS driver in training. The mother and the daughter were deeply invested in their intimate bond and were quite proud that they were each other's "best friend." The mother's careful cultivation of Jenny's future musical career, however, was a source of both intimacy and considerable friction. In chapter 6, we meet Eric (the Shins), a sixteen-year-old boy who was barely managing to graduate from high school at the time; we learn of the anguish that this was causing his businessman father and his mother, who owned a nail salon but had once been a radio announcer. Finally, in chapter 7, we meet Jun-Ho and his family (the Hyuns)—a recently immigrated family living in a modest apartment. The Hyuns were busily trying to secure an economic foothold in the United States, with the father working as a computer technician and the mother laboring at a dry cleaner. Whereas the other four families featured in this book were long-settled immigrants whose children had been born in the United States, Jun-Ho's family provided a contrasting case of a recently arrived immigrant family whose stories, nevertheless, continue the Korean diasporic aspirations for cosmopolitanism and opportunity presented by the American dream.

We end the book with concluding thoughts about what we ultimately learned from our long engagement with a segment of Chicagoland Korean American immigrant families. Taken together, our survey and ethnographic data reveal that Korean American families were not, as many have believed, marked primarily by tensions among Asian immigrant parents and their children regarding acculturation. In fact, parents and teens were often on the same page about the challenges and difficulties of navigating the racialized landscape in the United States. Foremost in the immigrant parents' minds were their children's psychological well-being and character, which would help them feel secure and comfortable in the United States. In turn, the teens, while sometimes experiencing distress over being racially stereotyped or angst over their sense of cultural belongingness, were fortified and supported by their parents to forge their own paths. These parents and children were actively grappling with how to claim their places within a suburban American middle class with resilience and with generosity toward each other's dreams and desires. By following five Korean American immigrant families with teens over a period of some seven–eight years, we were able to observe the families weathering various moments of self-doubt and anguish and settling into their distinctive, if somewhat unexpected, places within suburban middle-class America.

1

Family Context

Emerging Adult and Parent Perspectives

David was a twenty-year-old college student who was born in South Korea and immigrated to the United States at age six with his Christian missionary parents.[1] He described a childhood and early adolescence that was rife with clashes with his immigrant parents. He spoke of his parents fighting frequently with each other and not being involved in his life. Having seen his studious older brother suffer from considerable parental pressure to achieve academically and to become a doctor, David described himself in adolescence as "a bad kid" who smoked, drank, used recreational drugs, and hung out with "gang bangers." However, upon entering college after years of longing to escape his parental home, he came to see things a bit differently: "I think once you get older, you kind of realize how much you love being home. And it's like you start missing your parents and, I don't know, you just start growing up and maturing." And from this vantage point, David redeemed what he had earlier perceived as his parents' parenting failures by attributing them to their "Korean culture."

Korean American Emerging Adults' Perspectives: Redeeming Immigrant Parents

David was one of the nineteen Korean American college students whom we interviewed at the University of Illinois for our first study together.[2] As we began to develop our plans for this initial anthropology-psychology collaborative study in the early aughts, Nancy was also in the process of completing her ethnographic work with Korean American college students at the University of Illinois and their families. She was listening to a group of young Korean Americans' attempts to make meaning out of their college experience—a uniquely Korean American–centered experience in which all their nonacademic lives at college were spent with Korean American friends, family members (i.e., siblings and cousins), and church—in relation to their families' immigrant aspirations and the liberal ideals of an American education. Nancy's work was eventually published as a book in 2009 (*The Intimate University: Korean American Students and the Problems of Segregation*). However, her fieldwork had raised some new questions about the psychological well-being of the immigrant Korean American families she featured in the book, so much so that she decided to spend a year affiliated with the psychology department to study clinical psychology.

Sumie, having recently arrived as a new psychology faculty member at the University of Illinois with a long-standing interest in Asian American mental health and family processes, was fascinated by Nancy's observations about occasional references made by her Korean American college students to their immigrant parents as unstable and "depressed." Nancy noted that when she interviewed these immigrant Korean American parents for her fieldwork, there were hints that the parents were indeed suffering psychologically in some ways, but Nancy felt ill equipped to pursue questions about mental health and well-being without additional understanding of psychology. We wondered to what extent Korean American students' mental health may be tied to their immigrant parents' suffering. Our initial interests, then, centered on intergenerational family dynamics and the relationship between Korean American students' psychological functioning and their perception of their parents' (and, more broadly, their families') psychological well-being.

To explore these questions, we surveyed and interviewed college students at the University of Illinois about their perceptions of family and personal well-being. We initially began with the aim of surveying Korean American college students from Chicagoland suburbs and comparing them to White American peers who had attended high schools from the same middle-class suburbs. We added South Asian American college students, also from the Chicagoland suburbs, when we realized that it was difficult to parse our preliminary results as reflecting culture/race differences or immigrant/nonimmigrant family differences. Because South Asian Americans, another post-1965 Asian immigrant community, constituted a sizable presence both on campus and in Chicagoland communities, we thought they would make for an apt comparison group. The campus study survey ultimately sampled 104 Korean American, 102 South Asian American, and 93 White American students, a pool from which we recruited a smaller number of interviewees.[3] In thinking about how our Korean American college students might view their immigrant parents, we took particular note of Pyke's (2000) study of the narration of immigrant family life among thirty-four Korean American and thirty-nine Vietnamese American immigrant emerging adults in California. Pyke's analysis had revealed that the narratives of the overwhelming majority of these emerging adults included some negative portraiture of their parents and their immigrant upbringing. By and large, the emerging adults in Pyke's study viewed their Asian parents as overly strict, emotionally distant, uncommunicative, not openly affectionate, or otherwise deficient in comparison to the "normal American family," a phrase that referred to the imagery of White, middle-class American families that the Asian American young adults had gleaned both from television and from the families of their non-Asian friends. Pyke surmised that Asian American young adults' inclination to critique their immigrant family through the ideological lens of the "normal American family" (which is loving, egalitarian, and harmonious) reflected these Asian Americans' aspirations to become "Americans," even as they were racially marked. We were curious to see whether similar narratives about what was "normal" as "American" would emerge among our Korean American and South Asian American interlocutors.

The results of our initial foray into mixed-method research foretold the complex but fascinating scholarly road ahead for us as an interdisciplinary pair. Our findings in the campus study as well as the Chicagoland study diverged somewhat from the previous portraits of Korean American (and Asian American) family relationships as inevitably conflicted. In short, we found that Korean American college students in our campus study responded to questionnaires in a way that could be "read" as painting a portrait of Korean immigrant families as dysfunctional, especially when contrasted with the responses of their White American and South Asian American peers. Yet, our data also showed a surprising lack of association between Korean American students' perception of their family as dysfunctional and their own level of individual distress. In contrast, for White Americans and South Asian Americans, family

Contrast with South Asian

dysfunction and individual distress were significantly associated (see appendix for a summary of the survey methods and findings).

The interview narratives hinted at a similar disjuncture between difficult family relations and the Korean American students' individual distress, which contrasted with South Asian American students' narratives, which tended to connect their personal well-being to their family relations. What surprised us the most about the Korean American interviews, even as we were conducting and discussing them in weekly research meetings, was these emerging adults' lack of anguish as they described growing up with family hardships—including in some cases extreme challenges such as having been held up at knifepoint while working at the family store. In fact, many of the Korean American narratives seemed to fit what personality psychologist Dan McAdams and colleagues (2001) characterized as redemption sequences, namely, stories of negative experiences that nonetheless lead to positive outcomes. That is, unlike the prevailing view in the literature that negative experiences with family (especially in the form of an acculturation gap) continue to register as distress, these Korean American emerging adults were actively constructing an alternative story about their immigrant upbringing. Across the nineteen cases, we found that slightly over half (ten out of nineteen) of the Korean American emerging adults we interviewed employed these redemptive narratives.

Moreover, the narratives of Korean American emerging adults, while acknowledging the psychological toll that their immigrant upbringing had taken on them, were not constrained by the widely held portrait of an ideal "normal American family." Instead, many Korean American emerging adults talked about their families in relation mostly to other Korean American families that they knew from high school or church, and they described having come to appreciate their parents' efforts and deficits as part and parcel of immigration. What we found runs against the grain of Pyke's portrait of Korean American and Vietnamese American young adults who continued to derogate their immigrant parents and immigrant childhoods as not "normal." In our campus study, Korean American college students did indeed respond to survey questionnaires in ways that might be interpreted (at least from the perspective of Western ideas about healthy family functioning) as dysfunctional. Yet our analysis revealed that these students were also able to both intellectually and affectively distance themselves from this negative stance. Many of the students articulated an understanding and sympathetic view of their parents. Instead of echoing a hegemonic "normal American" family ideology, the students viewed their parents through more nuanced, ethnic perspectives. As an example, let us return to David—the college student introduced at the beginning of this chapter—who told of a difficult childhood and adolescence but was now sympathetic to his parents' lack of understanding and involvement. He said,

> I don't think they really *failed* to do it [i.e., be involved in his and his brothers' lives]. It's just they're very ... I think my parents, as well as a majority of other Asian American parents, failed to do something like that. Like they don't really know how to get involved in their children's lives as well as American parents do. So I think in a way ... but I can't even really say it was a *failure*, it's just a part of the *culture* so ... *and if it's part of the culture then that's just the way it is.* (emphasis added)

David elaborated on this culture-based redemption in his accounts of his older brother, who, at the time of the interview, was unemployed and hanging out at home. David matter-of-factly reported on his brother's apparent depression as being a result of parental pressure; interestingly, though, he defended his parents, chiding his brother for his inability to assert himself in the face of the pressure:

> *I don't wanna blame my parents,* you know. 'Cause it's just they just push for [pause] what [pause] like they want their children to have a very secure life and, and like in Korean society being a doctor is a very, is a very secure job. It's a hard job you know? You have to be very studious as well as very diligent. ... When our parents came over here they work very hard, you know? They came over with nothing, and they made a very big impact on, um, the minority influence in the States and that's all because they were diligent. *And that's kind of like the way they think.* And they think that if you study hard and do well for yourself in college, then you know? It's just like being a doctor is just like one of the positive ... like one of the roles like. It's just something that's very like well known to them. ... [H]e [David's brother] knew that he could've done what he wanted to do. I mean, no matter how my parents push him, he knows that

in the end it's his *choice*. . . . On his part it was more of his *fault* than it was of my parents 'cause it's his *choice*. (emphasis added)

Just as David had redeemed his childhood isolation in the first quotation above, here he forgave his parents for the pressure they placed on his brother by attributing it to their immigrant reality and mindset. David's inclination to forgive his immigrant parents was evident in other Korean American college students we interviewed. In fact, ten out of nineteen students narrated a positive change story in which their view of earlier immigration-related parent-child conflicts had been resolved (Kang et al. 2010). However, three students rejected the redemptive narrative and remained noticeably troubled by family shortcomings. These students were aware that others might expect them to stop harboring resentment toward their immigrant parents, but they were resolute in refusing to do so. Their self-conscious rejection of redemption suggests the extent to which narrative redemption is normative for this population of first- and second-generation immigrant young adults.

Take, for instance, Paul, an eighteen-year-old American-born son of a salesman father and an accountant mother, who lamented a childhood with little love, and most of all with a father whom he thought of as unable to play a proper fatherly role. Paul described his father's perpetual dissatisfaction with him while growing up. In the passionate statement that follows, Paul explained that while he is implicitly expected to forgive his immigrant father's parenting transgressions in the name of cultural understanding—that is, redeem him in just the way that the others had managed to do—Paul concluded that he just could not bring himself to do so.

I mean, I've always tried to *understand* that, you know like, I'm automatically different because I'm a minority and that our values and culture are a lot more different than typical American culture and I've always tried to *understand* that [our family was different] because I have no choice. . . . I've always been like, "Let me think about it *from his perspective*." You know, like, "Why is he saying this?" "Why is he doing this?" blah blah blah blah blah [sigh]. . . . To an extent, Koreans aren't quite as heartless . . . [but] you don't have to keep doing that over and over. I mean, there's some times, where you can just be lenient and be just like, "Ok, I probably should say this . . . but [in] this instance, I'll just let it go and I'll just make him feel comfortable." (emphasis added)

With "blah blah blah blah blah," Paul gestures toward the redemption narrative—and the sympathetic understanding of immigration—that he himself is not quite able to muster. Paul describes his own attempts to understand his father's perspectives and motivations, and his father's seeming unwillingness to reciprocate and meet him halfway. He continued:

> You're coming to America as a Korean immigrant. You don't know anything about America. You have, nothing you . . . everything you know is Korean. . . . But sometimes I think that like he has an obligation almost, especially raising a family who are [i.e., American] . . . both of which [i.e., children] are born in the U.S. that he has to show both Eastern and Western values.

With these remarks, Paul made clear again that while he might sympathize with his father's difficulty as an immigrant needing to bridge discrepant worlds, he could not chalk up all his family strife to the hardships of immigration. Across the nineteen interviews, Paul and the two other Korean American students without redemption narratives stood apart in their residual bitterness about their childhood and immigrant upbringing.

The three "unredeeming" students aside, the Korean American emerging adults in our campus study had, by and large, come to "normalize" or "redeem" their immigrant family experience through empathy and understanding of their parents' ethnic and immigrant circumstances. Importantly, even in the cases in which the students themselves could not quite muster complete empathy, it was clear that they knew the co-ethnic script. That is, redeeming narratives appeared to be a master narrative within the Korean American communities in which these students were embedded. We would add, though, that the students who seemed most distressed appeared also to be using "Korean" and "American" to draw sharp distinctions between themselves and their parents.

The interviews offered us a partial answer to the puzzle of the Korean American student survey data: the apparent disconnect between

redemptive
sequence of
storytelling

flaw
in sample

individual well-being and family functioning. The relatively lower family functioning reflected in the survey data was, in many ways, borne out by the students' interview narratives of growing up in immigrant households with parents who were not always fully present, and these physical or psychological absences made for many psychological challenges and conflicts. However, at the same time, we found that many of the Korean American emerging adults managed in some way to redeem their immigrant families even as they detailed the considerable stress of their childhoods. As we have illustrated, this redemption was consistent with what some scholars have described as a redemptive sequence of storytelling (McAdams 2001; McAdams et al. 2001). Through storytelling, Korean American emerging adults narrated how it was that their reckoning with the past allowed them to feel closer to their parents.

We leave open the possibility that the inclination to redeem their immigrant parents may not be as strong for those young people with rockier transitions to emerging adulthood. We acknowledge that these Korean American college students represented a select group of "successful" young adults by virtue of having gained admission to a top state university. However, we also wonder if perhaps the passage to college and college itself (whether it be the physical and psychological distance afforded by going away to college, or the peer and institutional support that students are given to explore their ethnic identities) shaped these Korean American students' reflections, allowing them to "normalize" their immigrant families. As we thought about these findings, we alternatively wondered whether it was possible that these reassessments of immigrant family life begin earlier in adolescence. And, having heard only the students' side of the story, we began to wonder about Korean immigrant parents' perspectives on the particular challenges of raising their children in the United States. It was these questions that motivated us to plan a study with Korean American teens and their parents in the hope that we might observe immigrant family dynamics as they unfolded "in real time."

Korean American Parents' Perspective: Parenting in the Global Flux

Before we turn our attention to the Korean American families, it is important to understand the discursive landscape in which Korean

American immigrant parents were navigating their parenting challenges. To offer a sense of this landscape, we trace three broad strands of
"conversations" about culture and parenting in the 2000s that together
serve as context for understanding the work of the five Korean American
families we followed in depth. The first of these discourses is the caricature of regimented Chinese "tiger" parenting made infamous by Amy
Chua's 2011 book, *The Battle Hymn of the Tiger Mother*. The second is
the scholarly and lay discourse about the sizable educational migration
of South Korean primary and secondary students to English-speaking
nations that peaked around 2007. The Korean American communities
in Chicagoland, where our study took place, as well as the University
of Illinois, where we were located at the time of the study, experienced an
influx of these Korean *chogi yuhak* (translated as "early study abroad")
students during the course of our study. We trace the conversations that
occurred at the intersection of the settled Korean American families and
the recently migrated students and families from Korea. The third is the
conversation in ethnic media and among Korean American immigrant
parents about how best to prepare their Korean American children for
success in America. These discourses shed light on the larger social and
cultural landscape against which Korean American parents and teens
in our study were making sense of their own family's stories about what
makes for successful Korean American lives.

caricature
educational migration
success

Tiger Mother and Parenting Anxieties

We were grappling with our survey and ethnography data when the
national debate about culturally specific parenting exploded with the
publication of Amy Chua's 2011 book, *Battle Hymn of the Tiger Mother*,
which was preceded by an excerpt from the book provocatively titled
"Why Chinese Mothers Are Superior" that was published in the *Wall
Street Journal*. As with many other scholars and commentators (see,
e.g., Hau 2015), we take issue with Chua's well-publicized work premised on what she describes as culturally distinct "Chinese" and
"American" parenting regimes. A casual reading of the book suggests
that for Chua, Chinese-ness is little more than the antics of aggressively
upwardly mobile immigrant parents hell bent on producing children
who can realize the American dream. In Chua's characterization, "tiger"

cultural distinction

parenting is a hard-knocks regimen of delayed gratification, unyield-ing discipline, and shaming tactics (with considerable elbow grease on the part of the parents) intended to fortify the child's character and to produce adults capable of withstanding the interminable hard work and sacrifice required to achieve success at the highest possible level. Throughout the majority of her book, Chua portrays herself as a supremely confident parent, self-assured that her extreme parenting regimen would replicate the academic and career success of her immi-grant parents as well as her own success. Chua's foil, Western parenting, is another stick figure: a race-to-the-bottom, child-centered parenting in which children's frail egos rule the roost and make for little more than mediocre adults, unable to achieve excellence in the United States, let alone to compete with a meteoric China.[4] It is this backdrop of American anxieties about the rise of China as a world economic power that arguably occasioned the book—and probably accounted for its commercial success.

None of the Korean American families with whom we engaged for our study, however, enjoyed Chua's confidence in their parenting in gen-eral or in a parenting strategy that they labeled as "Korean" or "Asian." A remarkable feature of the *Battle Hymn of the Tiger Mother* is its virtual silence on race and class, which are contextual factors that emerged so prominently for the Korean American families we feature in this book. The "Chinese" parenting Chua describes is in fact drenched in her own considerable class capital as an upper-middle-class Ivy League law pro-fessor and as a high-achieving, Harvard-educated daughter of well-educated parents. Chua's husband, also a law professor at the same Ivy League law school, is a White Jewish man who grew up in an educated, upper-middle-class family. A discussion of race is largely absent from Chua's book; interestingly, there is no recognition that it will ever matter to Chua's children that they are biracial Asian Americans. A search of Chua's book for any word associated with race ("race," "racial," "racism," "prejudice," and "discrimination") produces exactly one mention in an episode about family travel with her parents and her sister: "The seven of us would travel abroad together in a giant rental van. . . . We'd giggle as passersby stared at us, trying to figure out our weird *racial* combina-tion. (Was Jed the adopted white son of an Asian family? Or a human trafficker selling the rest of us into slavery?)" (87; emphasis added). This

Silence on race & class

passing and giggling reference to race speaks profoundly to the work's general silence on the matter.[5]

That Chua's book struck a popular chord with the lay public and in scholarly communities in the United States and even in China is, however, not surprising. Ours is a historical moment in which many parents worldwide worry about the futures of their children (i.e., their employment and well-being)—an anxiety that Chua preyed on. Although the book was touted as a reflexive and humorous work of self-criticism, Chua's smug confidence—and her seeming imperviousness to her children's saying that they at times "hated" her—that is maintained in the narrative until the climactic mother-daughter fight made the book ripe for outrage.[6] The tiger mother hoopla erupted while we were in the thick of writing this book and mulling over data on Korean American parents for whom nothing about parenting was as clear as it seemed to be for Chua. Indeed, the parents in our book did not enjoy unified, unwavering, confident parenting philosophies. For the most part, they were not parents who could afford elite private schools, foreign travel, or private music lessons to usher their children into Ivy League educations, nor could they imagine raceless, classless futures for their children.[7] Unfortunately, Chua's "tiger parenting" meme has bequeathed to Asian American youth (and their parents) yet another racialized stereotype of Asian Americans as a model minority group, this time oddly and provocatively wrapped up in anxiety about China's rise. Our quibbles with Chua aside, there is no question that her book spoke to middle-class anxiety both in the United States and beyond; indeed, there was considerable interest in the book in Asia as well.[8]

South Korean Education Comes to Chicagoland

With hindsight, we have come to think of this book's most concentrated research period in the mid-aughts as a moment in which ideas about effective parenting—specifically, how to marshal family resources on a global scale in order to position children for successful adulthood— were in transition both in the United States and beyond. For the Korean immigrant parents in the United States, most visible were the rising numbers of South Koreans who were electing to send their children to the United States for precollege study abroad. Commonly referred to as "*chogi yuhak*" (early study abroad), it is a flexible, global educational strategy in which children study abroad at primary or secondary schools in English-speaking nations for short-term education before college (Lo, Abelmann, Kwon, and Okazaki 2015). Because it takes considerable and coordinated efforts and financial resources for parents to orchestrate a precollege study abroad—often involving extended periods of transnational split households—this educational migration strategy was seen as a lens through which to understand the cosmopolitan desires as well as anxiety of South Korean parents regarding their children's future economic opportunities (Abelmann, Newendorp, and Lee-Chung 2014).

At issue, of course, are the desires and motivations that compelled South Korean parents to engage in this transnational education strategy by sending their teens to primary and secondary schools in the United States. The popularization of early study abroad among South Korean children was driven by the anxieties of both the South Korean elite and its middle class about their children's futures, as well as loosening of regulations within South Korea that allowed for legal educational migration (Okazaki and Kim 2018). Following the neoliberal education reform in the 1990s and the International Monetary Fund crisis in 1997, South Korean families were becoming keenly aware of the necessity to prepare their children for a rapidly globalizing world, which in turn motivated them to pursue opportunities overseas for their children to acquire the English-language mastery and cosmopolitan experience valued in South Korean education and employment (Shim and Park 2008).

In the initial years of Korean early study abroad (circa mid- to late 1990s), South Koreans had thought of an overseas stay in the United States as a respite from their own intensive childrearing regimes; at that time, the United States was the primary destination and was known for educating the whole child and thus for appreciating children's diverse capacities (Kang and Abelmann 2011). By the mid-aughts, more and more Korean *chogi yuhak* returnee families began reporting in South Korean media on the enormous challenges and disappointments they experienced overseas, and it was becoming increasingly apparent that the United States too was a competitive system and that the elite American education was out of reach for nonelite South Korean students (Kang and Abelmann 2011). However, the notion of sending precollege children abroad had become sufficiently popularized and practiced by middle-class South Korean families that a large number of Korean students of wide-ranging academic abilities continued to arrive in the United States throughout the early 2000s. For many of these students, study abroad was less about acquiring social capital for a successful future in South Korea and more about getting a second chance or a fresh start in a new land after failed schooling experiences in South Korea (Williams 2015).

It turns out that our Chicagoland study's initial data collection had coincided with the rapid escalation of South Korean early study abroad students, although at the time when we were most actively in the field collecting data from teens and parents, our research team had not realized the extent of the phenomenon. In 2004, at the beginning of our Chicagoland study, South Korean early study abroad was in the escalation phase: indeed, 2002–2003 was the year with the greatest percentage increase of such migration, which would peak in 2006 and wane dramatically in the aftermath of the 2008 South Korean currency crisis and the global economic downturn (Okazaki and Kim 2018). The increased presence of *chogi yuhak* students from Korea was felt in Chicagoland as well as in east central Illinois where the University of Illinois' flagship campus was located. Some younger, primary-school-aged Korean students were residing with their mothers in the so-called wild geese (*kirogi*) family arrangements, in which the father typically remained in South Korea working to support his children's education abroad while the mother and the children lived abroad for a period lasting from a few months to several years. Private boarding schools in Chicagoland and in Champaign were taking in increasing numbers of Korean international high school students (Williams 2015). And as we will see, unaccompanied high-school-aged students from Korea were ending up at some of the same public high schools as the American-born children of Korean immigrant families in our study, populating the ESL (English as a Second Language) classes, and in some cases even living with the families of their Korean friends and neighbors (as fee-paying boarders or as relatives).

In our fieldwork, we encountered many recently immigrated Korean high school students who were now studying in American high schools, including some who had migrated from South Korea to the United States with their parents and siblings. The line between family migration and early study abroad became blurred, especially as long-term Korean immigrant parents echoed similar narratives about why they were raising their children in the United States (i.e., escaping the South Korean educational system and providing greater educational opportunities for their children) as the Korean parents who had planned short-term *chogi yuhak*. Indeed, the most recently immigrated among the families featured in this book—the Hyun family—told us explicitly that they opted to emigrate as a whole family precisely because they could not afford to maintain two households (one in South Korea and one in the United States) for early study abroad. Similarly, Nancy and Jin-Heon observed tense relations between the Kohs and their considerably more prosperous early-study-abroad niece from Korea, who enjoyed luxuries that the Kohs would never have been able to afford in South Korea, let alone in immigrant America, where they were living quite modestly.

As our fieldwork unfolded, so did considerable tensions between Korean Americans and these short-term educational migrants at middle schools and high schools in the Chicagoland area. The families in this book, regardless of their own year of immigration (which ranged from 1980 to 2003), could not help but be aware of some of the ways in which globalization was changing their homeland and, in turn, the recent immigrants from South Korea bringing their neoliberal ideas about parenting into their Korean ethnic circles. The increasingly visible student mobility between South Korea and the United States was another context in which it had become increasingly nonsensical to speak of "American" and "Korean" parenting regimes. In 2001, the U.S. Congress passed the No Child Left Behind Act, inaugurating a testing regime in American K–12 education that would have been very familiar to immigrants or short-term migrants from East Asia. Even as South Korean education migrants were arriving in droves to escape the hypercompetitive academic culture of Korea, it was East Asian test scores—impressive South Korean results among them—that politicians and the media touted to goad the American public about the extent of the U.S. educational crisis. Notably, South Korean media tend to downplay Korean students' consistently high achievement on the Programme for International Student Assessment (PISA), a worldwide scholastic test, casting it as a negative reflection of excessive competition, "examination hell," "education fever," and extensive privatization of education (Waldow, Takayama, and Sung 2014).

Two Dialogues about Race and Korean American Parenting

[Church Conversation]

We now turn to two mid-aughts dialogues about parenting in Korean American communities that reflected the messy mix of domestic and global ideas about how Korean American parents should raise their children in the United States. We understand these conversations to be revealing of the competing ideas that parents in this book were juggling in the mid-aughts and beyond. The first dialogue we describe comes from a series of Korean American ethnic media features about parenting and education that appeared in the past decade. The second dialogue took place in the course of our fieldwork, in which members of our research team were participant-observers. This community dialogue, which took place in 2004, was occasioned by a presentation that Nancy made at one of the Korean Catholic churches in Chicagoland where we administered the survey to parents and teens and also recruited families for ethnography. Upon revisiting both of these conversations, we were struck by how conscious Korean American parents were about the tenor of both global and local trends in academic competition. The Korean ethnic media treatment of parenting issues revealed educators' and parents' concerns about raising academically successful, globally competitive, *and* emotionally healthy Korean American adults. The church conversation both reflected and contested the larger national (and transnational) parenting discourse of the day.

ETHNIC MEDIA CHIDES KOREAN IMMIGRANT PARENTS

The sociologists Zhou and Kim (2006) had pointed to the powerful role that ethnic media plays in explaining and unraveling the ins and outs of the American educational system to Chinese American and Korean American immigrant parents, thereby shaping their community discourse around education, success, and achievement. For Korean American communities, Zhou and Kim cite two major Korean newspapers that are circulated widely in the United States (the *Korea Times* and *Central Daily*), both of which have weekly sections devoted to education, featuring average SAT scores of local high schools, American college rankings, college admission requirements and strategies, and general parenting advice. The Korean ethnic papers also translate and publish major education-related articles that appear in mainstream English

holistic Korean parenting

newspapers and magazines. We examined a sampling of education and parenting articles that appeared in the national and Chicagoland Korean-language media outlets in the mid-aughts as another strand of background dialogue about education and parenting that was happening at the time when our research team was engaging in intensive data collection.

Overall, parenting and education articles in Korean American ethnic media reflected the tension between the persistent ideas of American liberal education and a transformed, globalized, competitive, American educational market. There were also signs of ambivalence felt among Korean American parents and educators as to how much to push for rigorous academic preparation versus valuing each child's individuality, creativity, and passion. On the one hand, the journalists and the experts chided immigrant parents for their attempts to reproduce South Korean parenting in the United States, urging them to think instead of their children's happiness and of the range of opportunities and values that the United States promised beyond elite education. On the other hand, the media and the experts aimed to instruct Korean American parents that South Korean–like competition was the new normal for American college admission, especially at elite and selective colleges. We observed that, at least in this type of public conversation about educational and parenting strategies, the media was freely dispensing cultural glosses such as "the Korean way" or "the American way" of parenting children.

For example, in December 2005, the *Korea Times*' U.S. edition (published in Los Angeles and disseminated in Korean American communities around the United States) reported on a panel of experts in Southern California assembled by the *Korea Times* to discuss how to raise successful children.[9] Among the panel was an elementary school principal with a PhD in education, a vice principal at a high school, and the president of the Korean Parent Association at a local high school. The reporter from the newspaper introduced the forum with the following pithy preamble: "More than [worrying about getting into] university, educate your children to live well after they graduate!" The female reporter described the scores of South Korean parents willing to travel across the ocean to get their children out of South Korea's college entrance examination–based education system into the American education system, but she also reminded Korean American parents that "college entrance is getting competitive in the U.S. as well. From dawn till the wee hours of the night many American students are told, 'Study! Volunteer! Prepare for your SATs!' And parents are sending them to [after-school] academies, educational consulting centers, and so on." The reporter continued with a description of Bush-era changes in which American education is becoming ever more test based, "so much so that it is coming to resemble South Korea!" Some of the educators acknowledged that the competition for college entrance has, indeed, heated up considerably, such that it was even difficult for students to gain admission to UCLA and other well-regarded public universities.

The panelists reprimanded Korean American parents for engaging in "the Korean way of parenting" that narrowly focused only on standardized test preparation and gaining admission to Ivy League and other elite well-known universities (e.g., Stanford, MIT). While there was acknowledgment that Korean American students were succeeding in obtaining good grades and high test scores, the overarching message was that these academic achievements were not sufficient. The panel's focus on childrearing encouraged Korean American parents to think beyond elite college admissions to consider a broader set of skills that their American-raised children might need to succeed in the future. With these communication skills in mind, Korean American parents were also advised to be open to interacting with, and encouraging their children to be socially comfortable in, the U.S. multicultural society. The high school principal on the panel noted that the problem is "not only that Korean parents are only satisfied with an A, but that because parents don't know how to listen to their children's problems, the kids become isolated and don't get in the habit of expressing things to their parents." Korean American parents were also faulted for their ignorance about the breadth of American academic excellence across a range of higher education institutions, which caused them to steer their children away from elite liberal arts colleges (e.g., Williams College) and universities (e.g., Duke University) that were less well known among Koreans, which in turn increased academic pressure on their children to aim for only the most selective schools. The panelist advised parents to educate themselves about American education and to burst the bubble of their many misconceptions and biases.

Another educator on the panel advised immigrant parents to educate their children for a twenty-year global horizon. He described the imperative for Korean American young people to become "globally gifted" and to be "the kind of person who can compete in the global arena." Describing a range of soft social skills, the educator went on to say that those best poised to succeed are "able to convince people of their ideas through intelligent expression; and make efforts to learn new things, to be able to accept new ideas and resolve conflicts." The educator said that many Korean American high school students seem to be lacking in communication and relationship skills.

Social skills

This theme of socioemotional development, quite apart from global competition in the United States and everywhere, appeared in other articles in the same newspaper. For example, take an article published in 2007 in the *Korea Times* reporting on a special seminar in response to the Virginia Tech massacre perpetrated by a Korean-descent college student.[10] In the article, a lawyer was quoted as saying, "The Korean value system that emphasizes the 'best' can produce great people, but at the same time it leaves behind many young people who can't handle the pressure. Now is the time that we must learn the value of being 'ordinary people.'" The considerable anxiety and horror experienced by Korean American communities around the nation—that the most horrific mass killings on American soil in recent memory was perpetrated by a Korean immigrant student with good grades and a quiet personality—morphed into a public discussion about how Korean immigrant parents must focus less on grades and more on the emotional well-being of their children.

Communication

A 2011 article in a Chicago Korean American publication, *Chicago Kyocharo*, showcased a newly published book (in Korean) that compiled essays written by eight parents of Korean American students who attended Harvard.[11] The *Chicago Kyocharo* article featured one case from the book, that of Mrs. Byun Yun-Suk, who named good parent-child communication as the key to her daughter's success. Mrs. Byun was quoted describing her mother-daughter relationship in this way: "[I have been] treating my daughter like a friend since she was a little girl. We thought through everything together. I was at her side, knowing what her concerns were, and how she was developing her values." We observed that this book, which was published in Korea for a domestic audience eager to learn how to parent a Korean child toward the ultimate success of gaining admission to Harvard, nevertheless promotes a more relationally intimate form of parenting. In this way, the Korean book featured in ethnic media for the Korean American immigrant families fit squarely into the popular genre of parenting memoirs published in Korea in the 2000s by South Korean parents whose children engaged in early study abroad (Abelmann and Kang 2014), which described the considerable social and cultural tensions surrounding global parenting strategies. We found the Korean ethnic media's interest in this book to be of particular interest precisely because of the contradictory messages that it sends about Korean American achievement. On the one hand, the book's singular focus on Harvard admission diverges from the larger Korean American experts' and journalists' message to Korean American parents to broaden their families' college horizons beyond a narrow set of elite institutions. On the other hand, the book's parenting advice seems to steer parents away from a harsh and unrelenting focus on studies and toward more holistic, socioemotional parenting.

All in all, our glimpses into Korean ethnic media messages on parenting seem to strike a similar note. Experts encourage Korean immigrant parents to remember that the American education system is different from the Korean system in two ways: to some extent the American system is kinder and more variegated, but the parents must also navigate the American system with the whole-student approach and with attention to socioemotional learning in order to avoid worst-case scenarios (e.g., the Virginia Tech shooting). Experts and educators urge immigrant parents not to be so narrowly competitive, yet there are also frequent reminders of how competitive it is to gain admission to elite universities in the United States. On the whole, Korean American parents were constantly urged by ethnic media to examine and to amend their parenting strategies. And indeed, as we will detail in the family ethnography chapters, we found that the Korean immigrant parents in our study engaged in extensive and ruminative reflections about how to raise emotionally fortified Korean American children. And while mentions of race and racism were strikingly absent from these ethnic media education and parenting discourses in the mid-aughts, parenting around race and racial identity was a salient concern for many of our Korean American families as well.

COMMUNITY CONVERSATION AMONG PARENTS
AT A KOREAN CHURCH MEETING

As a part of the survey data collection, our research team approached various Korean American churches and service organizations in Chicagoland so as to gain access to their congregants and clients. In return, we offered to give presentations or to facilitate discussions about topics of interest to Korean American families, such as mental health, college experience, and so on. This was how Nancy came to present at a church PTA meeting on a late Sunday morning at a Korean Catholic church in a northwestern Chicago suburb after the survey was administered to the parents. Nancy spoke in Korean for some thirty minutes to a gathering attended by about fifty parents, her remarks premised on the lessons learned from her then in-progress book manuscript, *The Intimate University: Korean American Students and the Problems of Segregation*, in which she had analyzed the oftentimes ethnically segregated social lives of Korean Americans at the University of Illinois at Urbana-Champaign. As the University of Illinois was the likely destination of the children of many of the parents gathered, it was clear that the Korean American parents were eager to engage with Nancy and the graduate students (Euna and Jin-Heon) from our team. The open conversation (carried out entirely in Korean) that ensued after Nancy's remarks centered largely on the parents' concerns about how to foster their Korean American children's positive ethnic identity. [12]

We realize now—though we did not fully appreciate it at the time—the extent to which the theme underlying the community conversation at the parents' gathering that day was about race, specifically about their children's comfort with mainstream (White) America, even though the discussion was laced with references to "Korean" and "American" people and values. At the time, we had been particularly struck by the quiet comments of one of the mothers who would later join our study (Mrs. Koh, chapter 3), but we were surprised to see that many other comments also touched on race and racial comfort levels. First to speak was a mother who mostly praised her own daughters' successful American integration but also indicated a concern about the future costs of her daughters cultivating an exclusively non-Korean American social circle. She noted that her high school sophomore and college sophomore daughters, who had arrived in the United States only five years earlier, did not seem willing to make any Korean or Korean American friends. However, this mother also admitted that initially, upon their arrival in the United States, she had told her daughters not to socialize with South Korean people so that they would learn English more quickly. She described her concerns in the following manner:

> Since then, my children naturally distanced themselves from Korean people. My older child even went to a small private college in order to not attend the U of I [where it is well known that there are many Koreans]. Because my children associate with American friends, they tend to compare me with their [non-Korean] friends' parents. And they often say that I'm "too much" for them, with my excessive attachment to them. They say that none of their American friends' parents are like that. So I worry about whether my communication with my children will fade away.

A woman standing next to her interrupted to ask whether the speaker's daughters had friends at the Korean church, to which she answered that they did not attend church at all. She nonetheless continued this way: "But there are some advantages to [my children's ways] as well. My children's way of thinking is broader than the typical Korean way. But I have begun to think . . . friends are important, so I wonder if they will really be comfortable in this country?" Another parent then spoke—with nary a hint of unease—discussing her children's bicultural comfort level: she rested assured that they were able to absorb the "best of both worlds." She did allow that her children's co-ethnic comfort level was proving more important as they moved into adulthood:

> I brought my children [to the United States] when they were in 5th–6th grade. My children, in contrast to the two people who just spoke, socialized with many Korean people. I am really happy about that. They have been able to maintain their Korean language while also absorbing American culture. Both of my children went to private university in Boston. . . . But by socializing with American people, however, they realized that American people are not living the life they imagined. . . . I really tried to teach my children only good things about Korean culture,

and we still talk a great deal about Korean culture. I think of my children as having successfully absorbed the best of both worlds and as being able to draw on both as they live in this country.

It was at this point in the conversation that Mrs. Koh revealed her worries about her teen son's lack of confidence as a racial minority in the United States, fearing that her son might not have what it takes to make it in America. Empathizing with Mrs. Koh's anguish, another parent suggested the protective effects of cultural identification for racial minorities in the following way:

> I think that above all, we must teach our children a great deal about Korean culture. Even in school, we should do whatever we can to have them learn Korean if the option is there. If we make them proud of their home country, they will necessarily develop a positive racial identity over time. . . . If we teach our children well, they will remember that they are of Korean descent. And if we are successful, *they will suffer less pain over issues of racial identity.* (emphasis added)

The church PTA forum went on in this manner, with various Korean American immigrant parents offering a wide range of thoughts about the right mix of "Korean" culture and "American" culture for raising their visibly racial-minority children. Ultimately, what remained with us long after the meeting was the palpable anguish voiced by several of the parents over the difficulty of navigating their children through a racialized landscape toward a successful adulthood.

Korean American Families in Flux

Together, the ethnic media discourse in the mid- to late aughts and the church community's parent forum reveal the quite anxious parenting undercurrent that was running through Korean American communities during the time of our field research in Chicagoland. Whereas South Korean parents were still eagerly sending their children to the United States as early study abroad students to escape the unforgiving South Korean educational regime, the Korean American parents in our study did not have the luxury of confidence that their children's American

education would provide a quick fix to the ills of South Korean education, nor were they able to imagine that race would not matter to their race
children's American futures. And unlike the "tiger mom" Amy Chua, the
Korean American parents who shared their concerns and stories with
us were certainly not confidently valorizing the "Korean" way or the
"Asian" way of parenting as superior to that of American parenting. We
have introduced these glimpses from the mainstream and ethnic media
as well as a church setting as examples of the discourse that comprised
the local, national, and global contexts at the time of our study.

This book aims to illuminate how Korean American parents and
teens navigate immigrant America, attending to the convergences as
well as divergences across the data we collected over the years in this
mixed-method study: we have situated the quantitative (i.e., analyses of
parent-teen survey data) data within the larger ethnographic context,
and then drawn on the qualitative, longitudinal fieldwork with families.
To set the stage for the ethnographic portraits of five Korean American
families that form the core of this book, we next offer a lay of the land for
the Korean American communities in Chicagoland in the mid-aughts.

2

Community Context

Korean Americans in Chicagoland

On an early October Sunday, Lisa (an undergraduate researcher) and Euna (one of our graduate researchers) arrived at a nondenominational Korean church to engage in survey data collection. After the worship service, teens in the youth group escorted the researchers to the lounge area. While Euna went elsewhere to coordinate the parent survey administration for about ten minutes, Lisa engaged in informal conversations with some of the youths gathered there—almost all of whom were American-born children of Korean immigrant parents—asking them which town they were from and how old they were. It turned out that many of those gathered were young teens still in middle school or just beginning high school. The teens in turn asked Lisa what it was like being in college. Lisa answered, "The same thing you do now, but no parents," to which the teens responded, "Really? That is awesome! I don't really get along with my parents." Others chimed in, "[My parents] don't understand me," or "They don't listen." Lisa asked where they wanted to go to college, and most of them did not have any idea where they wanted to go. While the girls were a bit more vocal, the boys who spoke answered that their parents just wanted them to do well in school.

As Lisa distributed the survey, the Korean American teens asked how long it would take them to complete the survey. Lisa answered that it took most kids about forty minutes, and there was an audible groan. At first there was awkward silence, but as time progressed, the teens started to talk again. Some asked Lisa for clarification on words (e.g., "obligated"), and most of them said they simply did not know the answers to some of the questions, such as how old their parents had been when they came to the United States or how old they were now. While taking their surveys, the teens also kept on asking Lisa questions about what it was like to have a driver's license, and what it was like being on her own, not having to listen to parents, or not getting into trouble for coming home late.

* * *

On an early November afternoon, we were setting up for a related survey data collection at Valley Creek West High School, a well-resourced and well-regarded suburban high school with a graduation rate of almost 100 percent. We had arranged with Ms. Pak, the school's Korean liaison, to administer the survey to the twenty or so Korean ESL students who had signed up to participate. We flipped through the stack of parent consent forms that Ms. Pak had collected and were happy to see that over half of the forms had parent contact information, opening the way for us to contact parents for possible involvement in family ethnography. Around 3:15 p.m., as Sumie kept an eye out for the pizza delivery, two students arrived, a girl and a boy. They were extremely excited and clearly impressed that Nancy could speak Korean; the girl said that she had never before met a White person who could speak Korean. For the next several minutes, every new arriving student was told about Nancy's Korean-speaking ability, and newly arriving students seemed equally impressed, uttering "Ehhh!" to signal their delight. We found this whole episode rather amusing and endearing. Some students even began testing Nancy to see how far her comprehension went.

During the survey, the teens seemed to be talking to one another, frequently raising their hands to ask Nancy questions about the meanings of some words. Some students wanted to look at the English version just to see if they understood the Korean questions correctly, which suggested that some of the students were between languages and might not have known the harder Korean words. It became clear at some point that, because there were many students in this group who were not currently living with their parents, some of the family questions about their daily routines with their mother and father were difficult for some students to answer. We decided to ask each student, as he or she turned in the survey, whether the student lived with his/her parents or not. Their responses were really quite eye-opening with respect to the extent and variety of arrangements—mothers who shuttle back and forth between Korea and the United States, fathers back in Korea, a number of the students living with aunts, and at least one student living with grandparents.

* * *

The narratives of Korean American college students in the campus study offered glimpses of their immigrant parents, filtered through the retrospective lens of emerging adults, the majority of whom were living away from home. We were eager to take our research on Korean American immigrant families off the campus and venture into Chicagoland, where the overwhelming majority of our Korean American college students had spent their childhood and adolescent years. We also wanted to get to know Korean American teens and their immigrant parents while they were still living together in the same household. Although we brought our own disciplinary lenses (as a psychologist and an anthropologist) and our methodological expertise (quantitative and qualitative approaches) to the study, we worked actively to have the data from the survey and ethnography "talk" to each other. We were also eager to attend to both the local and the global contexts and to the bodies of scholarship on Asian American families, Asian parenting, and global citizenship. What emerged were portraits of ethnic churches that are challenged by various intrachurch dynamics, a suburban high school grappling with changing demographics and the often rocky integration of newcomer English language learners, and suburban ethnic enclaves of Korean American communities that are different in scale and intimacy from those of traditional urban ethnic enclaves.

Research Process in Chicagoland Korean America

Chicagoland has long been a destination for Korean immigrants. According to the 2000 U.S. Census, the state of Illinois was home to the fourth-largest community of Korean Americans in the country, with about a quarter of the state's population residing in Chicagoland (Yu, Choe, and Han 2002). However, the aughts saw a shift in residential patterns, with Korean American communities in California, Texas, and the East Coast states (New Jersey, Virginia, and New York) growing more than in Illinois such that, by 2010, the Illinois Korean American community had fallen to the seventh-largest in the nation. And starting in the 1990s, Chicago Korean Americans (especially families) had suburbanized rapidly into the northwest suburbs in search of good public schools (C. K. Kim et al. 2012).

Starting in the fall of 2003, our research team (ourselves, together with the five graduate research assistants) spent a great deal of time and effort to establish working relationships with Chicagoland schools and churches so as to be able to recruit Korean American adolescents and parents for the survey and family ethnography. To set things in motion, we crafted a press release about our upcoming study, which we had translated into Korean and sent to major Korean daily newspapers distributed in Chicagoland (*Chungang Ilbo* and *Hanguk Ilbo*) in late fall 2003. We and the student researchers made multiple trips to Chicagoland to meet with the staff at various Korean American service agencies and with clergy and lay leaders at various Korean American churches, to learn about the community and to request permission to recruit survey participants at their sites.

And although almost all our data collection efforts ultimately took place through Korean American churches for reasons we will make clear below, we sought contacts with secular institutions and key informants in Chicagoland that would give us a larger sense of the ethnic landscape. Upon our visit to one well-established social service agency (Korean American Community Services, or KACS, which at the time was the oldest and largest in Chicagoland) in what used to be the Koreatown business district in the Albany Park neighborhood within Chicago city proper, we learned that there were not many Korean American families who still lived in the city of Chicago because of extensive suburbanization save for Korean elders who remained. In fact, in order to provide social services to adolescents and families, this agency was sending its staff to suburban outposts.[1] And as much as we strove to collect survey data from urban families as well as suburban families and from non-Christian or non-Catholic families (and in the end we did manage to collect youth survey data from one nondenominational church and one secular social service agency, both located in the city of Chicago), we had to contend with the reality that the majority of the Korean American adolescents were located in the northern—and to a lesser extent, western and southwestern—suburbs of the city and that the majority of the community was affiliated with Korean churches. Our experience is supported by an analysis of the demography of Koreans in Chicago in 2000, which found that over 85 percent of children between the ages of five and seventeen lived in the suburbs rather than in the city (Kim, Park, and Choi 2005).

On the receiving end of the suburbanization, which was to a large extent driven by families searching for good school districts for their children and for home ownership, were communities in northern and northwestern Cook County, extending into Lake County to the north. In describing the history and demography of the suburbanization of the Chicago Korean community, Kim, Park, and Choi (2005) described the costs of these immigrant aspirations. To be able to afford home ownership in these affluent suburbs with good school districts, Korean immigrant parents often take on self-employed small entrepreneurial work. Indeed, Korean Americans in the United States are notable for their high concentration in self-employment. The 1990 U.S. Census data (cited in Yoon 1997) indicated that the self-employment rate of Korean Americans, at 24.3 percent, was the highest among U.S. ethnic groups. In Chicagoland in the 1990s, the rate of self-employment among Korean American men was 32 percent (Rajiman 1996, cited in Raijman and Tienda 2003).

Korean American small businesses are concentrated in niches: it was estimated that by the late 1990s, Korean Americans owned 80 percent of all dry cleaners in Chicago (Jo 2005). Korean Americans also dominated beauty supply stores, especially on the South Side of Chicago, that served primarily African American clientele (Jo 2005). Another notable occupation for Korean immigrants is in nursing, and there were estimated to be about twelve hundred Korean nurses in Chicagoland in 2003 (M. J. Kim 2005). Of the five Korean American families featured in this book, four families were small business owners or worked in Korean-owned businesses, operating a dry cleaning shop, a nail salon, or a video rental shop; and in one family, the mother worked as a nurse. These features of Korean American demography are significant for family life, as many Korean American small entrepreneurs operate mom-and-pop shops with no other employees, often in locations far from their homes, requiring long-distance commuting and long hours spent away from their families.

To get a sense of the community from the perspective of mental health professionals who work with it, Hyeyoung interviewed Dr. Kwon, a clinical psychologist whose office was located in the old Koreatown neighborhood in Chicago city proper. Dr. Kwon provided testing services for Korean American families whose children were struggling in school, and she shared her observation that Korean immigrant parents tend to not discipline their children very strictly but instead allow a great deal of freedom—a parenting style that Dr. Kwon thought was associated with attention deficit and hyperactivity among her young clientele. Dr. Kwon also shared her concern about the new group of recently immigrated affluent Korean students who were sent overseas by parents for precollege study abroad. Although it did not appear that Dr. Kwon was working directly with these *chogi yuhak* (early study abroad) students, she was clearly aware of the "stir" these newcomers were creating in the community with their extravagant lifestyle and lack of adult supervision.

That many Korean American second-generation children also spent a great many of their childhood days in the absence of parental contact and supervision was noted by a young Korean American social worker from KACS. This agency, a comprehensive social service agency located in the city proper, had sent Ms. Nam to their satellite office in the north suburbs to do school-based social work and outreach at two local public schools. She told Jin-Heon and Hyeyoung that while the majority of Korean American children in the area do well and learn to be independent at an earlier age in the absence of parental supervision, the students she sees in her counseling work tend to be those who are recently immigrated and are struggling with language barriers at school. Ms. Nam explained that although these students feel isolated and incompetent at school because they cannot speak English well, the students do not feel free to disclose their school problems to their parents because their immigrant parents' hardships and sacrifices are all too visible to them. Ms. Nam had also observed that immigrant parents are not able to be involved hands-on with their children's schooling because of their long work hours and their lack of familiarity with American schools. Ms. Nam also shared that she sees a different form of emotional problems among second-generation Korean American students and their parents, where there are intergenerational conflicts surrounding communications and perceived lack of mutual respect between the parents and

two- and three-story buildings, arranged in quadrangles around parking lots and expanses of grass fields, with walkways throughout and a man-made lake. Nancy could not help but approach a couple of different entryways to the buildings to note the names on the buzzers. Nancy estimated that there was about one Korean surname per entryway to six–eight apartment units, not quite the estimate of upward of 70 percent Korean residents given to our team by Ms. Nam, the social worker who works with public schools in the district.

Nancy, Grace, and Charse walked about the grounds in the hope of encountering some Korean immigrant families there. They approached a Korean couple (whom Nancy spotted because the woman's walk was "distinctly Korean" and suggested a more rural origin within Korea), whom they were able to engage in a conversation. Nancy's speaking to them in Korean seemed to help the couple ease into a casual conversation with a group of three strangers, and little by little, the couple shared that they had been living in the complex for about four years, that the husband was a CPA, and that they had two sons. The couple indicated to Nancy and Grace that the complex is "a place that people come to leave," a starting place for new immigrants so their children can attend the renowned high school. They suggested that if our team really wanted to meet the recently immigrated Korean students and the parents, we must make contact with the Korean PTA and the ESL program at the local high school.

Indeed, our research team did follow through with this excellent suggestion to contact the school. Much to our delight, the principal of the high school in question was welcoming—and quite proud of how well his school had done in reaching out to Korean newcomer students. The high school principal also allowed our research team to recruit survey participants through their ESL program, and as a result, we were able to engage a recently migrated Korean immigrant family who resided in this apartment complex into our family ethnography project. Because of this, our research team paid multiple visits to this so-called Korean ghetto over the years.

The High School

Sumie interviewed the outgoing principal of Valley Creek West High School two weeks prior to his retirement after a long career as an educator and school administrator. Mr. Jones had graduated from the University of Illinois in 1964 and then had served in the United States Army for two years, thirteen months of which he had spent stationed in Dangkok-dong, north of Seoul. Soon after he returned to the States, he obtained his master's degree and a teaching certificate on the GI Bill and had worked at the same high school from 1968 until his retirement. He had served as a social studies teacher, academic dean, and student activities director, and had spent ten years as an associate principal and twelve years as the principal. With such a long career in the same high school, he was certainly an excellent historian of the school and the changes that had accompanied the recent decades. He had been interviewed back in 2000 by a local Korean newspaper, and his work at the school with the Korean American families was featured in an article.

An affable White American man from Illinois who had fond memories of his military stint in Korea during the Korean War, Mr. Jones professed a cultural affinity toward Koreans. Perhaps because of his personal interest and generous spirit, on the eve of his retirement after thirty-seven years working at the same high school, he welcomed our research team to the school, allowing us access to his Korean American liaison (Ms. Pak) and facilitating our getting permission to collect survey data from their Korean ESL students. Two of our ethnography families' teens were attending this school, and he permitted our graduate researchers to shadow these students for one day. He told us about various accommodations that his school had crafted in response to the demographic shifts (e.g., hiring a bilingual Korean liaison to interface with the parents). At the time of the study, the school population was estimated to be approximately 12 percent Korean. Although Korean speakers had been the most populous in the school's ESL classes, the numbers had waned in recent years and been overtaken by Spanish-speaking students.

Mr. Jones spoke at length about the increasingly driven climate of the school, populated by children of "very high-powered" upper-middle-class families. He noted that compared to when he started his career in the 1970s, today's students are much more stressed. And compared to high schools in more middle-class districts, the students at his school were much more inclined to study hard and hold themselves to a high bar for achievement. He noted that in the 1990s the number of Korean American students at the school began to grow, which was a new phenomenon for an area that was lacking in cultural diversity. He shared that he had allowed a separate parent organization for Korean Americans to form so that the school staff could talk to them about cultural differences between the American high school experience and the immigrant parents' expectations; he had also partnered with a Korean American social agency to make use of their translators and to make referrals for various services (including mental health). As he talked, his knowledge of the social ecology of the local Korean American immigrant families was readily apparent. He described the parent-child conflict born out of language gaps and differing expectations and the immigrant frustrations that had begun to be visible at the school, as well as the interethnic tensions between newly arrived ESL students from South Korea and the American-born Korean American students, a theme we will encounter in a number of chapters. He also spoke of his awareness of the central role of ethnic churches in the lives of Korean American families and even the tensions between the English youth ministry and the Korean ministry for their parents. By the time of his retirement, Mr. Jones had seen that the local Korean American families at the school had become more acculturated on the whole and required less attention from the school staff, and that many Korean American students had become integrated well into the fabric of the school; he proudly announced, in fact, that the homecoming queen that past season had been a Korean American girl. His school was now experiencing a rather sudden influx of Latino students (6 percent of the school), and there was a sense that he and his staff—having gone through the process earlier with Korean American families—knew how to connect with the students and their immigrant parents.

Our team was introduced to Ms. Pak, the Korean liaison on the staff of the school guidance department (though she is not a counselor herself), whom Mr. Jones had directed to assist us with recruiting recently arrived Korean students into our study. Ms. Pak's job was to serve as a liaison between the school staff and the non-English-speaking parents of Korean ESL students. She indicated that almost all her contacts with the Korean families took place over the phone, given the busy schedule of Korean immigrant adults, who work long hours—and she surmised that the reluctance not to have face-to-face contact with the school might also stem from the possibility that some of the Korean students and families might be skirting the law (e.g., having an undocumented status or not actually residing in the school district). Ms. Pak herself was born in South Korea, had immigrated as a young child along with her parents, and had attended Valley Creek West and the University of Illinois. Although she had majored in business at Illinois, she had decided to switch the course of her career to teaching. While attending graduate school to earn her teaching certificate, Ms. Pak had taken on the job as a Korean liaison because she felt her own past as an immigrant (and her family having hosted a cousin who came from Korea to the United States at age fourteen and went on to a university and law school in the United States) resonated with issues facing the families of Korean ESL students.

The Churches

While we gathered ethnographic data about the Korean American community and key secular institutions and landmarks, we were also mindful of the demographic of Korean Americans being overwhelmingly Christian and active churchgoers. Kim and Kim (2002, quoted in D. B. Lee 2005) had estimated that 70 percent of Korean immigrants were affiliated with Korean churches in the Chicagoland area; and as of 2003, there were 268 Korean churches in Chicagoland (D. B. Lee 2005). Because family members tend to attend the same church, we reasoned that we would have a greater chance of collecting data from teens and parents from the same families by administering surveys at churches on Sundays after worship services.

In this phase of building goodwill and being introduced to the Chicago Korean American community, we were greatly helped by the sociologist Kwang-Chung Kim and his wife, Shin Kim, who were not only the foremost scholars of Korean American churches and Korean American immigrant families (Hurh and Kim 1990; Kim, Kim, and Hurh 1991) but also a pair of respected elders in the Chicagoland Korean American community whose professional and social reaches within the ethnic network were considerable. This affable couple, whom Nancy had met through her research with Korean Americans in Illinois, were quite willing to make personal introductions to the senior pastors at various mega-churches in Chicagoland. These personal introductions by the Kims to the gatekeepers and stakeholders in the Chicagoland Korean American community boosted our credibility, as Nancy (a Korean-speaking White professor) and Sumie (a Japanese American professor with no Korean language ability) were a pair of outsiders to the community. In some cases, the Kims visited the pastors at the churches with us, and before and after visits, they regaled us with back stories of the churches, the people, and the latest trends in Korean American churches.

Our engagement with various Korean churches included our bilingual graduate researchers' attendance at various Protestant adult and youth worship services, youth group retreats and fundraisers, Catholic masses, and lunches with the congregants after the services. Through these visits, we learned that there were, in fact, multiple ministries within the same church and these ministries sometimes can have fraught relations with one another. Typically, the Korean-language ministry led by the senior pastors (most often immigrants themselves) ministers to the immigrant adult generation while the English-language youth ministry (led by a more youthful minister—in one church we encountered an African American youth minister) preaches to the 1.5- or second-generation adolescents. This fact, that parents and adolescents are often quite separate in their worship and study even while attending the same Korean American church, later became a significant source of challenge in our survey data collection. (We ended up with fewer families in our survey in which we had the data from both the parents and the adolescents even though the surveys were administered on Sundays after the service in the same building.) Such internal divisiveness and conflict, which frequently plague Korean churches, have been documented by scholars, who also critique Korean churches for their tendency to be self-contained and self-serving but in a fairly conservative, patriarchal way (e.g., see D. B. Lee 2005).

This point—that churches tend to be at the center of the ethnic social network for many Korean Americans in the community, and yet they are not entirely meeting the psychological needs of the congregation—was repeated by Ms. Nam, the young KACS social worker we interviewed, as well as by a number of the Korean American families we encountered through the course of our fieldwork. Ms. Nam told us that she had designed a mental health intervention program for Korean American youth and approached local Korean churches for support, but many large Protestant congregations turned down her proposal. We also saw, in one of our ethnography families, that they ran right up against this lack of responsiveness to their troubled son when they tried to reach out for help from their own church members. In fact, that this family's mother had been desperately searching for some sort of psychological help for her son within the confines of the church—and approached Hyeyoung at the church the family attended after taking our parent survey filled with questions about psychological functioning—was the impetus for our ethnographic engagement with this family.

In our visits with Protestant church pastors—many of which were immediately followed by the Kims' astute commentaries and analyses of the church dynamics—the tensions between the Korean-language adult ministries and English-language youth ministries were quite palpable. We remember quite clearly one visit with a cynical youth minister who was simultaneously critical of his youth congregants, whom he portrayed as "rich kids" who were not genuinely motivated to practice Christianity, while also sympathetic to the youths' displeasure with the immigrant generation's demands (both the demands of the immigrant parents on their teens and those of the Korean senior minister on the Korean American youth minister). We also learned from both senior and youth pastors of their concerns about brewing tension among English-speaking second-generation Korean American youth and the increasingly sizable contingent of Korean-speaking recently immigrated youth in their congregations. Some of the larger churches handled this by creating separate English and Korean services for these youths, while smaller churches that attempted to bring together these youth into the same service and youth groups were less successful in retaining the second-generation youth. In retrospect, these tensions we observed at Korean churches hinted at the larger Korean American community's struggles with the question of how the older, more settled immigrant generation of Korean American adults must accommodate the changes within their community as their American-born children become emerging adults and as more recently immigrated Korean compatriots with more cosmopolitan sensibilities join their institutions and populate their neighborhoods. As well, we later came to see how Korean American youth ministries can shape the lens through which the adolescents view their immigrant parents' family strategies, as in the case of the Hyun family.

The Family Survey

By June 2004, we had secured agreements with a handful of Korean American churches and a service organization, thanks to the patient trust-building church visits of our graduate researchers. Agreements at other survey sites followed in the summer and fall. From our initial engagements with the church pastors, we had learned that the Korean American churches in the area, especially the large Protestant churches in the suburbs, were frequently solicited with requests from multiple scholars and students for survey participation, as there were a number of Korean and Korean American students at local Christian seminaries who were conducting scholarly projects on Korean American churches (not to mention researchers like ourselves). In fact, there were six Korean-run seminaries in Chicagoland that offered instruction in Korean language as of 1999, in addition to ten seminaries run by mainline Christian denominations that also enrolled Korean seminary students (D. B. Lee 2005). The clergy were understandably wary and reluctant to have their congregants participate in yet another survey study. We thus worked hard to build working relationships in which we contributed to the congregations in some way. We found that once the agreements were secured, the participating churches were quite helpful and welcoming to the research activities (including ethnographic activities in the second year). We had also prepared, pilot tested, and translated into Korean the parent and youth versions of the paper-and-pencil survey.

We had completed the majority of the survey data collection by early fall of 2004. In all, we collected survey data at two Protestant churches, four Catholic churches, one nondenominational church, one community-based service agency in the Koreatown neighborhood in the city of Chicago, and one ESL cohort at a suburban high school.[3] We sought to diversify the pool of Korean American families with respect to their religious denominational affiliations, different geographic sites within Chicagoland (including some locales within the city of Chicago as well as northern, western, and southern suburbs that vary in relative affluence), and immigration history (seeking both established immigrant families with American-born teens and more recently immigrated families with teens). Although it would have been ideal for us to recruit more Korean American survey respondents from non-church-affiliated settings, we were not able to find many secular organizations frequented by Korean American teens and immigrant parents of teens. By and large, the majority of Korean immigrant parents completed the survey in Korean whereas the majority of Korean American teens completed the survey in English. (The only exceptions were the Korean American teens we recruited through the high school ESL program.)

Survey collection at churches typically involved members of the research team making multiple trips to each church as participant-observers to get to know the setting. Nancy sometimes accompanied the graduate researchers to church activities where the parents were present and made presentations or led discussions at church PTA meetings or parent groups. The graduate researchers, almost all of whom were Christians themselves, attended worship services, ate meals after services with parents, and observed church youth retreats and church youth activities (e.g., car washes to raise funds for youth activities). The survey data collection typically was arranged at each site to take place after worship services on Sundays, as it was customary for many families to spend time in fellowship with other congregants in the early afternoon after worship services. We had crafted a short PowerPoint presentation (in Korean and in English) to discuss the premise of the research project, which the graduate students made to the groups of parents or youths who had gathered as volunteer participants. The slide presentation was based largely on the data we had gathered from the University of Illinois campus (described in chapter 1), in which we highlighted preliminary survey findings about the large role that religion and family played in their self-identity, their reports of dissatisfaction with their family communication and family dynamics, and a handful of direct quotations from Korean American college students about what it was like growing up with immigrant Korean parents. It seemed clear that the presentation, having resonated for the listeners, was an effective recruitment tool. The presentation ended with our request for their participation in the survey. The final slide showed the ways in which we envisioned the survey contributing (e.g., to humanize portraits of Korean American families, to correct institutions' and policymakers' misunderstandings about Korean American families, to help schools and colleges better serve Korean American students, to learn from the Korean American case about how other immigrant families adapt to America, to understand the future of Korean

American communities and the next generation). We typically offered a small lunch (*dduk* or *gim bap*) to parents who responded to the survey, and youth were offered ten-dollar gift cards as tokens of appreciation for their participation in the survey. We worked very hard to gather parent and adolescent data from the same families, but this proved to be a fairly challenging proposition because many parents and their teen children did not attend the same church. Some parents' busy work lives also made it difficult for them to stay after worship services to complete the survey.

The Survey Questionnaires and Findings

We collected survey responses from 101 Korean American parents (71 percent of respondents were the mothers) and 205 Korean American (104 male, 101 female) youths. The parents ranged in age from 38 to 54 with a mean age of 45, whereas the youth ranged in age from 13 to 19, with a mean age of 15.7. Tables 2.1 and 2.2 summarize the demographic

TABLE 2.1. Demographic Background of Korean Parents (N = 101)

Parent Age	Mean 45.0 (SD = 3.7), Range 38–54
Parent Sex	
Male	29%
Female	71%
Parent Marital Status	
Married	95%
Separated	1%
Divorced	4%
Year of immigration to the U.S.	Median = 1986 Mode = 1986 Range = 1969 to 2004
Highest education	
Elementary	2%
Middle	3%
High school (technical)	11%
High school (college prep)	10%
Two-year college	16%
Four-year college	46%
Postgraduate	8%
Residence	
Rent	12%
Own	83%
Religious Affiliation	
Protestant	44%
Catholic	56%

TABLE 2.2. Demographic Background of Korean American Youth (N = 205)

Youth Age	Mean 15.7 (SD = 1.4), Range 13–19
Youth Sex	
Male	51%
Female	49%
Parent Marital Status	
Married	86%
Separated	3%
Divorced	4.5%
Widowed	2.5%
Single	4.0%
Place of Birth	
U.S.	69%
Korea	31%
Age at immigration (n = 64)	Mean = 11.0 (SD = 4.2), Range 1–16
Age 1–5	18.8%
Age 6–11	23.4%
Age 12–14	37.5%
Age 15–16	20.3%
Family Residence	
Rent	23%
Own	78%
Religious Affiliation	
Protestant	52%
Catholic	48%
Buddhist	<1%

characteristics of the parents in the survey and the youth in the survey, respectively. The data for the parents represent 83 unique households because 18 couples both took the survey. The data for the youth represent 184 unique households because 20 sibling pairs (and one sibling triad) took the survey.

Table 2.3 shows the main instruments we used in our survey, along with sample items and how findings using these scales can be interpreted.

Teen Survey Data

In the campus study (featured in chapter 1) we had found that Korean American college students reported significantly higher depressive symptoms than did their South Asian American and White American

TABLE 2.3. Overview of Survey Instruments

Name of instrument	Psychological construct	Sample items	Interpretation of the scale
Vancouver Index of Acculturation (VIA) Korean (Ryder et al. 2000)	Identification with Korean culture	"I often participate in my heritage cultural traditions."	Higher numbers indicate higher level of identification
Vancouver Index of Acculturation (VIA) American (Ryder et al. 2000)	Identification with American culture	"I often participate in mainstream American cultural traditions."	Higher numbers indicate higher level of identification
The family AP-GAR (Smilkstein et al. 1982)	Level of satisfaction with family	"I am satisfied that I can turn to my family for help when something is troubling me."	Higher numbers indicate higher satisfaction with family.
McMaster Family Assessment Device (FAD) General Functioning subscale (Miller et al. 1985)	Overall family functioning	"In times of crisis we can turn to each other for support." "We can express feelings to each other."	Higher numbers indicate perception of worse family functioning.
Satisfaction with Life scale (SWLS) (Diener et al. 1985)	Global satisfaction with one's life	"In most ways my life is close to my ideal."	Higher numbers indicate higher life satisfaction.
The Center for Epidemiologic Studies Depression Scale (CES-D) (Radloff 1977)	Frequency of depressive symptoms in the past two weeks	"I was bothered by things that usually don't bother me." "I felt sad."	Higher numbers indicate higher psychological distress

peers. Yet, it was only in the Korean American group that their individual distress level was *not* correlated with perception of family functioning. That is, the more White American and South Asian American college students evaluated their family to be dysfunctional, the more depressive symptoms they reported, whereas Korean American students' individual distress symptoms were not statistically associated with their family functioning scores. We were intrigued by the emerging adults' "disconnect" from their assessment of their immigrant family past and wanted to see if similar patterns would hold for the 205 Korean American teens in Chicagoland. Table 2.4 shows the zero-order correlations among the scores on family functioning and distress/well-being scales in the high school sample.[4]

TABLE 2.4. Correlations among Teens' Report of Family and Individual Distress

	Family APGAR	FAD-General	SWL	CES-D
Family APGAR	—	−.75**	.52**	−.39**
FAD-General		—	−.47**	.41**
SWL			—	−.48**

**Correlation is significant at the 0.01 level.

Here, we see stark differences from the college study: in the Korean American teen data, family functioning and distress/wellness variables were highly correlated with one another. Levels of subjective well-being (as assessed by the Satisfaction with Life Scale) were positively correlated with satisfaction with family functioning (assessed by Family APGAR) and negatively correlated with perception of family dysfunction (assessed by McMaster Family Assessment Device–General) as well as distress (as assessed by the Center for Epidemiologic Study–Depression Scale). Similarly, levels of distress (CES-D scale) were negatively correlated with satisfaction with family functioning and positively correlated with perception of family dysfunction. What we are able to glean from these figures is that, unlike Korean American college students, whose levels of individual wellness/distress were not associated with their sense of family functioning, Korean American high school students' individual wellness/distress was associated with the way they viewed their families.

The parent data shed light on whether immigrant Korean parents' personal well-being or level of distress was associated with the way they perceived their families to be functioning. As shown in table 2.5, the correlation pattern among Korean American teens was also seen for the Korean American parents we surveyed. Like their adolescent children, the immigrant parents' own assessment of their families' functioning was associated with their individual well-being. Taken together, the patterns of correlations among Korean American teens and parents in Chicagoland suggest that individual-level sense of distress and wellness were very much associated with the way they perceive their families. Those teens and parents who felt satisfied with their family (e.g., communications,

TABLE 2.5. Correlations among Parents' Report of Family and Individual Distress

	Family APGAR	FAD-General	SWL	CES-D
Family APGAR	—	−.68**	.51**	−.49**
FAD-General		—	−.28**	.46**
SWL			—	−.53**

**Correlation is significant at the 0.01 level.

support and understanding) were also more likely to feel satisfied with their personal lives and felt less distressed.

Moving from the indirect comparison between our adolescent data from Chicagoland and the campus study, we now turn our attention to the family-level comparison within the Chicagoland families. Having collected parallel survey data from both adolescents and parents, we wanted to see to what extent the data from our Chicagoland Korean American families were consistent with existing psychological literature on Asian American families with adolescents.

Parent-Teen Survey Data

The larger survey sample of 205 adolescents and 101 parents helps us gather a broad sense of the Chicagoland Korean American community in which our ethnographic participants were living and working. To allow our survey data to speak more directly to the prevailing psychological and sociological literature about the putative link between the acculturation gap and distress, we needed to structure our data to carry out analyses that compared parents and adolescents from the same family. To this end, we identified sixty-three families for which the data were available for at least one youth and one parent from the same family.

Table 2.6 shows the mean scores for the Korean parents and youth on family and psychosocial distress variables. The right-most column in table 2.6 displays the paired t-test statistic, which indicates whether the average differences between the parent and the youth scores on these psychological scales were statistically significant. These parent-youth comparison results reveal an interesting pattern. That the adolescents score much higher on the American acculturation scale than

TABLE 2.6. Means and Standard Deviations for Parent and Youth Pairs

	Parent	Youth	*t* statistic
VIA-Korean	6.55 (.92)	6.96 (1.37)	2.27*
VIA-American	4.88 (.86)	6.78 (1.13)	12.07**
Family APGAR	15.15 (2.19)	13.59 (3.57)	3.19*
FAD-General	1.95 (.30)	2.19 (.49)	3.53**
Satisfaction with Life	21.19 (5.92)	20.48 (6.50)	.66
CES-D	10.96 (6.14)	20.75 (11.31)	5.74**

*Paired differences between parent and child scores are statistically significant at p < .05.
**Paired differences between parent and child scores are statistically significant at p < .001.

their immigrant parents is not particularly surprising, as it is consistent with existing literature (Juang and Umaña-Taylor 2012). Somewhat surprising is that the adolescents' scores on the Korean enculturation scale are slightly higher than those of their parents. Thus on these indices of cultural identification, the Korean American adolescents not only appear to be bicultural but also identify with Korean culture even more than their parents do. As we engage with the ethnographic portraits of the immigrant families, we will come to better understand that the immigrant parental generation had, at best, ambivalent feelings about their connections to, and identification with, Korea and Koreanness; after all, the immigrant generation left Korea partly because there had been some personal dissatisfaction with their lives in South Korea. Nonetheless, the statistically significant differences between parents and adolescents on both American acculturation and Korean enculturation scales in our sample allow us to confirm that, at least on these conventional questionnaire-based indices of acculturation, there indeed are the so-called intergenerational acculturation gaps on American acculturation among the Korean American families we surveyed in Chicagoland.

While this pattern of the adolescents identifying with the Korean culture just as strongly as (or, in this case, even more strongly than) the parents may seem counter to the portrayal of an intergenerational culture gap in terms of "Koreanized" parents and "Americanized" children, scholars have recently begun to problematize the acculturation-gap research as too simplistic. For example, Telzer (2011) argued that the acculturation gap should be conceptualized in more specific ways (e.g., do the differences lie in the parent or the child being higher or lower on heritage or host cultural values, language, or behavior?). Costigan and Dokis (2006) also pointed to the often-understated findings that many parents also acculturate fairly quickly to the host culture and that the large parent-child acculturation gap is not inevitable. Waters et al. (2010) had also found that dissonant acculturation (in which parents and children do not have fluency in a common language) occurred only in a small minority of immigrant families.

Our data also allowed us to test for the basic form of the acculturation gap–distress hypothesis. Because there were differences in the scores between parents and adolescents on American and Korean cultural dimensions, we created a "difference score" index by subtracting adolescent scores from parent scores. We then examined whether the difference scores—which we might fashion as a proxy for the degree of distance between parents and adolescents—on American and Korean cultural dimensions might be related to family functioning and individual distress. Table 2.7 displays the correlations between the parent-youth difference scores on Korean and American acculturation scales and individual scores on life satisfaction and depression measures.

As shown in table 2.7, the parents' depressive symptoms (as measured by the CES-D) were not correlated in any statistically meaningful ways

TABLE 2.7. Correlations between Parent and Youth Responses

	VIA-American difference	FAD difference	Parent SWL	Parent CES-D	Youth SWL	Youth CES-D
VIA-Korean difference	.32*	−.14	−.17	.03	.30*	−.08
VIA-American difference	—	.12	−.05	−.03	.23	−.13
FAD difference		—	.00	−.11	−.32**	.45**
Parent SWL			—	−.48**	.05	−.10
Parent CES-D				—	−.10	−.08
Youth SWL					—	−.45**

*Correlation is significant at p < .05.
**Correlation is significant at p < .01.

to the acculturation gap on either dimensions (VIA-Korean difference, VIA-American difference) or on parent-child differences in the way they view family function (FAD difference). However, for the youth, the VIA-Korean difference (i.e., the extent to which the parent and youth differ on identification with Korean culture) was modestly but significantly correlated with the youth's life satisfaction. Also noteworthy is that the intergenerational gap in perceived family functioning (i.e., parents rating the family as more functional than the youth do) were moderately correlated with youth life satisfaction and depressive symptoms, with the greater gap contributing to more negative well-being for youth.

To summarize, the acculturation gap indices in our sample did not appear to be meaningfully associated with parent or adolescent distress for the most part. That is, although family members' survey responses did reveal glimpses of parent-child acculturation gaps and individual distress, by and large they did not conform neatly to the acculturation gap–distress literature. In the family ethnography chapters that follow, we show that the parents and adolescents did talk about what in their family lives was "Korean" or "American," just as the parents who attended the church PTA meeting described earlier readily invoked these terms and ideas as frames of reference for their parenting dilemmas. However, we also learned that these cultural reference points stood for much bigger ideas about race and ethnicity, and what it meant for immigrant racial minorities to navigate the uncertain terrains between their ethnic "Korean" community and the racially stratified "American" society.

The ethnographic chapters will demonstrate the extent to which the meanings and significance of "Korean" and "American" are practical concerns rallied to fashion a healthy Korean American adulthood. As we have seen, acculturation does not make for a particularly meaningful predictor of individual functioning. While comprised of very different data and seemingly talking about very different matters, our quantitative and qualitative data both hint at the reconciliatory work that Korean American teens and parents do to keep their families working. The redemptive narratives that Korean American emerging adults shared with us in the campus study may have their roots in the preceding years when parents and teens were still residing together. The Chicagoland surveys show parents and children less at odds with each other than we might have imagined—and with the acculturation gap not working in the way the literature may have suggested. In the ethnographic chapters, we will show that while there are indeed tensions in all of the families, their fault lines are seldom clear with respect to the Korean versus American contrast. Instead, what we observed were often practical—and sometimes anguished—negotiations between the immigrant parents and their American-raised youth over how to navigate racialized America.

Engaging the Family Ethnography Informants

The final survey data included responses from 205 adolescents and 101 parents. The families who agreed to be a part of the ethnography project came to us through different pathways. At the end of the survey, each respondent was asked to indicate whether she or he would be interested in potentially being contacted with information about other parts of the research project. There were sixty-three families in which at least one adolescent and one parent took the survey. From this list, we identified a subset of families to recruit into the ethnographic component of our study. Because our initial project goals included understanding the process by which parents and adolescents negotiate family hardships (a question that arose from our campus study), we were particularly interested in reaching out to families whose survey responses suggest some form of parental or adolescent distress or parent-child disagreement about how their families were functioning. In addition, we reached out to the parents of families who approached us at church gatherings either after the data collection or at group meetings with the researchers. In some instances, the parents were motivated to seek us out because they had specific concerns about the well-being of their adolescent children, and in other cases the parents approached us to tell us about parenting strategies that they felt were working well for their families. Despite our efforts to identify some families who were experiencing difficulties, we think that the book reveals remarkable instances of resilience and successful negotiation—the very processes that we were able to observe over time. In all, we contacted eleven families to gauge their potential interest in participating in the family ethnography project, and eight families initially agreed to start the project. However, teen participants in two families decided not to continue with the project after an initial introductory meeting with one of the graduate researchers. Although the parents in these two families were eager to continue contact with us, we did not engage these two families in the family ethnography project. By the end of the two-year period, we had gathered initial family ethnography data from six families who allowed us into their lives for sustained data collection, which typically lasted between six and ten months.

Four graduate student researchers (Grace, Hyeyoung, Jin-Heon, and Euna) served as the primary contacts for the six families who became our ethnographic informants, but our ethnographic fieldwork with families was often conducted by teams of researchers, depending on the nature of the encounter or a visit. For example, we first encountered the Chung family in the field when Grace and Hyeyoung visited their Korean church to administer the surveys, and Hyeyoung agreed to be the primary contact for this family. The initial series of phone contacts between Hyeyoung and Mrs. Chung resulted in an invitation for the team to visit the family in its Chicagoland home. Nancy, Grace, Hyeyoung, and Jin-Heon all visited the family, and what was initially envisioned as a brief introductory visit with the family turned into a five-hour dinner in their home. And while Hyeyoung carried out the bulk of the interviews with various members of the family in the first year and acted as a participant-observer of family activities at church, home, music concerts, and the like, Jin-Heon visited the father a number of times at his shop. A team of graduate and undergraduate researchers also hosted the Chung family's visits to our campus (the University of Illinois at Urbana-Champaign) as the older daughter, Esther, considered her college choices. We had a lovely dinner with Mrs. Chung and her son Doug at a restaurant in the Chicago suburbs. And although Esther ultimately chose to attend a university in a neighboring state, Doug enrolled in our university a year later, allowing us to meet with him on many occasions on campus during his undergraduate studies. Our encounters with the other four families followed a similar pattern, with graduate and undergraduate researchers having extensive contacts with each family during the intensive ethnography period between 2004 and 2006, followed by our multiple follow-up contacts with each family in the subsequent years. It is not an overstatement to say that the ethnography data for each family were gathered as a truly collective effort.

During the initial two-year period during which the team was collecting family ethnography data, the research team members wrote fieldnotes as soon after each encounter with any members of the ethnography families as possible and posted the notes on a shared data archive. All members of the research team reviewed and commented on the field documents, making for a robust archive of data and reflection. A typical fieldnote might have four or five researchers commenting on, or asking questions about, the data and others' observations. In some instances, we audiorecorded the ethnographic encounters with the permission of the family, and we transcribed those recordings. Throughout the duration of the two-year period, the project team also met weekly for two hours and culled field research notes on interviews, participant observations, and survey administration in a web-based data archive. After this two-year period of primary data collection, we—with occasional assistance from graduate researchers—continued to gather follow-up data with many of the families through e-mail, phone, and in-person visits. We were unable to maintain contact with one of the six families and were not able to gather any follow-up data. This book, then, features the five families whose stories represent divergent answers to the question of how Korean American parents and teens make their families work. The family ethnographies reveal both the moment-to-moment flashpoints in Korean American immigrant family life that unfolded *and* the narrative, meaning-making work performed by families that spanned the crucial years of transition from adolescence into emerging adulthood.

3

Ben

Parenting for a Racialized America

On one early December evening, Nancy and Jin-Heon visited with the Koh family during Ben's high school senior year. The urgent topic on hand was Ben's college applications, and Mr. and Mrs. Koh eagerly sought Nancy's and Jin-Heon's opinions about the American college admission process. By then, Ben had already been accepted to two out-of-state public universities and was waiting to hear from the University of Illinois at Chicago. However, Mrs. Koh was clearly frustrated with Ben's lack of diligence and ambition and with his high school GPA being too low for admission to the flagship campus of the University of Illinois despite high SAT scores. He had apparently refused to take honors courses and had gotten by in high school spending only about twenty minutes each evening on homework. Mrs. Koh, skeptical of his college application essay, which centered on his volleyball, church, and leadership activities, had Ben show it to a college guidance expert at their church to help improve the essay. Meanwhile, Mr. Koh—the more laid-back of the two parents—was impressed with Ben's essay, as he thought it appealed to the American regard for leadership. To us, this scene crystallizes some of the central parenting struggles for the Kohs—that is, how do you raise a Korean American boy who is interested in sports and is academically unambitious?

* * *

We described earlier how we came to meet Ben Koh's mother at a Korean Catholic church PTA gathering. The parents assembled there were almost entirely immigrants from South Korea whose children were American born. The meeting was well attended, with about fifty Korean American mothers and fathers in the room as well as several clergy members. Nancy spoke in Korean about her own research on

Korean American undergraduates at the University of Illinois, synthe-sizing research findings as well as her own thoughts about how Korean American students can maximize their college educational experience. Following Nancy's forty-five-minute talk, the audience came alive with comments and questions.

Amidst the many active exchanges that ensued, for the three members of our research team assembled there (Nancy, Euna, and Jin-Heon), it was Mrs. Koh's question that most stood out: hers was the most emo-tional and personal, and it was hard hitting and disarmingly frank about race in America. Even among a number of quite personal comments volunteered by the parents in the room, her admissions struck us as somehow more raw. Her story and query were not thinly veiled "hum-blebrag" about children, as had been the case with some of the other parents' remarks. When the research team later reflected on this rather remarkable moment, we all agreed that Mrs. Koh and her family might make for a valuable addition to our ethnographic study. As it turns out, the opportunity came our way because Mrs. Koh had approached Euna—who had introduced herself as a doctoral student in counseling psychology and had answered questions related to mental health and counseling at the meeting—soon after the church meeting with further questions. In this manner, the research relationship with the Koh family emerged easily from this public forum.

What did Mrs. Koh reveal about her eldest son, Ben, at the church parent meeting? She began her comments by stating that she had two children—Gene was in sixth grade and Ben was in eighth grade at the time—and that they had formerly lived in the city of Chicago but had moved to East Creek, a Chicago North Shore suburb known for its out-standing public schools.[1] She added that it had been hard for her boys to make friends following the family's move but that after some time, Ben began bringing home a few "American" friends. Mrs. Koh was troubled to observe that her son seemed to be subservient to these friends, acting as if he felt the need to cater to them. "Instead of just thinking of them as friends, he seemed to think he needed to 'serve' them," was how she put it. Some of this, she surmised, was about the difficulties of needing to fit into an already well-established social circle of youth in East Creek who had known one another since they were youngsters, the difficulty of "squeezing into the middle of strong friendships." However, Mrs. Koh felt frustrated and angry to find her son acting this way and ventured a very racial interpretation of the situation: that Ben "was not psychologically strong enough to think of White American friends as 'real' or 'good' friends" who were his equals. In passing, she also mentioned that the White children in question were Jewish. She told the parent group that she had purposely made efforts to "distance" Ben from those children. Addressing both Nancy and her fellow parents assembled there, she asked, "How can I solve this problem?"

Mrs. Koh would later share with Euna what it was about Ben's behavior that had struck her as subservient. In one instance, she had watched Ben comply when one of his friends had "ordered" him to fetch him a waste paper basket when the boys were hanging out at her house. For Mrs. Koh, that her son would comply in this manner spoke to his—and more largely Korean Americans'—lack of confidence as members of a racial minority interacting with Whites in the United States.

Over the course of our research engagement with Ben's mother that year and in following years, she returned occasionally to the observation she shared that day, but more often she spoke of the general matter of Ben's well-being in the United States. It was above all Ben's psychological well-being that, time and again, most seemed to concern Mrs. Koh. She was enormously worried about his future—anguishing, in particular, over whether he had what it took, constitution-wise, to "make it" in America. Mrs. Koh went so far as to venture a diagnosis that Ben's retiring manner and lack of self-confidence were inextricably tied to what she viewed as ethnic self-loathing (especially prevalent among Asian American boys, according to Mrs. Koh), and that his low ethnic self-regard was born from his experience of racism against immigrants in the United States.

As we came to know the family, we discovered that Mrs. Koh's worries about Ben were hardly an isolated issue. Her angst, as it turned out, touched on her own and her husband's immigration histories as well as her concerns about her husband's temperament. In Ben, Mrs. Koh could not help but see the constellation of personality features that she also saw in her husband and that she believed made their immigrant lives in America so challenging: his passivity, shyness, and even femininity. (Upon meeting Mr. Koh, Jin-Heon also concurred that Mr. Koh did not speak or behave like a typically "macho" Korean man of his age. However, Euna also observed him to be fairly extroverted outside the home. On one dinner outing with Mr. and Mrs. Koh at a seafood restaurant, Mr. Koh even engaged extensively in an English conversation with a friendly waiter.) Yet, Mrs. Koh's reflections make clear that immigration is an intergenerational project and that when parents reflect on the ways in which the United States acts upon their immigrant children, they necessarily think about their own immigrant story and in particular about their own racial experiences. We found that parents' concerns about race were echoed in one form or another across the families we meet in this book. However, Mrs. Koh—at the time of our initial encounter with her family—had most vocally expressed the parental anxiety of Korean American immigrant parents: "Does my family have what it takes to thrive in this country?"

Ben and His Place in the Suburbs

Soon after the PTA meeting at her Korean Catholic church, Mrs. Koh took the initiative to call Euna to ask for help with two issues: Ben's "immaturity in social settings" and her own psychological issues, foremost her anxiety. For a good portion of the initial year that we interacted with Mrs. Koh, Ben's friendship with one particular White friend was foremost on her mind. For example, about five months after the church parent event, Mrs. Koh observed that the same friend seemed to have grown away from Ben. She shared her worries with Euna that *she* might have had something to do with this rupture in her son's friendship, as she noticed that the friend's mother—who had once been quite kind to Ben and often took Ben on outings along with her son—had changed her tone with Mrs. Koh as well. Several times Mrs. Koh wondered aloud to Euna, "Was there anything that I did wrong?" and fretted about her own possible contribution to the dissolution of her son's friendship. She later revealed that the friend in question was also the son of their middle school baseball coach and that Ben had not been selected for the team— another matter that had seemed relevant to the strained friendship of the boys. On another occasion, Mrs. Koh related a story about Ben having gone to a party at his friend's sumptuous home. Only an hour into the party Ben called home and asked to be picked up. She found him on the curb, "not with the host, but with another kid." Something had transpired, she surmised. She said to us, "I plan to ask him about this before he goes to college. I know he won't tell me, but why shouldn't I [ask]? Don't you agree?" What struck us was the poignancy of an immigrant mother fretting in a rather meddling way about every detail of her teen son's social life, as if her ruminations about these teenage interactions would somehow provide a clue as to how to help her son develop a better social repertoire with his "American" peers.

To Mrs. Koh, the family's move from the city of Chicago to suburban East Creek seemed to have contributed to her son's problem. In her thinking, Ben (and to a lesser extent, Ben's younger brother, Gene) seemed dogged by race and a sense of inferiority in the new suburban setting. In (multiracial) Chicago, her boys had been leaders, but in (White and "Jewish") East Creek, both their standing and their confidence had been shaken, and the boys—especially Ben—had come to feel "small." Ben had been a top academic student at his former school in Chicago, and his brother, Gene, had been the "most famous boy in the school!"—by which Mrs. Koh meant that he appeared to be socially well respected and well known. Importantly, in the city Gene had seemed to possess what Ben now desperately lacked: "self-esteem *as a Korean American.*" Chicago, Mrs. Koh reminisced, waxing nostalgic, was where Gene brought *kimchi* fried rice and Korean snacks to school and insisted that his friends try them. But in the suburbs, even Gene had told his mother that East Creek "isn't the sort of place where you take *kimchi* fried rice to school." Yet, at home, Gene was still quite interested in Korean food—a fact clearly relished by Mrs. Koh. In one of the home visits, Euna ended up going to a Korean grocery store with Mrs. Koh and Gene to buy *SunDae* (순대—Korean sausage) and *Jokpal* (족발—steamed pigs' trotters) that Gene was craving, and the three of them shared a hearty Korean meal together. Although Ben did not want to go to the Korean grocery store, tempted by *Jokpal*, he joined Euna and Gene and Mrs. Koh at the dinner table. (Euna recalled that Gene and Euna ate a lot while Ben ate little.)

As for Ben himself, he once told us that he preferred East Creek over Chicago but admitted that he had become quieter with the move. He explained that when he first moved to East Creek, he felt shy being a new kid at school. Although he was no longer new, he "got used to being quiet" at school. Yet, in the initial year of family ethnography in which the various members of our research team (including Euna, Nancy,

Jin-Heon, and Sumie) visited with Ben, he did not strike any of us as socially inept or lacking in self-regard. Although he was not especially talkative and was never the one to initiate conversations with us, including on one occasion when we took him to a lunch in the neighborhood without his parents, he came across as a polite but fairly typical teenage boy who would rather be playing sports with friends than spending time with university researchers. Ben's inclination to retreat to his bedroom on our research visits to the family home did not strike us as especially unusual for a teen boy. And indeed, Euna's interactions with him suggested that, while he was a little slow to warm up to her at first, especially in one-on-one interviews, he became fairly comfortable interacting with her, sometimes even speaking Korean with her.

Upon the first home visit, Euna found Ben and Mr. Koh watching a TV re-broadcast of a professional football game together. Euna made valiant efforts, using her limited knowledge of sports, to start conversation with Ben. At age fourteen, Ben seemed quite interested in various sports (e.g., football, basketball, baseball, and golf), and his two best friends (who were White) also shared interests in the same sports and had similar tastes in movies. When Euna asked him what he would like to be in the future, Ben stated—without hesitation—that he would like to become a baseball player. Euna followed with a question to him about whether his parents knew about his dream career, and Ben told her that his parents were supportive of his dream. Mrs. Koh had also told Euna that watching her sons play baseball games in the summer was one of the most fun and thrilling activities for her. Although Mrs. Koh did not initially understand why American parents are so enthusiastic about their children's sports, by the time we had met the family, Mrs. Koh had become a great fan of various sports herself. (Later on in high school and college, Ben chose volleyball as his primary sport.)

And yet, Mrs. Koh was very sensitive about Ben's social comfort level, including his relation to all things Korean. Interestingly, with us Mrs. Koh always referred to Ben by his American name but to Gene with his Korean name, Min-Jun, perhaps acceding to Ben's self-image as an all-American boy. She wished that Ben "could be like Min-Jun, always proud of being Korean, devouring Korean food and books." She was sensitive to the fact that while Gene was willing to speak to her in Korean in front of his friends, Ben never uttered a word of Korean in the presence of his friends. Ben also confirmed to Euna his lack of interest in making friends with other Korean Americans, insisting that "[t]hey [Korean Americans] are just different, they just don't do the same things" as his friends and he did, referring to sports. Ben communicated this apparent lack of interest in Korean culture, Korean history, or Korean identity to Rich, a Korean American undergraduate researcher who chatted with him after a team of researchers went to see his baseball game.

Mrs. Koh fretted over Ben's vulnerability in the East Creek crowd. Discussing an upcoming Christmas holiday party at the home of one of the boys' non-Korean friends—she too had been invited but was inclined to bow out: "I'd love to go, but after a few rounds of simple conversation, I'll run out of things to say and then I'll just feel awkward"—and she was worried about the gift exchange for the boys. While Ben was quietly preparing gifts for his friends even as she was quite sure that the friends would not reciprocate, her younger son inquired with each of his friends about their intentions about gift exchange and was proceeding accordingly. Mrs. Koh intimated that Gene's approach, in contrast to Ben's, to this social event was the more rational, resilient approach. With her proclamation that "[a]s for us, we are people who do such things" (i.e., prepare gifts for others), Mrs. Koh seemed to be indicating their family's uneasiness in settings like East Creek (or maybe the United States). Again and again, Mrs. Koh returned to the discussion of Ben's passivity and lack of confidence, traits that—not inconsequentially—she thought he shared with his father. Because Mrs. Koh's worries about Ben's well-being and temperament were so central to our initial contacts with her, various research team members paid particular attention in our interactions with Ben to any hints of maladjustment. Uniformly, our individual and collective impressions suggested that Ben was an average teen boy who was into sports, was not especially gregarious or forthcoming, but was able to interact appropriately with his peers and strangers.

Although Mr. Koh did not express his concerns about Ben with nearly the same level of anguish or in as much detail as did Mrs. Koh, he also seemed mindful of Ben's fragile sense of identity. Mr. Koh told us that he often inquired as to the ethnicity of Ben's friends, to which Ben often protested, "Why are you so obsessed with knowing that?" It seems that Mr. Koh took that sort of response as speaking to Ben's own negative feelings about being Korean. He also wondered if Ben's downward turn in Spanish class that semester might also have been a matter of an ethnic complex. Ben had been the top performer in Spanish earlier that semester, but, his father ventured, because he was embarrassed to call attention to himself, be began to purposely answer incorrectly. Jin-Heon, a bit surprised at this interpretation, took pains to confirm that this was indeed how Mr. Koh was thinking about why Ben was not succeeding academically.

We see then that the Kohs were keenly attentive to Ben in a racialized America. While all parents fret about how their children are faring socially ("Do they have friends?" "Are they being bullied?"), Ben's parents, we submit, did so through the lens of race. One time Mrs. Koh described how it was for her *every day* as she waited for Ben at the school bus stop, hoping each day at 4:00 p.m. that he would *not* show up, that instead he might be off hanging out with friends after school. "Every day," she stressed. Building on just this wish that Ben might enjoy an easy social life (as a register of ethnic self-confidence in America), we turn now to the broader context within which the Kohs had come to envision a successful outcome of their immigration.

The parental anguish about Ben's lack of ethnic pride aside, Ben seemed keenly aware of racial stereotypes foisted upon him. As an eighth grader, he described his school as predominantly White, with about ten–fifteen other Korean American students in his grade and a smaller number of Latino and Black students. He told Euna, "It's hard to be an Asian American because they do expect me to be smart." Ben admitted that he is not an A student, and his friends would jokingly comment on this fact, saying, "How come you are not as smart as other [Asian Americans]?" Ben, uncomfortable with having his race called out, had no comeback for his friends other than to mutter, "I don't know." We sensed that, like his parents, Ben attended to these hints of racialization in his suburban context and his place within that complex racial landscape. However, unlike his parents, who were quite bitter about what they saw as racial slights and humiliations, Ben seemed to gravitate nevertheless toward friendship and identification with his White peers.

Immigration Travails

Whereas the first meeting between Euna and the Kohs was easily arranged soon after the church PTA meeting in November, it was not until January that Euna was able to schedule a second visit with Mrs. Koh. Actually, the quiet conversation between Euna and Mrs. Koh had only been accomplished with considerable juggling of schedules. Euna met Mrs. Koh at their new dry cleaning business and gifted her with flowers for the occasion, and Euna could feel that Mrs. Koh was charmed by this gesture. Mr. and Mrs. Koh had quickly settled into a routine in their new business as they shuttled back and forth, over an hour each way with no traffic, between their East Creek home in the North Shore suburb and the shop in a southwest suburb of Chicago. Mr. Koh began his morning at 4:30 a.m., making it to the store no later than 6:30 a.m. for the shop's opening at 7:00 a.m. Mrs. Koh, in turn, joined her husband by 10:00 or 11:00 a.m. after getting the boys off to school. One parent would then leave with time enough to meet the children after school at 4:00 p.m. at their home. The other parent would close the shop sometime after 7:00 p.m. (the official closing time, but not accounting for stragglers) and then head home.

That day, Mrs. Koh reveled in quiet conversation with Euna at the shop—albeit one interrupted time and again by customers—after she had refused her husband's plea that *she* be the one to go back home to meet the children that day: "Please, can you go today, I'm sleepy and I can't do it." Euna was munching on the remaining half of Mr. Koh's Subway sandwich and chatting when Mrs. Koh half-whispered, "I wonder if he's left already?" as if to signal that she had some important matters she wanted to discuss with Euna. The sandwich turned out to be an immigrant detail in its own right. As he was heading out of the shop, Mr. Koh offered it to Euna: "Don't be shy. Things in the U.S. are different than in South Korea. Here it's *even* okay to finish another person's leftovers!" Mr. Koh was one to take note of the many little things that spoke to the details of immigrant life.

It was then, in the lull of a late afternoon conversation, that Mrs. Koh told a small story, one that we relate here because it speaks to Mrs. Koh's palpable sense of the enormous difficulties of immigration. Just as she had wondered about whether her husband's personality was in part forged in the immigrant passage, she acknowledged that Ben was an immigrant baby, one (literally) conceived at the time of their immigrant transition, who might have borne the effects of her own psychological difficulties of the time. Mrs. Koh told Euna that her early immigration years had been quite difficult, and Ben, who was born in the midst of her immigration stress, inevitably conjured that pain for her—hence she wondered too about her own part in forming what she viewed as Ben's less-than-ideal immigrant personality.

We note that Mrs. Koh had an unusual way of beginning the story of those difficult years. In response to Euna's request to talk about how she and Mr. Koh had immigrated to the United States, she began with the declaration, "I love leisure!"—detailing that she enjoyed skiing in particular. She began with this as if to say that after she immigrated, there had been few pleasures. *Once*, though, in her very early immigrant days, Mrs. Koh went to great lengths to have fun. Ben was only three months old when she, her husband, her mother (who had flown in from South Korea to help care for the newborn), and Ben bundled into the car for a ski trip; her own mother had encouraged her to go ahead and take advantage of the fact that she could watch Ben so that the couple could ski. Mrs. Koh was disappointed when her husband announced that he didn't want to ski and would wait in the car. Baby Ben was bawling, "looking up at me as if he recognized my sadness and crying his eyes out." Although fully aware that the cards were stacked against her actually getting on the slopes, she was determined. Leaving the threesome behind—a crying infant, a doting grandmother, and a dozing husband— she headed for the slopes. As she shared this story, Mrs. Koh offered Euna coffee, recalling the many cups of coffee she had made as an office worker in her pre-immigration, younger, carefree years in South Korea.

That it was Ben's tears that made that ski run a portentous moment was fitting. She confided in Jin-Heon when he visited the couple at the dry cleaner that if not for Ben, she would have quickly returned to South Korea:

> It was December 12, 1988, when I arrived in Chicago. Chicago's Korean community was so country bumpkin-ish. I couldn't believe that *this* was the America that had always been so clean and bright in my imagination. It was so cold that all I did was squat by the radiator all day long. I cried and cried, just like I did on the plane and at Kimpo airport [in Seoul].

Mrs. Koh made a point of explaining, however, that hers was *not* a case of blindly following a man. She hinted to Euna that she came from a family without much wealth and longed to live overseas, where she had imagined an easier, more affordable life in which she would not feel pressured to live up to others' expectations:

> It wasn't that I simply believed in my husband and came to the U.S. I figured that if I came, there would at least be something for *me* to do. Of course, it wasn't that the stories of immigrants who visited South Korea had given me so much hope. [Once I arrived in the United States], there was nothing that could relieve my stress, not even a moment's peace of mind to even think about my circumstances. There was nothing to be hopeful about. There was no one, nothing I could lean on. . . . It was only days after I had arrived at my in-laws' home in Chicago that they handed me a box of cabbages and radishes, expecting me to make *kimchi*. But I had never made *kimchi* in my life. And they expected me to serve them delicious food. . . . So that was how I lived for some three or four or maybe six months.

As she recounted this story to Jin-Heon, she looked at her husband, who had been sitting by quietly. As if to put the finishing touches on her immigrant hardship story she said, "It isn't as stressful for more recent immigrants." Mr. Koh, who had been quietly (and perhaps defiantly) listening, eyes closed and arms folded on his chest, spoke up for the first time: "Nowadays the life of immigrants is well known in South Korea so people come knowing the reality [of things]." To this, Mrs. Koh added, "You know, eking out a living like that . . . that's why we couldn't break away from being anything other than laborers. I guess that's the reality that people who come these days have reconciled themselves to." By recalling how her own hopes for immigration had been brighter, she signaled the extent of her disappointment and disillusionment.

Euna later learned in a phone conversation with Mrs. Koh that, after those first few months of suffering, Mrs. Koh had headed home to South Korea, intending to file for divorce. However, she returned to the United States, it turns out, only because she had meanwhile learned that she was pregnant with Ben. That is why—with the memories of the early days of marriage and immigration—she told Euna, that her heart still pounded anxiously when she heard her husband returning from work, recalling how trapped she felt in her early marriage. And these sorts of honest admissions evoked some painful thoughts about Ben: that because of the circumstances surrounding his birth and the bitter memories of her early immigrant days, he had been the much harder child for her to raise. As we learned later, Gene had turned out to have an easy-going temperament, making his way in immigrant American with greater ease. Mrs. Koh admitted to Euna, "Even if they do exactly the same thing, if Min-Jun [Gene] does it I'm OK, but if it's Ben, I lose my temper."

We were somewhat surprised by Mrs. Koh's candor about her feelings toward Ben and Gene, but her hard feelings about Ben were clearly felt within the family dynamic. When alone with Euna, Ben (at age fourteen) admitted of his relationship with his mother that "it's not the best. My mom has a better relationship with my brother, not with me" and said that Gene was "mama's boy." Euna noted that Ben seemed annoyed by (and perhaps a bit envious of) the special bond between his brother and his mother. Yet, Ben also revealed that he felt closer to his mother than to his father and that he preferred not to reveal too many personal things to his parents. And Euna did observe some moments of tender teasing and affection between Mrs. Koh and Ben, especially around their two family dogs.

Hard-Knock Working Lives

The Kohs have not enjoyed easy lives in the United States. Above all, their work lives have never proceeded smoothly. A college graduate in South Korea, Mr. Koh nonetheless began life in the United States as a factory worker. He described himself as a "common laborer for an American factory, a *common* laborer." He continued for twelve years, toiling at a factory that manufactured an electronics part, one that he described as wrapped with delicate copper threads; he said that the work involving this electronics part was notorious in South Korea for being dangerous, but in the United States the work was, he marveled, "unbelievably" safe. Although he began at six dollars an hour, by the time he quit in 2000, his wages were up to eleven dollars an hour.

Next, the Kohs opened a dry cleaning shop in Lakeside Park, a wealthy North Shore suburb. It is common knowledge in immigrant Korean America that owning and operating a small business promises a greater income stream than nonprofessional labor; in her earlier research Nancy had found that Korean American wage laborers were self-conscious about not having ventured into small businesses. Mr. Koh described their first small business venture in Lakeside Park as "a bitter hell," and went on to say that he tried not to think about his time there and about all the money he eventually lost in that venture. Although Mr. Koh did not share the exact circumstances under which he and his wife later lost their dry cleaning store in Lakeside Park, there was a lingering bitterness. "There is really no way to recover, to undo the mess," he said. "I had never dreamed that I would [again] suffer as much as I had in the South Korean military," was how he summarized that suffering in the United States. At the time of the initial period of family ethnography, we sensed that the debt from the initial business failure was still monumental (a figure in the ballpark of a hundred thousand dollars).

The story of the Kohs' business failure in Lakeside Park, which we learned about piecemeal over repeated encounters with Mr. and Mrs. Koh, was—from their perspective—a dark tale of American racism and classism and of the enormous indignities of immigrant service labor. For the Kohs, integral to the story of their racial trials was their insistence that their Lakeside Park clientele had been mostly Jewish and the bane of Mr. Koh's existence. Mrs. Koh summarily referred to the days of the Lakeside Park dry cleaning store as "like living in Sodom and Gomorrah's time," among unrepentant sinners. It was the hypocrisy of their wealthy clients that seemed to have most infuriated them: that the "Jewish" clients brought in Prada suits to be cleaned but were cheap; that they drove Jaguars but nonetheless troubled the Kohs with discount coupons; and so on. In those years, Mr. Koh eventually retreated entirely from the front desk, unable to even face the customers he so disdained. Mr. Koh's most incendiary remarks about Jewish customers always turned back to his own hurt: "We were *so* humiliated by them. They know just how to treat people as inferiors." There were also specific incidents that rankled, such as the time when a "Jewish" customer accused Mr. Koh of having stolen a Rolex watch that the customer had left in the pocket of a garment. "They look down on Koreans," Mrs. Koh offered. She also recalled that as Mr. Koh had written up the customer receipts, he had sworn under his breath (in Korean), "Robbers!"

In recovering from the failure of their Lakeside Park business, the Kohs took over from Mrs. Koh's sister-in-law a dry cleaning store in the southwest suburb—one with, they surmised, greater prospects. It was this southwest suburb's more middle-class Irish American clientele, in stark contrast with the difficulties of working with Lakeside Park elites, that gave them hope. This was the dry cleaning store where Euna and Jin-Heon were invited to spend time with Mr. and Mrs. Koh in the initial year of our ethnography.

When we caught up with the family in 2008 just as Ben was applying to college, their financial situation seemed precarious. By then, the Kohs had lost their second dry cleaning business, this time after having been taken to court for back rent they owed. Theirs was a case of being caught in the subprime mortgage crisis, as they had taken a second mortgage on their East Creek home to take over the business from Mrs. Koh's sister-in-law. With no health insurance, they told us that they "eat well and tell ourselves that we can't get sick." In fact, they had already weathered a medical crisis without health insurance in the past. Mrs. Koh told us that at the time of their second business collapse, she had ended up in the emergency room in a state of near paralysis. The moment she could move, she was determined to walk away, keenly aware of the bill increasing for every second she lay there; a Korean immigrant nurse friend, however, insisted that she needed to rest a bit. The scant three-hour visit to the emergency room resulted in an eight-thousand-dollar bill, one she told us she had just finished paying off.

In 2008, Mr. Koh had just begun driving a school bus as well as working as a limousine driver. It was the promised $750 signing bonus that had prompted Mr. Koh to drive a school bus; the large incentive was offered because few people are willing to drive such a big vehicle. Although Mrs. Koh let us know how little he was making as a school bus driver by asking us to guess "how much a week" ($290), Mr. Koh added that the work is important because there are cases in which parents sue for bus driver negligence. Indeed, their financial straits aside, Mr. Koh did seem proud of his early morning and afternoon shifts.

Indignities of Suburban Living

Our reader will recall that when Mrs. Koh spoke up at the church meeting about Ben being pushed around by a peer, she had described the peer as Jewish. Just as Mr. and Mrs. Koh were convinced that their Lakeside

Park dry cleaning clientele who had so humiliated them were Jewish, they had also perceived their neighborhood of East Creek as also overwhelmingly Jewish. Actual population statistics suggest a sizable but still numerically minority Jewish population in both towns. In fact, when Euna pressed Mrs. Koh privately about the matter, she admitted that Ben's friend in question "might have been Italian." Mrs. Koh herself seemed aware that the extent of her sensitivity to racism was unique in her circle. She recounted once sharing her thoughts about racism with another Korean immigrant who simply said to her, "What do you expect, that's how things are"—as if to imply, "Why the big deal?" Yet, with both Nancy and Sumie being Jewish (although we doubted that the Kohs were aware of this fact), the harsh tone and content of Mr. and Mrs. Koh's utterances in the fieldnotes and interview transcripts were admittedly jarring; we did, however, appreciate that Mr. and Mrs. Koh's apparent antisemitism was inextricably caught up in the indignities of working in the service labor sector and living in upper-middle-class suburbs.

When we began our family ethnography, it was immediately apparent to us that the Kohs' house was one of the smallest and least distinguished houses in the neighborhood. This, of course, is not an uncommon pattern in which Korean immigrants make their way to wealthier suburbs that are known for their better schools and reside in the least expensive housing options in those areas. The inside of the Koh home was equally undistinguished but functional, with no apparent effort at home decor. In this way, the Koh family's living situation was most similar to that of the Hyuns, another family we feature in this book, who were renting a two-bedroom apartment in a large complex of apartments managed by a Korean American company that was located in the same school district.

Mrs. Koh described her tenuous relationship with the predominantly White and (she thought) Jewish neighborhood. When she moved into her East Creek home three and a half years before we met the family, she went to pains to visit and deliver ice cream to her new neighbors, a gesture that she thought would work similarly in both South Korea and the United States. One neighbor woman refused to come to the door, ostensibly because the neighbor was "busy with the children." Mrs. Koh, however, took this as a personal affront. And although Ben and Gene eventually became friendly with the children from that house, Mrs. Koh told us that the parents continued to refuse to greet her on the street.

She took a moment to share a detail with Euna that revealed the burden of her own defenses—and intermittent seething—as she managed her daily life in the suburbs: "When I see those kids, I mutter 'those brats' [저 새끼들—*saekki*]." She also shared stories of overt racism such as another Korean American neighbor's front door being egged and her own front door having had ice cream hurled at it (an incident that she reported to the police, who agreed that it had been a racially motivated incident).

A persistent theme across our meetings with the Kohs was their class standing, not only in relation to an imagined (Jewish) American upper-middle class but also in relation to their sense of mainstream Korean America. At her first visit to the family home, Euna found the parents—but not the sons—eating a certain kind of sausage (순대—*SunDae*), a somewhat low-brow Korean fare. Mrs. Koh asked her, "Are you OK eating *this* sort of food?" assuming that Euna would not be comfortable with this humble fare. Euna took note that her rapport with the parents seemed to get off to a nice start when she happily gobbled up the sausage on her plate. (And in fact, Mr. and Mrs. Koh took such a liking to Euna that, at one point, they even offered to give her a wedding dress that was never claimed by a customer at their dry cleaning shop—despite Euna having no immediate plans to wed at the time of this ethnography.)

The move from urban Chicago to suburban East Creek had been a challenging one for the family, as it had also landed the family in Korean American company beyond their comfort zone. When describing her reticence to show up at the boys' school, she mentioned that her boys had called attention to their parents' English as markedly inferior to that of other Korean American parents at this suburban school. For Mr. Koh, above all it was their new suburban Korean Catholic church that was off-putting. He was explicit: the fellow Korean parish members seemed to somehow signal to the newcomers from the city that the old-timers were so much better for having suburbanized earlier. For this reason, Mr. Koh had not been a regular attendee at the church, and Mrs. Koh had mentioned that people at the church had been wagering on when *he* would finally show up at church (Mrs. Koh and the boys began attending first)—a year was the bet. Not surprisingly, he was offended, but Mrs. Koh interjected, "It's entirely my fault, I should have never told you" about the bet. Later Mr. Koh told Euna that it was only for "family peace" that he attended the church at all.

In fact, on the evening of Euna's first family visit with the Kohs (which started in the midafternoon), Mrs. Koh was hosting a small church gathering at their home (many Korean immigrant churches are organized this way) with eight guests. When it was almost his turn to read from the Bible, Mr. Koh left the table abruptly, at which point the group began to question whether he left in protest or simply to fetch his glasses. They gave up on pestering him about the Bible passage but later asked him to join them in singing a hymn until he finally requested plainly that they leave him alone. Mrs. Koh described Ben's similarly uneasy relationship with his peers at the church as part and parcel of her husband's ambivalence about the Korean American community. Against these class and religious tensions within suburban Korean America, and in spite of the Kohs' professed troubles with their "Jewish" neighbors and clientele, the Koh family seemed eager to find their place within White America.

Almost a year after we had begun our ethnographic encounters with the Kohs, we learned that Ben was dating a White girl, and we were a bit surprised that neither parent seemed particularly concerned. Mr. Koh echoed other Korean immigrant parents in this study with his thoughts about more socially competent (White) "American" children. Mrs. Koh, for her part, was proud that Ben and his brother were playing baseball in East Creek. She underscored her point: "There are six hundred kids playing baseball in East Creek, and Ben and his brother are the *only* Korean kids!" Mr. Koh spoke of his observations this way: "While American adolescents are innocent and pure, Korean adolescents size one another up and are overly indulged."

As we put the finishing touches on this book, the Kohs were still in the same house in East Creek. But even four years earlier, Mr. and Mrs. Koh had shared with us that they thought of their days in that home as numbered, and they imagined moving to a smaller apartment. In fact, at one visit we found a "for sale" sign, half exposed, leaning against the house, and we could not help but notice a broken window. We learned from the Kohs that at the time, the house was worth less than the combined mortgages of the house and their business and that they had been considering a short sale rather than face a foreclosure. By placing themselves in a service industry within a prosperous community and locating their home at the lower end of an affluent suburb, the Kohs had come face to face with particular American racial and class realities, ones that had profoundly colored their immigrant lives.

Like Father, like Son

On many occasions when she met alone with one of our researchers, Mrs. Koh elaborated on her thoughts that her husband was ill suited to the challenges of immigrant life. Once Mrs. Koh recalled a humorous indication of her husband's underwhelming persona: as a young woman in Korea, even after becoming engaged to Mr. Koh (who was already in the United States at the time), she had forgotten about her engagement and mindlessly consented to be introduced via a matchmaker to other eligible bachelors. To Mrs. Koh, Ben's problems were in part those of his father, although it was not entirely clear whether she meant to blame genetic disposition or an intergenerational immigrant transmission. She harped that Mr. Koh was "far too detail oriented" generally, and embarrassingly so about domestic matters, such as fretting over what size can of sweet potatoes to buy or doting on the children by bringing them snacks.

For his part, as if to personify his wife's often feminized depictions of him, Mr. Koh agreed that he was inclined to sit by quietly as his wife ranted about one thing or another—in much the way that he remembers his mother sitting by quietly as own his father wielded his authority. He told Jin-Heon (when they met alone) that his wife had once accused him of being the sort of person who "needs nothing other than himself, *kimchi*, newspapers, and a telephone." He admitted that she had him pegged accurately and that, in fact, he had lived without making even a single friend in the United States. Although he imagined that with the right person he could nurture a friendship, he told Jin-Heon that such had not been the luxury of his immigrant life.

Late in our ethnography, after the Kohs had already weathered two successive business failures, Mrs. Koh told us that their relationship had fared much better after they stopped co-running the business. Working together, they "fought all day long," was how Mrs. Koh recalled it. Nancy and Jin-Heon could not help but laugh at some of her recollections of Mr. Koh's shockingly nonchalant work ethic. Although derisive, the stories seemed also a tad endearing—a fine line that many of Mrs. Koh's accounts of her husband seemed to straddle. One was about Mr. Koh's delivery of an expensive tuxedo to a customer's home: too "lazy" to wait for someone to arrive home, he hung the tuxedo on the railing of the family's back porch. When the customer later reported that the tuxedo was not where it was reportedly left, Mr. Koh went back to the home to find that it had blown off into the woods, and he had to dry clean it all over again. Even in her many-years-later account, Mrs. Koh was incredulous: "How was it that he had come to think that one could make money without really working?"

Mrs. Koh's "diagnosis" of Ben's problem was that like his father, he was neither social nor ambitious enough to thrive in America. Furthermore, she hypothesized that these characteristics were hatched from a combination of immigrant suffering, the ravages of American racism, and the indignities of class with the move to the wealthy suburb where Ben did not quite fit in. For Mrs. Koh, then, the most important thing was to fortify Ben's emotional and psychological health so as to ready him for the challenges of adult American life as a racial minority. To her, this meant that she had to abandon the "Korean" focus on educational success or on preserving Korean cultural identity and to focus on his general well-being. And by the time we caught up with the Kohs in 2008, some four years after our initial encounter, both parents had become quite confident in what they came to think of as their somewhat maverick ("American") approach to raising their sons.

Ben's parents, in a word, had prioritized his social development over academics. Mrs. Koh once reported with satisfaction that Ben's priorities had shifted from middle school to high school, with friends and fun taking the upper hand. "I let him have fun, rather than nagging him about his academic performance." "Friends and fun mean," she added, "that he isn't being left out." However, she continued that she did take note of the fact that he was still timid with girls, even "passive," while the others of his peer group seemed to be actively approaching them. Ben also confirmed to us that his parents did not put much pressure on him to do well in school. When a group of us (Nancy, Jin-Heon, and Sumie) chatted with Ben over lunch after he had completed his freshman year in high school, he admitted that his classes were easy but not especially interesting and that he only spent about an hour each day on homework. (Although one hour each day greatly exceeded Mrs. Koh's estimate that he only spent twenty minutes each day on homework, this still struck us as a fairly light load. Valley Creek East High School, which Ben attended, is considered to be a top-rate public high school with over a 90 percent college-going rate. Mrs. Koh later told us that Ben was not taking any honors or advanced classes.)

Of course, none of this is to say that Ben's parents were entirely uninterested in his schooling. Even when it came to schooling and the matter of how they might prod his progress, it was his self-esteem that they decided to safeguard above all. Here they join the American mainstream (as well as Korean American educators featured in ethnic media) in the notion that self-esteem is critical to academic performance in both the short and the long run. For her part, Mrs. Koh asserted that the American context, and Ben himself, demanded this sort of parenting. So, for example, she said that even when faced with bad test results and in an instant when "I was about to explode with anger, I just said 'Good job!'" Ben, she explained, had complained that "Korean parents expect too much of their kids, always wanting them to get all As, while Americans don't." Mrs. Koh laughed when she told us that as a high school student, Ben dreamed first of becoming a baseball or football player, with becoming a lawyer as a back-up plan. Similarly, with Euna, Mrs. Koh cracked up over the fact that Gene as a middle schooler was dreaming of working in the pet section at a local grocery chain. When the laughter subsided, she came to the real punch line: "Studying isn't something a person does forever, but isn't personality what's really important?" The laughter in these instances was a reaction to how different things were in the United States and Korea: both Euna and Mrs. Koh knew it would be unthinkable in South Korea to imagine people celebrating anything but academically based achievement and professional accomplishment.

As for Mr. Koh, he described a policy of total silence on the matter of Ben: even if he was entirely unsatisfied with what was going on, he had taken to saying nothing. Mr. Koh described Ben as having set clear limits on what he was willing to do academically: "Don't push me, a C is fine, and I'm not going to go to any after-school classes," he had said, anticipating what his father might suggest. While Mr. Koh was not entirely at peace with the idea of letting a C slide by, he confided to us that "the American style of parenting [i.e., focusing on the whole child rather than only on academic performance] is more rational and worthy than the Korean one." Ben also let us know that he was aware of being raised differently from his Korean American peers. He told us that his parents were mindful of the social challenges brought on by the move from the city to the suburbs and that his parents had let up on caring so much about his academic performance. All they would say, he reported, was, "Do better next time and work harder!" to which he said he typically answered, "I'll work harder next time." Immigration success for Ben's parents, then, was indexed by their sons' mental well-being and self-confidence.

When we met the family toward the end of Ben's final year at high school, Mrs. Koh was reconciled to the fact that Ben would not, after all, pursue what had been a shared dream of attending the University of Illinois' flagship campus downstate (where we were on the faculty at the time). In fact, just the week before our meeting, Ben had received the news of his rejection from Illinois. She felt that Ben himself was suffering a bit as he reconciled with the fact that many of his school friends were heading there. Ben's mother seemed resigned: after all, despite her coaxing, Ben had refused to take an SAT prep course or to raise his GPA by taking honors classes. (That he had tested pretty well on the SAT without studying only underscored for her his laziness.) She mused about her everyday domestic landscape: she stands at the sink washing the dishes; she glances to the right and one of her sons is goofing off on the computer (if it is Ben he lets her see it; if it is Gene he goes to the trouble to hide it); and she looks to the left and the other one is watching TV.

As Mrs. Koh told us about Ben's rejection from his top college choice, we could sense a mild sense of despondency—that all the immigrant indignities they had suffered had only resulted in this less than ideal outcome—even as at other moments it was clear that she had prided herself on her family's perhaps more enlightened approach to immigrant pressures. Mrs. Koh admitted that while she thought of herself as different, she still harbored some of the "typical Korean" desires for her children: academic success, first chair violin in an orchestra, and the like. At one point, she even shared a far-fetched idea of sending her boys to Seoul National University to study dentistry, as she had heard that some of the top Korean universities were admitting students from overseas to study exclusively in English. (After speaking with Jin-Heon and Nancy and realizing how far-fetched this scheme was, Mrs. Koh did not pursue this idea.) Her irritation at Ben, who seemed entirely unambitious in her eyes, had apparently festered throughout his high school years to the extent that by the time Ben was in his senior year of high school, she spoke of being ready for Ben to go away to college "because I can't stand even looking at him" and being reminded of all her struggles to get Ben to apply himself academically.

Returning, one final time, to the incident that Mrs. Koh had raised at the church PTA event, Mrs. Koh told us some years later that a number of parents present at the church event that day had phoned her in the aftermath of her public comments. One of the parents and a friend suggested that perhaps she had misinterpreted Ben's behavior. That friend had offered that perhaps Ben's apparent subservience was no more than his being nice, just as Mrs. Koh was also nice, the friend continued. Mrs. Koh then began to observe *herself*, noticing that indeed she *was* kind to people and became increasingly convinced that this was probably exactly what had been at work with Ben. It is unlikely, given the tenor of the many talks with Mrs. Koh over the years that we had known her, that she had grown entirely unconcerned about matters of Ben's personality and self-esteem. However, this exchange offers a window into the considerable psychic toll exacted on immigrant parents. Mrs. Koh was nothing short of an ethnographer herself, observing Ben and wrestling with frames of analysis as she both took stock of the situation and in turn fashioned a parenting response for her American-born teen against a racial landscape colored by her immigrant experience. It is this entire process, one replete with observation, calculation, and self-conscious strategy, that we dub here "parenting for a racialized America."

In the process of raising her two American-born sons in an affluent suburb, Mrs. Koh also created a place for herself in the community. When Jin-Heon and Nancy visited the family in the waning days of Ben's high school career, Mrs. Koh joined late because she had been called in to Ben's school to discuss the possibility of forming a Korean PTA—by then 16 percent of the students at her sons' high school were Korean. Mrs. Koh had meant to decline; she didn't want the "headache" of it, and she figured that the school's request for her to get involved may have come because she was one of the most frequent users of the school's translation services. That Mrs. Koh had perhaps emerged as a particularly vocal parent—recalling as we did our first encounter with her—did not, of course, surprise us. She also divulged that with Ben's relatively active participation in the school sports teams, she had become more active volunteering at school (e.g., working the concessions at games, etc.) than most of her co-ethnic peers. And when it came down to it, she was convinced of the need for a Korean PTA to address Korean teens' lack of self-confidence, their emotional issues, and their need for academic support. She laughed recalling that at the first organizational meeting, it was only the academic support needs that piqued the interest of the Korean immigrant parents gathered there ("their eyes lit up").

Jin-Heon and Nancy were more than surprised when Mrs. Koh brought up the example of Seung-Hui Cho (of the Virginia Tech campus mass killing, which by then had occurred over a year and a half earlier) to give steam to the more emotional issues of Korean American boys such as social introversion, pent-up feelings, and the like. Evidently, to all of this, the school counselor had added depression. We were a bit speechless that Mrs. Koh drew an analogy between rank-and-file Korean American high schoolers and mass murderer Cho (the very equation that even the U.S. media had, for the most part, cautiously avoided). Perhaps what surprised us most, and perhaps was part and parcel of Mrs. Koh's willingness to take on the Korean PTA, were her accounts of Gene. Four years after our initial encounter with the family, Mrs. Koh had registered changes in Gene that dissolved her earlier sense of him as the easy child whom she did not have to worry about in the immigrant landscape. Gene had, she said, recently become "timid" (*sosim*). She had been particularly surprised—recalling a similar incident with Ben—that fairly recently, Gene had called her from a party wanting to be picked up early because kids at the party "weren't playing with me." Mrs. Koh in very plain terms let us know that she took this to mean that Gene was beginning to realize his racial difference. Nancy then asked Mr. Koh if he agreed with his wife's assessment, and he obliquely indicated that he was not of the same mind. The boys' social comfort was, after all, Mrs. Koh's obsession but not Mr. Koh's.

Coda: The Sports Strategy Pays Off

In our very final meeting with the Kohs on a pleasant late summer evening, we were impressed by Mrs. Koh's answer to our query about her sons' racial resilience at that time. Even as the litany of past racist incidents rolled off her tongue with ease, she told us that she hoped these matters were easier for her boys at this point. In her moments of reflection, she remarked about her own personal transformation. In fact, Mrs. Koh now wondered how much of what she had perceived earlier as Ben's constitutional timidity was due to her own worries. She told us a story about visiting the Holy Hill National Shrine of Mary in Wisconsin (a Catholic site) twice, once when the boys were little and then again more recently with now college-aged sons. There are steep steps at the Holy Hill that those making the pilgrimage must descend. She had remembered that Ben as a child had not been able to walk down the steep steps out of fear. Now as an adult Ben was able to walk down. She interpreted this as a sign of his greater confidence and maturity. We cannot help but note that her worries about Ben's confidence were intimately tied up with her worries about his masculinity and racial comfort level.

Our final meeting ended on a happy note, as Mr. and Mrs. Koh shared the latest news about the boys. They were both studying at the University of Illinois at Chicago in "practical" majors (accounting) and playing on the volleyball team. Mr. and Mrs. Koh's parenting strategy, which had focused on building the boys' confidence and a sense of belonging through sports participation, had apparently paid off. Mrs. Koh proudly noted that Ben already had a job lined up at a prestigious accounting firm, and that this job had in fact materialized because of his chance encounter in an elevator at his summer internship with a former volleyball teammate who had a connection at the firm. With the boys now on a seemingly smooth pathway toward successful adulthood, Mr. and Mrs. Koh both looked youthful and content about their lot in life as immigrant parents and with the choices they had made.

It would be easy, at a glance, to see the Koh family's "sports strategy" as an assimilationist strategy, but we know that the story is much more complex and subtle. The parents were keenly aware of racism (partly born of their own sense of having been discriminated against), and they had reasoned that their Korean American boys would need confidence to navigate the racial landscape. Building social networks through sports was a means to develop this confidence. Whether the boys remained culturally Korean was not the issue at hand, but their confident racial identities as Korean American males were at the heart of the project.

racism

seems so far that racism = social marginalization or unrealized multiculturalism

4

Doug and Esther

An Exit Strategy

What struck us about the Chung family from the start was the clarity of their immigrant vision and the purposeful, strategic ways in which the parents sculpted their family life accordingly. Of all the parents we encountered, Mr. Chung articulated—and in many ways his family appeared to be achieving—the American dream. Like the Kohs, Mr. and Mrs. Chung were keenly aware of racism, and their parenting strategy was born out of their desire to make it easier for their children to navigate the racialized landscape. The Chung family, however, had higher income on account of the mother's profession, as well as seemingly fewer worries about their children's psychological constitutions. Their parenting strategy, then, was to create a social environment for the family that would promise social comfort with the White mainstream culture. The parents' own class striving struck a very White American chord. Although they belonged to a Korean American church, the parents had themselves wanted to acculturate and become "American." As we will see, the parents referred repeatedly to their ability to interact with non-Koreans. Contrary to the acculturation gap–distress literature that would have immigrant parents holding firm on their Koreanness and the U.S.-born children insisting on their Americanness, both the parents and the children in this family seemed to embrace their Americanness and showed less apparent concern about being culturally Korean. However, despite considerable effort on the part of Mr. and Mrs. Chung to make their children's race a nonissue, both children paved a pathway through college and emerging adulthood in ways that reflected considerable awareness of their racial status.

The family of four, with two older teens at the time of our initial meeting (Esther was seventeen, Doug was sixteen), lived in a spacious, artfully decorated home in a quiet and well-manicured suburban neighborhood far north of Chicago, blocks from the shores of Lake Michigan. When the children were thirteen and fourteen, the parents made a strategic move from Valley Vista to the predominantly White town of Tall Grove. (Valley Vista is an affluent suburb populated with many Korean American families, including the Park family. Valley Vista is also adjacent to East Creek, another affluent suburb, where the Koh family lived.) The move was conceived and orchestrated by the father as *the* way for the family to "make it" in a racialized America, and the family members worked not only to echo but to actualize the father's vision. And yet, just weeks into our family ethnography, we began to see that family consensus can be much more fragile or fleeting than meets the eye. And even as members of the family narrated their consensual family story, each story revealed small contradictions between family ideals and lived realities. Over the years, we were able to observe how easily the family's consensus was disrupted when their teens began to question the goals and assumptions of what we dub the Chung "family project" of exiting the Korean ethnic bubble and becoming American.

Particularly noteworthy for the Chung family was that parents and teens alike articulated a consensual parenting strategy. The four family members described to us unified goals and a shared understanding of the means by which to realize these goals. It struck us that the Chungs seemed to embrace a self-conscious assimilationist strategy, one that has been well documented in the scholarly literature.[1] Interestingly, this family's American dream—which on the surface mirrors the familiar climb of immigrant mobility through education—was narrated through the parents' sense of themselves as an atypical Korean American family uninterested in, and perhaps even a bit critical of, other Korean American families who centered their lives around ethnic trappings (the Korean "ethnic enclave mentality"). For example, the parents took special pride in the family's intellectualism and cosmopolitanism. And even though Mr. Chung worked as a small entrepreneur, owning a video rental shop in a scruffy town bordering the city of Chicago, he prided himself on playing classical music and opera as the background music in his shop. Over the course of the family ethnography, both teens were eventually admitted to and enrolled in two prestigious Big Ten universities, such that the parenting strategy appeared to have paid off. Ironically, it was at these universities—icons of the family's upward mobility—where the Chung children's lives began to diverge from the scripts of the family project.

The Family Project: The "American Dream"

The big move in question, from Valley Vista to Tall Grove, was tied up in ideas of cultural assimilation. The parents made a realistic calculation that their children would grow up to become Americans and that there was little reason for the family to cling to "Korea this, Korea that." So, they elaborated, they were not the sort of Korean American family that subscribed to Korean-language newspapers, watched only Korean dramas on TV, listened only to Korean music, belonged to a Korean American mega-church, worked in the Korean ethnic economy, and so on. The parents took pride in the fact that the mother (as an intensive care unit nurse) and the father both worked outside of the ethnic sector "servicing Americans." The parents felt that their working with "Americans" made them more open-minded and cosmopolitan than other Korean Americans who worked primarily in the ethnic sector. With the move to a northern county, their children would grow up in a largely White neighborhood and attend largely White schools, experiences that would ready them to navigate their way through White society. The White school, the parents calculated, would be the ideal site for the children to gain the necessary social skills and the motivation to pursue prestigious and high-paying occupations (namely, medicine or pharmacy) in their upward occupational trajectory. Their children, they hoped, would not be handicapped by the language barrier that had made for the humiliating racial discrimination that the parents, especially the mother, had faced.

So the parents left Cook County (where the large majority of Koreans in Chicagoland live) and moved to an overwhelmingly White school district across the county line. The student body at the high school that Esther and Doug attended, according to the data provided by the school on their website, was 98 percent White at the time of our ethnography. And while the church they had joined after the move was still an ethnic Korean church, it was importantly *not* a Korean mega-church with thousands of members and the "typical" ostentatious line-up of luxury cars crowding the church parking lot on Sundays. And indeed, we observed in our several ethnographic visits to the church that it was a smaller Korean church with an African American youth pastor and rather ordinary cars packing the parking lot.

The family moved into a three-thousand-square-foot house in a fairly new subdivision near the lakefront. The parents were proud of their daily hour-long walks in the neighborhood, friendly neighbors, and a backyard garden where they grew flowers and vegetables. Upon our visit, the research team saw that the home was immaculate and carefully decorated with many paintings, beautiful family photos, decorative plates, and other objects; the home decor struck us as reminiscent of a glossy magazine image of a gracious American home. Interestingly, it was Mr. Chung who had lovingly collected the decorative art objects that were displayed throughout the home, most fussily lining the tops of the kitchen shelves; Esther let us know that she found the careful home decor somewhat embarrassing and that her father had in fact collected many of the objects at garage sales. Although the parents described the move as foremost about "White" environs for their children, there was no question that they were enjoying some tangible trappings of success. With the large house (which they may not have been able to afford in more expensive Valley Vista) near the lakefront, the parents were also realizing their own immigrant dream.

Mrs. Chung's Story

Mrs. Chung's narration of her family origin in Korea is marked by a sense of her family's exceptionalism and cosmopolitanism. Remarkably, her father had studied abroad at Kyoto University in Japan (one of the most prestigious universities in Japan) in his youth in the 1920s. Under the threat of communism, Mrs. Chung's parents left what would eventually become North Korea and resettled as refugees in a small rural village in South Korea, where they eked out a living as poor tenant farmers. As she told the story of their harrowing escape southward, Mrs. Chung emphasized the special treatment that her parents received along their journey because they were recognized as well-educated intellectuals, "head and shoulders above 'typical' Korean families." Despite the economic hardships, Mrs. Chung's parents managed to instill intellectual values in their children, and Mrs. Chung herself was an outstanding student. Mrs. Chung's distinction, her excellence, and her ambition enabled her to escape the crumbling agrarian economy of her rural hometown and enter a nursing school, as did so many other poor but smart girls from South Korea at the time. One of her older sisters had also become a nurse and had immigrated to Germany, and Mrs. Chung chose nursing with immigration in mind. However, Mrs. Chung also indicated that her drive to excel destined her to some frustrations in her early career. She found the nursing education in South Korea to be a disappointment; it was not the intellectual experience she had sought but instead was filled with rote memorization of English-language nursing texts. Likewise, her early nursing job in Korea was unsatisfying as she was placed in custodial servile positions rather than in jobs in which she could develop professionally. It was after several frustrating years that Mrs. Chung decided, in 1980, to immigrate to the United States along with her parents, to pursue a more fulfilling career in nursing.

By the time our team met the family, Mrs. Chung had achieved a high level of professional status in her career as a highly skilled nurse with a specialization in neurological and cardiac ICU care at a prestigious hospital in Chicago. The road to her professional achievement was filled with humiliation and indignity, much of which she considered to be related to her lack of English fluency. Determined to master the new language, to move up in her career, and to find a secure economic foothold in America, she and her husband worked around the clock as new immigrants with their American-born children. On various occasions, Mrs. Chung commented to our research team members about how her generation of immigrant Koreans (including herself) had made many sacrifices for their children and that it would be well worth the effort if their children could become well established. In a particularly poignant episode during this period in her life, she recalled that she used to try to read bedtime stories to her young children—as she had imagined a "good parent" should—but that she was so physically exhausted that all she could muster was a cursory read of the beginning and the end of children's books, skipping the middle. Although this was a story about parenting that was by then many years in the past, it was clearly painful for her to recall the inevitably half-baked way in which she had attempted this parenting ideal.

Underlying Mrs. Chung's drive to improve her English, and for her children to master the language, was the vivid memory of her early

years in the United States. She told Hyeyoung that it was "so very difficult in the beginning." First were the problems of communication: "not
being able to make yourself understood . . . what should I call it, alien-
ation? And because I couldn't communicate, I didn't have any friends
either." She painted an earlier, and still lingering, image of herself as
plagued by a chronic and pervasive sense of paranoia. She struggled to
understand what others were saying but in turn was met with humiliating treatment ("They say things like, 'I need to speak someone who can
speak English' [in English]. . . . They say that right in your face. Both
patients and doctors! I was completely ignored and 'discriminated' [in
English] against." She recalled her preoccupation with the fear that others at her workplace were talking, laughing, and complaining about her.

Language continued to be a salient dimension of her life, although
less so in her work life as she rose in her professional ranks and more in
her personal life. At our initial meeting, she mournfully confided that
she could not "talk" to her children about anything meaningful, that the
only thing she and Doug talked about was baseball, which they watched
together on TV, and that she was unable to give Esther the advice she
would like to give as a mother. And soon after Mrs. Chung had revealed
this to us, we would hear from Esther and Doug that they too felt they
could not communicate easily with their parents—were unable to talk
about anything "deep." At one point the children had attended an extracurricular Korean-language school sponsored by their church for a few
years, but they did not want to continue and the parents did not insist.
(Over time, however, the depth of communication between Doug and
his mother appeared to evolve. When we spoke with Doug as a college
student, he told us that in the years following our initial encounter with
the family, he and his mother would come to talk about many things, at
great length, besides baseball.)

While firm in her sense that she and her husband had raised their
children to be "American," Mrs. Chung quietly conceded that even
if their children were not linguistic minorities, they were still racial
minorities. Nonetheless, given her own bitter memories of language-
related discrimination, she was confident that at least her children's
English fluency would protect them from overt discrimination. She
added that in the medical field, prejudice around one's nationality or
ethnicity matters far less than one's ability (granted, one must also be

fluent in English). She felt that racial minorities could make it in the United States if they chose professional careers that rely on "knowledge and skill."[2] (Ironically, Mrs. Chung, having achieved a high level of specialization in her nursing profession, expressed her shock at the "working-class attitude" of American nurses who expressed little ambition for their children.) Although she was explicit that she did not want to force her children into the medical professions, she was keenly aware that her children—especially her daughter—felt the pressure anyway. She said, "[Esther] says she feels that from us. To 'compensate' [English] for our hardship, she wants to give us happiness." She let on that her husband was much more singular in his belief that medical professions were the best path for his children and that he chided Esther for her interests in literature and Doug for his in teaching.

In reflecting on her life as an immigrant who had spent roughly half of her life in Korea and half in the United States, Mrs. Chung expressed that in her heart, she felt a sense of comfort whenever she returned to South Korea for a visit. However, she also admitted that she felt at sea in South Korea, surrounded by an unfamiliar and high-tech modern country. At the time of ethnography, it had already been some ten years since she had visited South Korea, and we sensed that she thought of herself as a country bumpkin in cosmopolitan Seoul.

The Chungs' assimilation strategy aside, our conversations with family members over the years revealed shifts in the conversations about being Korean in America between Mrs. Chung and the children. For example, Doug told Nancy and Sumie that he used to not like his mother telling and retelling the same story of his grandfather "throwing some guy off the cliff" during his harrowing trip out of North Korea. However, as Doug grew older, he came to see this as an interesting part of his family's legacy. Doug surmised that although his parents had always stressed the importance of becoming established in this country, his mother was proud of her Korean heritage. Doug recalled his mother telling him to always remember that he had a bit of Korea in him. We understand that Mrs. Chung had strived to achieve a delicate balance in her parenting strategy of supporting her children's positive cultural identity as Korean without acceding to the ethnic-enclave mentality of a Korean American community.

Mr. Chung's Story

Mr. Chung immigrated to the United States in 1984 through his family. The youngest of the six children, one of his older sisters, had first immigrated as a nurse and was accompanied by Mr. Chung's mother, who became the primary caretaker for the sister's children. Mr. Chung had aspired to immigrate to the United States and had worked hard to learn English while he was still in Korea. He recalled a particularly poignant memory of visiting his White American male English professor's home in Seoul during a hot summer day. He waxed nostalgic about the cool air blowing out of the air conditioner at his English professor's home and the taste of the American drink Fanta, "so cool and delicious." He smiled as he recalled, "Wow, I still can't forget the taste of Fanta. There was Korean Fanta [at the time], but the taste was different. With the air conditioner that I thought every house in America had, and Fanta, I came to think these were the trappings of an American." Mr. Chung had majored in business at a college in Seoul and worked for one year in an investment company, but as soon as his mother's invitation for him to join her in the United States was approved, Mr. Chung moved to the United States. The following year, he was introduced to Mrs. Chung through his sister, and they married.

In our interactions with the Chung family, Mr. Chung seemed to be the family figure with the most singular vision of how he and his family would achieve the American dream. Mr. Chung's first work in the United States was at the post office. He recalled that a post office job was one of the best that Korean immigrants could secure. (And in fact, there are still many Korean workers in post office jobs—particularly the midnight shifts—in the Chicago suburbs.) However, Mr. Chung decided to leave his post office job after seven years partly because he saw that other Korean immigrants running small businesses earned more money. He also shared with Jin-Heon that his African American supervisor at the post office assigned him tasks that his White American coworkers disliked doing, a practice that he understood to be racially discriminatory. He said, "Here [in the United States] typically post office workers are less educated, less substantial people." When he announced to his coworkers that he was leaving the post office job, he recalled their surprise because they imagined all postal workers staying at the post office until retirement. Here, his critique of unambitious American coworkers echoes the critique earlier voiced by Mrs. Chung about her fellow nurses. These immigrant parents constructed a narrative of themselves as determined workers who strove to rise above the humiliation of racial discrimination amidst the mediocrity of "working-class" American coworkers. Although Esther and Doug understood the tales of parental hardship as evidence of sacrifice for the sake of their upward mobility, it was also clear that these career strivings were, in and of themselves, important to the parents' identities.

Mr. Chung's work as a proprietor of a video rental shop, which he had occupied since 1991 after two years in a different location, had complicated meanings for both him and his family. As aforementioned, it was important to him that his was a small business with a non-Korean customer base. During a visit to Mr. Chung's shop, he said to Jin-Heon, "As you have seen here, my customers are all Americans. I have not seen a single Korean coming to rent American movies." However, as Jin-Heon sat in the shop for a three-hour stretch, he noted that Mr. Chung's customer base was ethnically quite diverse. Of the approximately twenty to thirty customers who came to the shop, many were African American, Latino/a, and Southeast Asian American. It seemed that while Mr. Chung aspired to live and work in a "mainstream America" that is primarily White and English speaking, his work life was populated by largely working-class and middle-class multiracial (and often immigrant) Americans in a scruffy neighborhood just north of Chicago. To Mr. Chung, however, that his business did not cater to the Korean ethnic community spoke to his successful foothold in the mainstream American society. His non-Korean customer base also meant that Mr. Chung could look to his customers for information about the American way of life and how one gets ahead. For example, he recounted his conversations with a high school counselor customer about the kinds of students who are sought by prestigious private universities such as Stanford and Brown. He also eagerly introduced Jin-Heon to one of his regular customers, a political science professor at a local college.

For a time during the first year of our ethnography, Mr. Chung and Esther were enamored with Stanford for its location and its prestige and were quite disappointed when she was not admitted in their early decision. He was explicit about his parental strategy (to move the family out of the Korean ethnic enclave) and believed that whichever campus Esther ultimately attended, she would immerse herself in the White world instead of seeking out Korean American friends. He felt that if his children were to have all Korean friends, it would be harder for them to live in "mainstream society." (In this vein, he was at odds with many other Korean immigrant parents' efforts to expose their children to "Korean culture.") He was happy that Esther had "successfully made all American friends after moving to the neighborhood, except for a Korean lawyer's daughter." He was less pleased about Doug's choice of friends, who, he surmised, were Latinos who lived in low-income apartment complexes with working-class parents.

Mr. Chung's proclamation of his "American" customer base aside, we would later learn that his video shop was adjacent to two shops (a dry cleaner and a nail salon) that were also Korean-owned. Mr. Chung confided in Jin-Heon that he sometimes liked to visit with the Korean dry cleaning shop owners and chat in Korean. He explained that speaking in Korean relieved his stress. (Unfortunately, the dry cleaner had gone out of business at the time of our last visit to Mr. Chung's store.) The contradictions between his idealized America and the lived reality of his life strike at the heart of the tension of Mr. Chung's immigrant life. That is, he remained vigilant against the performance of Korean identity for himself and his children, yet he nonetheless admitted that it is actually difficult for an immigrant to live, day in and day out, completely outside of the ethnic community. And while he strove to articulate a coherent parenting strategy for raising his Korean American children to be comfortable in "mainstream" America, our conversations revealed sometimes competing ideas about the realities of race and class.

Mr. Chung, we sensed, had not had an easy life. By everyone's accounts, he had worked extremely long hours all through his adult life. His video rental business already appeared to be suffering in the mid-aughts with the introduction of streaming videos, and he had had to downsize his business during the economically demanding years of having both children in college. And while the trappings of his life (his home, neighborhood, apparent good health, successful emerging adult children attending top public universities, and so forth) seemed, on the surface, to suggest that he and his wife had much to be proud of, it seemed to us that he continued to long for a better life.

Esther: Dutiful Accommodation

We learned early on in our ethnographic encounter that the family's move—and with it their assimilation strategy—had exacted some psychological costs. In fact, Mrs. Chung appeared to have had some misgivings about the move, as Esther had been dead-set against the idea and then despondent about having had to leave behind a tight group of girlfriends in Valley Vista. Doug told us that he had even warned his mother about Esther's depression and how teens these days even commit suicide over these sorts of emotional events. However, Esther told us that while the move was initially difficult for her (she never admitted to the turmoil that other family members reported on), she now appreciated her parents for having had the foresight to move the family out of the ethnic enclave. She offered, with hindsight, that she thought of the move as "broaden[ing] her horizons." For example, she joined the school swim team because she thought it would help with her social transition to the new school, which she said she never would have done had she stayed in her former school district. And she added that her White friends in Tall Grove were more "sophisticated" and open-minded than her Korean American friends in Valley Vista. With this retrospective gloss, we think of Esther as accommodating to her parents' strategy— even to the point of expressing gratitude—at least while she was in high school. At the same time, we also saw in Esther's relationship with her parents a certain kind of sadness at the lost emotional intimacy and the inability to fully communicate. Esther and her brother had gotten the big-picture message from their parents about the "family project" of a successful immigrant path; yet as the years passed, the emotional distance between Esther and her parents seemed to grow along with her divergence from the path to success that had been carefully tended by her parents.

During the initial ethnography period in which we had the most active contact with Esther, she at times struck us as a dutiful daughter whose vision for her future seemed consistent with that of her parents. She was academically successful and had a social circle in high school of mostly non-Korean friends. Once, while waiting for Esther's violin recital to begin, Mrs. Chung told Hyeyoung that Esther was very "humble and respectful to her parents" and that Esther did not like to boast. Mrs. Chung also thought of her daughter as a very compassionate girl who tended to gravitate toward friends who were less fortunate than she (such as a friend with a disability).

Tensions and disagreements between Esther and her parents were most often hinted at rather than overtly expressed. For example, Mrs. Chung insisted that she had never told Esther of her own desires that she might become a doctor, but it seemed that Esther "read" her parents' faces and simply understood that they dreamed of her pursuing a medical career. Mrs. Chung in turn read Esther's face to know that Esther felt pressured by her parents (and that she might have other desires), yet she did not explicitly encourage Esther to pursue other careers. Perhaps compounded by their mutual sense of a language barrier, a helpless paralysis seemed to characterize their silent and sometimes anguished (mis)communication. And in fact, Esther seemed, in many ways, to embody the implicit message of the Korean immigrant parental strivings. Esther recalled that as a young child, she hardly ever saw her father at home because of his long work hours at the post office or at the video rental shop. She explained that because he was never home, she had developed almost an abstract idea of her father—"invisible [and] God-like." She made clear to Hyeyoung that it was *not* that her parents pressured her to do well in school but that she was always conscious of their "presence"—echoing exactly what her mother had surmised. We note the elevated status of her father in her eyes, absent and yet a motivating force in her life.

Esther also revealed to us that both of her parents had worked long hours for as long as she could remember, and she felt that her parents' diligence deserved to be reciprocated by her own hard work. When she and her brother, she told Hyeyoung, were very young they were cared for by their paternal aunt and uncle, and at some point, their maternal grandmother had moved in and lived with them for several years as their primary caretaker. From Esther's perspective, in addition to the language barrier between her and her parents, she remembered her parents not being home very much from the time she was very young. Gradually, she described, it became more and more difficult to talk to her parents. It seemed to us as if the parents and the children in the family had never established the bases (the time, the place, and the common language) for communication. Once, Esther told Hyeyoung about a time as a junior high school student when she experienced a crisis of confidence in her Christian faith and a swirl of existential questions about death and the afterlife. Esther recalled struggling to decide whether to talk to her parents about her religious confusion but ultimately choosing not to confide in them because they "would not understand." These small, poignant moments speak to what we describe in this book as the psychic toil—the *family work*—of immigrant life.

We also got a glimpse of this emotional distance from the mother's perspective. Although Mrs. Chung felt that she would have been able to give better advice to Esther on intimate topics (such as sexuality) if it were not for the language barrier, she also felt that she and Esther shared a sense of mutual respect. Mrs. Chung told Hyeyoung that she thought of Esther's personality as exacting and as one not swayed by emotional attachments (*chông*). Mrs. Chung recalled Esther as a young child packing for a sleepover without asking for any help. In another memory, Mrs. Chung remembered Esther as a three-year-old child vomiting from some mild food poisoning yet telling her mother, exhausted from long hours at the hospital, to just leave a bucket beside her bed and go to sleep.

From Mrs. Chung's perspective, their fragile mother-daughter relationship was not only a matter of the language barrier but also a matter of important personality differences. Mrs. Chung had wondered if she had had a hand in Esther's independence, having always been a working mother and having had Doug a scant fifteen months after Esther. From early in life, Esther was cast as the mature older sister. Mrs. Chung related that when Esther and Doug were in a nursery school, Doug was shy and did not want to attend but Esther seemed fine. Mrs. Chung had then assumed that the transition had been an easy one for Esther. It was only much later that she found out how nervous Esther had been about the nursery school but that Esther had endured the stress in silence so as not to worry her. This portrait of Esther's dutiful stoicism—at that very early age—contrasted with Mrs. Chung's stories of Doug, with whom she described an easier relationship.

Early in our family ethnography, Esther echoed her father's critique of Korean Americans in Valley Vista. She related to Hyeyoung that back in Valley Vista, Korean American students thought of themselves as better than everyone else, a mentality expressed in comments such as "my problems are different from everybody else because I'm Korean and my parents are immigrants." She felt that Koreans in Valley Vista isolated themselves from mainstream society by only speaking Korean, telling Korean jokes, and buying certain brands. She recalled that Koreans in Valley Vista also used to say how much they hated Americans and how they thought America was "so stupid." Esther also added that her old Korean friends were overly concerned with "superficial" ideas of success (e.g., getting high grades, attending prestigious colleges) rather internal motivation to succeed. In contrast, her White friends received straight As because they were naturally smart and worked hard because it was something *they* (not their parents) wanted to do. Unburdened by a sense of being so unique, her White friends in Tall Grove seemed more open to discussing their inner experiences. Their openness about personal and sexual matters impressed Esther as a mark of maturity.

Given the family's overarching narrative about the significance of their move out of the Korean ethnic enclave into a Whiter neighborhood, it was somewhat puzzling to Hyeyoung that she had some difficulty engaging Esther in discussions about race and racism; alternatively, it is perhaps telling that Esther was unwilling to engage with racial topics given that Whiteness and, in this case, Korean American hankerings for White identification were necessarily unspoken, in much the way that the association between "American" and Whiteness was unarticulated. Esther reported that she tended to identify herself more as American than as Korean but that she also did not think much about race and ethnicity because she did not like the idea of seeing herself through these lenses. This said, she also described that on a daily basis she could "really feel" that others looked at her as an Asian American or Korean American even if there was nothing explicit. And in fact, when Hyeyoung and an undergraduate research assistant spent some time with Esther and her two high school friends during their visit to the campus of the University of Illinois in February of their senior year, Hyeyoung observed Esther's friends teasing her about presenting herself at school as "a nice Asian girl" in front of their teachers. Although this teasing and Esther's protests were playful, and one of her two friends doing the teasing was in fact another Korean American, we sensed that this might have been precisely the sort of daily event that reminded Esther, even by her closest friends, that she was racially "different." (Readers might also recall that Ben, in chapter 3, also spoke of similar experiences of having his race remarked upon by his friends in a joking manner.) Importantly, we note that Esther wrestled with racial stereotypes, and that even as she decried them, at moments she could not help but admit that many aspects of her life in fact conformed to the stereotypes. For example, while she was critical of the Valley Vista Korean Americans whose academic achievements were driven by familial and ethnic prescriptions rather than personal motivation, Esther also described herself as wanting to do well academically to please her family, especially her father, and said that her decision about which college to attend would be based on the cost and her parents' preference. Throughout the course of her college application process, Esther sometimes told us that her parents talked frequently about medical school whenever the family discussion turned toward college applications (in this case making the pressure more explicit), yet at other times proclaimed that she felt little pressure from her parents about her career path.

We see here the stuff of psychic toil: Esther tried very hard to accommodate her parental wishes and strategies, even as she admired her non-Korean friends' casual attitudes about education. Esther also spoke variously about the ethnic make-up of her social circle in Tall Grove. We did later learn from her father, as well as from her campus visit with friends, that Esther's closest friends in high school were in fact not all "White," as we had imagined given the family talk of assimilation to White society. Of her three closest friends, one was a Korean American daughter of a lawyer, another was of Spanish and Jewish heritage, and the last was of Jewish and Japanese heritage. Nonetheless, as with Mr. Chung's video rental store clientele (similarly more multiethnic than White), the fact that Esther's friends were not exclusively Korean was presented as a positive sign that she had achieved the social competence to navigate American society.

Our research team had most contact with Esther during her senior year of high school, during which the college application and selection process brought to the fore her family's ideas about education and "success." Although Esther won a handsome scholarship to an out-of-state Big Ten university and eventually enrolled there, we witnessed the sometimes-tense family negotiation around college (and career) selection. For one thing, Esther had initially been interested in going much farther away to school, particularly to California. The family in fact took a trip to northern California to visit Stanford. Mr. Chung was especially keen on the idea that Esther might attend a school in California; he fantasized that a California university education would make Esther more mature and open-minded. Soon after their visit to Stanford, the family also visited our campus "down state," and we hosted an informal tour for the family at two science laboratories and introduced them to some science professors and graduate students, per the family's request. Here, we observed that Mrs. Chung was the one family member who seemed to most relish visiting a large, bucolic campus and interacting with professors. For her, the visit provoked a sentimental reminiscence of her student days long ago. We sensed, though, that Esther was not especially interested in attending this in-state school that her two closest high school friends had already committed to attend. After this rather awkward campus visit, where the parents were clearly more interested than was Esther, we did not see her again except very briefly (Hyeyoung attended Esther's violin recital, a rather informal affair with a dozen or so mostly younger students, where she seemed tense and rather embarrassed by her lack of preparation), despite our considerable efforts to reconnect with her.

We later learned from Mrs. Chung, a year into Esther's college, that Esther had a very happy freshman year. Mrs. Chung beamed as she told us about Esther's two new close friends—one, a rich White girl from Greenwich, Connecticut, and another, an African American girl from a poor Brooklyn neighborhood. These new friends, epitomizing class and racial diversity, appeared to satisfy Mrs. Chung's hankerings for Esther's college "experience." Mrs. Chung marveled at how her daughter, whom she always saw as possessing a deep, quiet sense of confidence and maturity, was becoming a cosmopolitan intellectual, the kind of person who establishes intimate connections with a rich White girl and a poor Black girl all at once. It seemed that with Esther's new friendships, their strategic move away from the Korean ethnic enclave had indeed "paid off." Our subsequent updates about Esther came from Doug, who intimated that perhaps not all had been resolved for Esther, as well as from her parents. We sensed that she had some difficulty arriving at a decision regarding her career path, which may have been partly due to her more intense involvement in the church. It also appeared that, following her first year, in which she had befriended the two non-Asian friends—which had so pleased Mrs. Chung—her social circle at the university became almost exclusively Korean and Asian American. (Doug described visiting her at college and finding that "99 percent of her friends are from church—Korean and Asian.") Esther, who had always been much more religious than Doug, had joined a Korean campus ministry at her university, and her social life was becoming centered on her new affiliation as her religiosity intensified. Doug added that he thought Esther had not liked her high school experience very much because she felt ostracized for being an evangelical Christian. There were some hints from Doug that his parents had ambivalent feelings about Esther's increased religiosity. While they were pleased that she was religious, Doug hinted that the parents thought she was putting religion above everything else (including above the pursuit of a prestigious occupation and a family).

However, as Esther neared the end of her college education, we sensed less tension in the family regarding the educational *and* social outcome for Esther. Mrs. Chung revealed that she continued to see her relationship with Esther as being characterized by emotional distance, yet she also spoke approvingly of her daughter's grit, independence, and competence. It appeared that Esther had decided to become a physician's assistant rather than to pursue an M.D. degree so that she could do some creative writing on the side. Mrs. Chung told Nancy that she did not worry about her daughter. In fact, Mrs. Chung seemed not to be bothered by Esther's largely Korean social circle at college, as she spoke approvingly of Esther's Korean American college church friends as "pure" and "lovely."

Mr. Chung, on the other hand, still seemed not entirely resigned to Esther's career choice as a physician's assistant. In a conversation with Jin-Heon about Esther, Mr. Chung kept repeating, "I don't know [*jal moreuggesseo mwo*]" and "she will do whatever she needs to do for herself," accompanied by little sighs, hinting at his concern about her career decision. Mr. Chung also seemed somewhat unsettled by Esther's expressed interest in entering the Peace Corps after college in order to engage in charitable volunteer work. He appreciated that Esther's interests were driven by her religiosity and her Christian faith, which he approved of, but he nevertheless worried that her religious engagement might be somewhat excessive. However, because he himself valued regular church attendance and membership as a source of moral and spiritual guidance as well as social support, he seemed reluctant to voice his reservations about Esther's Christian faith.

In some initial conversations with Doug, we had treaded only very gingerly on the topic of Esther, as it seemed clear that an extensive inquiry into her life was somewhat off-limits and that Doug wanted to respect her privacy. However, across their years in college, it seemed that Doug and Esther were both communicating more with each other in general and that their religious differences had come into the open. Doug said that Esther "sees herself on a higher plane in terms of spirituality [i.e., than the rest of the family]." A month earlier, Doug had told Esther outright that he no longer went to church but asked her to keep this from their parents. Further, Doug detailed exactly the differences between Esther's and his father's religiosity. For his father, "church is more about church attendance; it isn't about knowing the Bible; it's just about something you do, routinely. It's how he approaches everything, 'you go every day, you do it.'" For his sister, though, "God and faith come before family and career," an approach that Doug thinks she shares with many co-ethnics of his generation. Korean American church appeared to have become a racial and spiritual comfort zone for Esther, which was why she had seldom come home during college and, when she had, had challenged the family on matters of spirituality and faith.

As for Esther's final plans to become a physician's assistant rather than a doctor, Doug described his parents' views on the matter this way: "If you are going into something medical then why not become a doctor. . . . [They] sort of feel like she is doing something that is less work." Esther, on the other hand, Doug continued, thought of her path as "something more fulfilling." Doug admitted that there was a part of his parents "that wants to go to church and mingle and say that my daughter is going to an Ivy League university to become a surgeon and bring that money to us" while "my sister wants to say I'm still going to do a medical career and make a decent living—so what's the difference?" Doug described his parents' initial reaction to Esther's career decision as "pressing the panic button as soon as they see her [in their minds] falling off a cliff— thinking 'we can re-motivate you to go to medical school.'"

Doug's Response: The Articulate Son

In contrast to Esther, Doug was cast by his family as being on a less certain path, especially during our first year of ethnography, with respect to both his social circles and his career trajectory. Esther told us about his cadre of high school friends who were all "ethnic" (meaning Hispanic), "rude," "loud," and "criminal." It was clear that Esther and her parents did not entirely approve of the company Doug kept and blamed the friends for breaking a stair rail in their house (which, Doug claimed, was caused by his friend's accidental slipping and falling on the stairway), ripping their sofa (for which Doug claimed responsibility), and being loud whenever they stayed over. Doug reported that his parents never had any problem with the few White friends that he had made.

Because Doug decided to attend the same university where we were professors, we were able to follow his college trajectory over the years. In fact, although he started out as a relatively minor player in our initial family ethnography, Doug ended up becoming the primary conduit between the research team and the family. We were impressed by his thoroughly good nature and the thoughtfulness with which he approached his education, his career, and his place in the world. Doug stayed a bit closer to home for college, attending the University of Illinois at Urbana-Champaign along with about fifty other classmates from his high school graduating class. (Doug told us later that the U of I wasn't a "choice" at all—it had been the only school to accept him.) We met Doug and Mrs. Chung for a casual dinner at a restaurant a few months before his enrollment at Illinois. At that time, Doug was already anticipating that his experience of attending Illinois—with its very large Korean American student body from Chicagoland—would be different from that of Korean American students hailing from more ethnically dense suburbs such as Valley Vista. He had already imagined that those Korean American kids from Valley Vista would have extensive but narrow interests in all things Korean and Korean American, while he saw himself as having non–ethnically marked interests such as the Chicago sports teams. At the time, we noted that perhaps Doug too subscribed to the family narrative of the significance of their move to the White suburb as a meaningful (and telling) life choice.

Back when we first met the family, when Doug was still a junior in high school, the family, including Doug himself, initially reported to us that Doug had weathered the move from Valley Vista to Tall Grove much more smoothly than Esther had. However, we came to learn from both Doug and his mother that his actual experience with the move had been quite difficult. Doug attended his new middle school for one year in Tall Grove, and he hinted that he had hated this new school because his new classmates were unable to accept anyone different from them. However, he had elected at the time to keep silent about his own struggles so as not to further burden his parents. Mrs. Chung revealed at the dinner with us and Doug that she felt terrible that she had been completely unaware of his difficulties that first year in Tall Grove. We argue that Doug's initial silence following the move was one of the ways in which the teenager accommodated to his parents' exit (i.e., from the ethnic enclave) strategy. And even as his mother expressed her regret, he seemed reluctant to name his middle school experience as one of racism, instead attributing it to his middle school classmates' "immaturity."

Doug did indicate that his favorite class in high school was a social science elective on immigration, a new course taught by a teacher who had been alarmed at the segregation—and apparent denigration—of Latino students who attended their largely White high school. Mrs. Chung beamed with pride in the fact that Doug had begun to take an interest in her past, was asking her about it, and was coming home telling her things he learned in the class. While discussion of sports had long been their primary bond, the mother-son relationship seemed to have deepened during Doug's senior year in high school. Perhaps, he later mused, Esther's having gone off to college had made for the turning point. Echoing her earlier pride in Esther's growth in college, Mrs. Chung took pride in her mature son, who had come to this point. And we also saw in Doug a teen transitioning into emerging adulthood, who was becoming keenly aware of how race and immigration played a part in his own life experience.

Early in his college freshman year, Doug made an admission of a sort to us that he had grown up envying other (White, upper-middle-class) kids at his high school, who occupied what seemed to be the comfortable and powerful position in society. These, it turns out, were the same classmates from his high school who entered Illinois with him but were leading a very different kind of college life by the time we met up with him, three months into his college career. These were the children whose parents and grandparents and other family members had attended Illinois, had grown up as Illinois sports fans, and had a family tradition and stories about the glory of being an Illinois alumnus. (Doug related how he had come to this realization, overhearing parents of his classmates say, "I am so glad that you are going to my alma mater.") These, as well, were children who grew up playing team sports (e.g., football, baseball). These were the children with inside jokes about events that had happened at their expensive summer sleepaway camps. And these were the boys who had once been his buddies but had begun to exclude him in their junior year of high school. They had made racial jokes that he had found offensive—by now a familiar refrain we were hearing from multiple Korean American teens—but his protests had been dismissed ("Don't be so PC."). He had become embittered by this sort of racial exclusion over the course of his high school years. He realized, he told us, that he had been "expendable." (Some years later, we revisited this conversation with Doug, who was tickled by this in the light of his considerably changed thinking on the matter. "I so don't think like that anymore," he said.)

Doug drew a contrast between the families of these White classmates and his own. He had to teach himself the game rules of popular sports. He had to contend with growing up in an immigrant household in which his parents were not fluent speakers of English, with a father who had experienced downward occupational mobility, and with both parents who worked long hours and could not teach him about mainstream American activities such as sports and fraternities. His parents could not regale him with stories of their glorious Illinois student days. Nor could they afford expensive summer sleepaway camps; as a matter of fact, summer camps were not even on his parents' radar screen. Doug talked about being a "self-taught" sports fan—an activity that his mother also took up in an effort to connect with the son. Although Doug did have a few cousins from his mother's side who had attended Illinois and were excited about his attending their alma mater, this was not the same stuff as the generational legacy of his White classmates. His cousins, it turned out, were religious Christians and their Illinois college lives had been centered on the largely Korean American campus church.[3]

Observing his White classmates at ease with their lot in society, Doug felt himself at the margins of this social circle looking in. He was aware that he was also at the margins of the tight-knit Korean American community at Illinois because he was not particularly religious and had not attended the same high schools or churches back in Chicagoland as the majority of Korean American students. Although Doug had tried going to the Korean American campus church that his cousins had attended, he faced the same type of social isolation there. The Korean American students had all known each other from "back home" and already had the inside jokes and references to things that he felt "alienated" from, such as Korean TV shows and Korean music. Indeed, he felt a considerable cultural divide between himself and most Korean American Christian students at Illinois.

Doug's revelation about his high school years—particularly his reflections on racialized marginalization—upended our sense that this entire family had been at one point united about the wisdom of the parenting strategy. The move away from a Korean ethnic "comfort zone" to a White suburb had made an impact on Doug's life, but not quite in the way that his parents had envisioned. It appeared that Doug had felt his social exclusion more acutely at his high school, but with a much bigger campus at Illinois, where he chose not to affiliate with his old classmates and other similar types, he felt free to explore and create his own social niche. In contrast to White classmates who frequently went "home" to Chicagoland on weekends, which to him spoke to their class privilege and a casual attitude toward college (i.e., it costs time and money to travel to and from campus to Chicagoland, thus a weekend trip is an indulgence), he was not in close touch with his high school friends. He reveled in the diversity of the people he had befriended in his dormitory. Whereas high school Doug may have eagerly looked forward to starting his own family legacy as an Illinois alumnus, college Doug had become less enamored with the White mainstream college experience.

Over his time in college, as we checked in with him approximately once a semester or so, Doug's thoughts about race and racism took on added layers of sophistication. He still recognized the same type of racism on campus that he had encountered in high school, which he was increasingly willing to name as racism. For example, there had been a campus incident in which a fraternity had hosted a party that played on racial stereotypes. Knowing some of the people at that particular fraternity, Doug was not shocked by this incident. However, he was upset about the general campus discourse that dismissed minorities as "using the race card." In reflecting back on his friendship with Mexican Americans, he recalled that he had felt a certain kinship with them during the final years of high school as they bonded over their experiences as racial minorities at an affluent and largely White high school. In high school, Doug recounted, Mexican Americans were treated in a "patronizing" way and were segregated into different (less academically rigorous) classes. In fact, Doug's freshman college roommate was the only Mexican American student from their high school to enroll at Illinois.

However, Doug began to sense the limits of such shared solidarity, as he and his Mexican American roommate began to have conflicts. He described to us a recent shouting match with his roommate. The roommate insisted that no matter how hard he worked, he would be taken advantage of by the mainstream society because he was Mexican. When Doug disagreed with his roommate's outlook, his roommate shot back that Doug was able to hold onto his work ethic (i.e., "work hard in college so you can secure a good job") because he, as an Asian, was closer to Whites than were Mexicans in terms of social status. This accusation felt counter to Doug's own sense of social marginalization from the White social circle. He suspected that his roommate had always harbored these racial theories but that they had not talked about the issue before in high school. He added that his parents would not be interested in this type of conversation about race. He told us that his parents had acknowledged mild racism that Doug had encountered at his high school but had advised him to ignore and overcome it. Now that he was on a large campus, Doug seemed to relish the possibilities of developing a new social self. He liked the fact that at this university, he could discuss race issues without being labeled "too PC" (even as there were talks of minorities using "the race card" when they protested racism), and he took comfort in having met other like-minded students with whom he could socialize.

One area that appeared to be a chronic source of conflict between Doug and his parents was his career choice. Even as a graduating high school student, he expressed an interest in a possible teaching career. He had been inspired by a history teacher at his high school and had hoped to follow a similar career path as a high school history teacher. His father had opposed this idea adamantly and had told Doug in no uncertain terms that "teaching is a woman's profession." Doug guessed that his father objected to a teaching career because it is not seen as a prestigious or respected occupation in the United States. Doug also surmised that his father viewed becoming a teacher as "taking the easy road" to life instead of working hard toward a prestigious occupation such as that of a doctor or a pharmacist. At one point, Doug worried that his father would try to use a guilt trip (about their immigrant sacrifices) to convince Doug to change his mind. He said that his father had made it clear to him and to Esther that the parents had worked very hard to get to "upper-middle-class" status and that they did not want to see their children's occupation and income move downward toward "middle class." As well, Doug came to see his father's wishes as a reflection of disappointments in the father's own work life. In a conversation with Nancy, Doug said,

> Dad still has this belief that I'm gonna go to medical school and he's always saying how excited he is . . . [I]t's frustrating when I think about it . . . but it's just the way he was raised . . . [H]e doesn't want me to—I don't know how to say it—turn out like him, so he's afraid. Expecting me to get into a good medical school 'cause, you know, I am going to a really nice college.

Of course, Mr. Chung's expectation that his children enter a prestigious professional occupation is not unique to this family; that many Asian American families hold this sort of academic expectation has been well documented (see, e.g., Lew 2006). In Doug's family's case, his aunts and uncles also reinforced this success narrative. For example, Doug talked of his cousin, an Illinois alumnus (and the son of his father's older sister, who had also immigrated as a nurse) who became a pharmacist. The pharmacist apparently hated his job but was paid well and had good work hours. To Doug's eyes, his father and the extended family aspired not just to "make it" in the United States (in the sense of securing a stable occupation) but to live in multi-million-dollar mansions in the affluent suburbs. Doug related an episode that occurred over the summer, as the father and son worked together at the video rental shop, when Mr. Chung pointed out an accountant's office near his video shop as an example of the kind of life he wanted for Doug: to have a nice car, work only four hours each day, five days a week, and get paid handsomely. Having worked extremely long hours all of his life and coming from an impoverished family in Korea, Doug's father envisioned the good life as being well off enough to be able to take days off at leisure to go to a Chicago Cubs baseball game, as he had seen this accountant do from time to time. Doug sensed that his father and his extended family wanted Doug to aspire to, and potentially achieve, such a level of wealth because he was "Americanized" and spoke fluent English. Doug had a slightly different vantage point. He explained to Nancy,

> [T]he Kennedys, the Roosevelts, they're always going to be really powerful in this country and I think that's what my Dad keeps forgetting. He keeps telling me these random success stories. And that is true, there are people who climb up all the way to the top, but it isn't as common as he thinks.

For Doug, the biggest chasm between him and his father came down to a future vision. While his father imagined Doug at the helm of an "American" family, comfortably enjoying the fruits of having "made it" in America, Doug thought it was "ridiculous" for his father to expect him to be the patriarch of a new American family. With these comments, Doug meant to bring race to the fore. Doug mused with Nancy that it is "important for Korean Americans to see themselves fitting into [the U.S.] racial pyramid." The American dream, he added, comes with an asterisk when one is an ethnic minority, and Doug was frustrated when others ignored this, among them his sister. "If I have kids," he said, "I am going to tell them this [i.e., race] is something to keep in the back of your mind: that you are not going to have it as easy as some other people."

More than halfway through his college career, Doug had decided not to get a degree in education (which would have led to teaching certification in secondary education) but instead to aim for an academic career as a college professor. There were several different reasons for this shift in his career aspirations, but almost all had to do with his college courses and experiences. It appeared that a part of the reason was that he did not feel comfortable with other education majors (who seemed very cliquish, "just like high school," sleeping through class and then going to a bar right after class). After volunteering his time as a tutor for a local public high school, he saw "how education in this country is screwed up. . . . [I]t is pretty bad." He had tutored students who were being taught math by a teacher with a degree in English, and students were repeating the same math course for the third time. He expressed some misgivings about whether he would really want to teach in a high school milieu where disciplining and controlling student behavior seemed to take precedence over teaching. In contrast, he found his college history courses intellectually exciting, and he felt inspired to pursue scholarship of the Korean colonial era or Russian/Eastern European history. It was clear that several university professors had been impressed with Doug and had encouraged him to pursue graduate study.

When Nancy talked with Doug about the active and purposive way in which he seemed to have managed his college education, he spoke of the professor in the first class he took at the university, who had counseled the students to be "radical," not in the political sense but in the sense of change, to be different from what one was in high school. To this, Doug added that when he thought about his parents' investment in his education, he might as well have gone to community college if he was not going to take full advantage of the breadth and depth of intellectual pursuits available at a top-rate university. The senior year in college found Doug counseling freshmen at the university to take advantage of professors' office hours: "I told them that you have to be more active—be more active as a person."

As for his parents, who were at first hesitant about his becoming a high school teacher, Doug felt that they now worried that he had given up sure employment. However, in another vein, they did appreciate the greater prestige of being a college professor; especially for his father, being a college professor (with a doctorate) would be a more "masculine" occupation as well. In our last meeting, Mrs. Chung had already begun, with a quiet delight, to reimagine Doug as the scholar in the family. She told Nancy about her nephew, who was a mathematician in Germany; he made occasional visits to the United States to give lectures. She wanted Nancy to know that Doug had always enjoyed her nephew's company and shared in his maniacal interest in things, as if to signal that Doug had the "professorial" disposition. Mr. Chung, however, had made it clear to Doug that his skill set would equally qualify him for law school—a three-year training with more promise than the approximately eight-year course of humanities graduate school. Indeed, the father-son relationship was one that seemed to still confound Doug. He revealed to us that his father's immigrant past was "something we don't broach" and that his father remained the "greatest enigma ever" to him in many ways. He saw his father as not having made peace yet with the reality of his children pursuing career paths and life choices that Mr. Chung had not envisioned for them. Whereas Esther was content to see her parents as now enjoying a nice vacation and walks by the lake, Doug continued to ruminate about his father's disappointments. Doug told us that he was particularly struck by his father's response as Doug asked him whether he was satisfied with his life. He recalled again how his father had shaken his head, as if to say, "Why would you even ask me that?" and then so dismissively muttered (in Korean), "Of course not."

Coda: Quiet Satisfaction

What do we make of Doug's assertion that the parental strategy (as epitomized by the exit from the Korean ethnic enclave) had not worked out exactly with respect to his ability to negotiate the White world? In our assessment, Doug had turned out, actually, to be quite a sophisticated observer of race relations and had had the kind of college experience that, in many ways, represents the liberal education that his mother had dreamed of (less so for his father, who wanted a more pre-professional education). And what do we make of Esther's social world, which had, in college, become almost exclusively Korean American? As high school students, both Esther and Doug had made accommodations in response to parental strategy (e.g., keeping silent about their own emotional struggles, echoing the narrative that the move was the key to their mobility, Esther's pursuit of a medical career despite her other interests). However, as Esther and Doug made their ways through universities, their social trajectories diverged. In a word, the family had gone to such effort to escape the Korean ethnic enclave, yet both Esther and Doug—each in their own way—had worked in college to leave the affluent White social circle behind in their lives. Doug summarized the trajectory of his family with four words: "*The strategy didn't work.*" He continued,

My Dad did not expect this at all—I assure you. It was naïve [of him] to assume certain results. . . . [but] he still stands by it. It's funny because I don't think he can check off a single item on that list of why he wanted to do it. It has been almost ten years: August 2011 will be exactly ten years [from the move].

We are hesitant, however, to simply conclude that "the strategy didn't work." Families, like parents' goals for their children, are necessarily works in progress. It would not do justice to the thoughtful Chung parents to dismiss their strategies or plans as having failed. The Chung family can boast well-educated children and a family of people who continue to work to communicate with one another, in spite of some linguistic and cultural divides. Indeed, relative to other Korean American families whom Nancy had portrayed in her *Intimate University* book, the Chung family was one for which things were working out very nicely. This is not, however, to say—as we have been stressing throughout this book—that theirs was a family without incident or struggle. The Chung family, from our admittedly quite partial vantage, is the work of considerable psychic toil.

In our observation, these turns in the road—the unexpected outcome of self-conscious assimilationist strategies—had extracted reconsiderations and accommodations from the parents. On the one hand, the parents had anticipated that race matters in this country but also believed that they could lessen the impact of racism if the children were raised in a mostly White setting, earned the right to participate fully in the White world, and were fluent English speakers. On the other hand, the parents seemed reluctant, perhaps even unwilling, to discuss the reality that Doug had been marginalized from both the White and the Korean American social circles. The Chung parents seemed to continue to believe that racism is a minor annoyance that could be overcome by achieving occupational prestige and living the good (affluent) life. Their emerging adult children, however, seemed to be seeking a greater meaning in their careers beyond the obvious trappings of upper-middle-class life. Mrs. Chung told Nancy that she tried to listen to Doug's racial analysis and tried to acknowledge his feelings even though she did not always understand what he meant. And it did appear that Mr. Chung was coming around to accepting Doug's career choice.

Jin-Heon visited Mr. Chung's video rental store some years after our first encounter with the family. Mr. Chung still appeared firm in his belief that "the move" was a correct one for the family and cited as evidence his memories of Esther (and, much later, Doug) thanking him for moving the family out of the Korean enclave. However, upon further questioning by Jin-Heon, Mr. Chung conceded that Esther and Doug appeared grateful mostly for the experience of having to adjust to a new social setting (and the maturity that accompanied this hardship), particularly in contrast to their former Korean American friends who had stayed in Valley Vista and remained comfortably ensconced in their familiar social circle. Esther and Doug appreciated that the move had given them skills and fortitude to navigate new social networks. Mr. Chung, then, was puzzled by Esther not keeping in contact with her non-Korean high school friends after she entered college. Mr. Chung revealed to Jin-Heon that the reason he had selected the White suburb to which he moved the family was that one of his former customers (a Japanese American woman with a Jewish husband and a biracial daughter the same age as Esther) had told him about her move from her former home near the video store to a new neighborhood. He thought highly of this customer and thought it would be ideal if Esther could have the customer's daughter as her close friend. And although Mr. Chung made efforts to engineer Esther's friendship with his former customer's daughter, he conceded that this friendship did not pan out as he had imagined. Mr. Chung related, "After getting into college, [Esther] seemed to cut all the relations off with her high school friends. It's strange."

In Nancy's chat with Doug at the end of his college years, Doug several times spoke of life's course in terms of unintended ("crazy") consequences. Doug reflected that one of the outcomes of the family move was that he "became a person who observed things." He spoke of this being "funny" because this had been nowhere in the plan. By extension, he credits the move with "pushing" him toward the humanities, a direction that was not always easy for his parents. Similarly, he reflected that the move was designed for Esther to adopt his father's matter-of-fact approach to religion but somehow instead ended up nudging her towards fervent and largely ethnically homogeneous religious practice.

In our most recent visit with Mrs. Chung, Nancy mentioned how well-mannered Doug was and how impressed we had been by the thoughtful way in which Doug had gone about his college career. Mrs. Chung then shared how a number of her husband's regular customers at the store had also made similar comments to Mr. Chung after having interacted with Doug during his work at the store over the summer. Indeed, as Jin-Heon was visiting Mr. Chung's store several months after Doug had worked his summer shift at the store, a White male customer asked Mr. Chung how Doug was doing. When Jin-Heon asked the customer about his impression of Doug, the customer told Jin-Heon, "Wow, yes, he's very kind and nice, just like his father." Mrs. Chung shared that her husband had told her sheepishly, "I guess we raised them well." (She added that her husband was never the type to brag.) As Mrs. Chung related her response—"Who knows if we even raised them?"—there was a quiet and lovely sense in which the Chung parents felt pride in how their children had turned out, even as their paths had taken some unexpected turns.

5

Jenny

A Music Strategy

Nancy and Grace's first meeting with Mrs. Park was a memorable one that spanned nearly four hours on a summer Saturday afternoon into early evening. Whereas Mrs. Park started out somewhat hesitantly—discussing details about her immigrant life in a matter-of-fact style and putting a positive spin on past struggles ("*il jang il dan*" or "everything has a good side and a bad side")—she became visibly joyful when the topic of the conversation turned toward her daughter, Jenny, who at the time was away at a summer music camp in a neighboring state. Mrs. Park smiled lovingly as she recounted stories about Jenny's compassionate personality and their close bond; for example, she recalled Jenny as a seven-month-old infant scooting over in a walker to offer a tissue to Mrs. Park, who had been crying after a fight with Mr. Park. Jenny, in turn, seemed to return her mother's affection by writing a letter home every day from her music camp. Over the course of the visit, Mrs. Park's phone rang several times, and she ignored the calls when discussing Jenny because she said she was having too much fun talking to Nancy and Grace. In the middle of this conversation, Jenny also called home from camp, and Mrs. Park eagerly picked up the phone. Nancy and Grace could not help but overhear Mrs. Park's end of the conversation with Jenny (in which she was speaking Korean and Jenny seemed to be answering back in English). As she hung up the phone with Jenny, Mrs. Park said, "I love you . . . miss you" in English. In this way, our research team was introduced from the start to the close, friendship-like bond between this mother-daughter pair.

* * *

In examining Doug and Esther's story earlier, we traced the somewhat complex way in which an assimilationist parenting strategy took some unexpected turns into the children's college years as Doug and Esther distanced themselves from some aspects of their parents' social mobility strategy. However, we also made clear that in many ways their strategy had worked—although the Chung parents would probably not have anticipated that Doug would have become so race conscious. The Chung family also offered a window on the workings of considerable language and religious differences between parents and children. And finally, the Chung parents and their emerging adult children each held different—and changing—ideas about the promises and the realities of their American lives. These intergenerational divides aside, we examined the ways in which the Chungs nonetheless "made family work."

Similarly, the Park family juggled competing ideas of ethnic and immigrant upbringing in the United States. This family at first made plentiful references to what was "Korean" and what was "American" about themselves in relation to the larger community in which they lived. However, as with other families, such references did not fall into the easy dichotomies of the parents wanting to retain Korean cultural identity and the children wanting to assume American cultural identity. On the one hand, particularly for Mrs. Park and her daughter, Jenny, an "American" upbringing stood for familial closeness, freedom, and a healthy and balanced life. They thought about these features as the fruits of immigration: a culture of family and childrearing that would have been hard to enact in South Korea. On the other hand, much of our interaction with Jenny's family—and as far as we could gather, much of Jenny's family's day-to-day life—revolved around Jenny's quite intense musical training and future. Considerable family time, thought, and resources were devoted to this project. What we dub this family's "music strategy" was a family endeavor to guide Jenny to a healthy and happy second-generation American life.

We viewed the music strategy as very much an immigrant project: first because the strategy called upon Mrs. Park's considerable orchestration, which on the surface may resemble Amy Chua's (and other Asian parents') draconian "tiger mother" efforts to drive her daughters toward achievements in classical music (Wang 2011); and second because the strategy was to some extent appreciated as one befitting an immigrant daughter, as it had her immigrant mother. An accomplished classical musician herself, Jenny's mother took a very intimate hand in the management of Jenny's musical life and her likely musical future. Mrs. Park had in fact come from South Korea to the United States in 1988 as a young adult to study piano performance at a conservatory in the Midwest when her husband was accepted into an MBA program in the same city; she and her husband are the only parents in our family ethnography to have begun their American sojourn as international students and to have earned advanced degrees in the United States (the only other U.S. degree holder was Mr. Shin, with a BA from an American university, who had emigrated from South Korea when he was in high school). We will see, however, that Mr. Park's rocky work history in the United States outside of the ethnic sector, and Mrs. Park's employment in the ethnic sector, albeit as a musician, contributed to their thinking about what sort of American career would make most sense for their American-born daughter.

The Park family, as with all of the families in this book, had been making family work but not without considerable psychic labor. Jenny and her parents wrestled to come to peace with what were probably quite normal teen/family trials. Although many of the children and parents in this study sought to be "good daughters (or sons)" and "good parents," Jenny and her mother both worked particularly hard to actualize these elusive ideals. While extremely proud of the intimate and very "American" relationship she shared with her mother, Jenny also sometimes described herself as suffering under her mother's arguably quite "Korean" musical regime, which made for a number of rough spots in Jenny's teen years and beyond. Above all, however, it seemed to us that Jenny and her parents—particularly the mother—were equally and intensely invested in making family work.

We begin with the family's social location—economically and ethnically—within their community. We then turn to mother-daughter intimacy, which turned on Jenny and Mrs. Park's consensus that liberal behavior—such as being able to talk about sex, and communicating openly about personal matters—is a feature of White, not Korean, families. At least in this respect, we hear an echo of Pyke's (2000) findings that Korean Americans think of open communication and open expressions of intimacy as the ideal "American" way that they hope to emulate. Notably, in Jenny's family, both the mother and the daughter realizing that her mother and father both hailed from wealthy Korean families. It was very clear that many of the perks in Jenny's life were thanks to her paternal grandparents' largesse: a thirty-five-thousand-dollar cello where most students at her level typically spent only six thousand dollars, an expensive sleepaway summer music camp, and youth orchestra overseas trips. When we first met Jenny, her father was holding down both an office job and a manual labor job on the side (we only learned this later; Jenny first told us that she did not know what the second job was). Jenny worried a great deal about her father and told us that she gave him shoulder massages and tried to work hard on the cello because she knew her winning music competitions made him happy. Speaking about how hard her dad was working and how "he is tired every day and doesn't have much energy to do anything," she said, "I just kind of feel guilty. I sometimes wish we could divide . . . our whole family's stress evenly." Jenny's mother was very aware of the extent to which her daughter felt burdened by the family's economic insecurity. Mrs. Park felt badly that Jenny did not especially enjoy shopping and could hardly bring herself to pick out something without first worrying about the price tag. When Jenny's seventeen-year-old cousin visited Chicago and shopped with abandon, Mrs. Park really noticed the difference. For her own part, Mrs. Park waffled on the family's economic situation: sometimes, she maintained that their economic woes were no different from those of any other Korean immigrant family; at other times, she told us that their family had been unable to amass wealth and enjoy leeway like many other immigrant families. With one voice both Mr. and Mrs. Park prided themselves on not caring as much about money as others—"why tie up your head with those details?" In this vein, Mrs. Park was proud to tell us that she had recently cut back on her weekend piano teaching and made family time a priority over money. However, despite their insistence that money did not matter as much to their family, it was clear that economic woes were ever present in their daily lives. When a good friend of hers built a beautiful new home, Mrs. Park told us she was envious and that she had even had a dream about that house.

When we took Jenny out for a late lunch during her junior year in high school, she was forthright about two things that set her apart: that her family had considerably less money than most of her high school peers (White and non-White), and that most of her friends were enjoying more carefree lives than she was in terms of time and money. When it came to her White friends, she observed that they had many fewer worries about their futures, even as they were not necessarily any more academically successful than Jenny. She told us that those White girls could be "frivolous"—that they could, for example, get wrapped up in thinking about makeup and such in ways that she could not. Jenny described her own less-than-carefree life this way: "I wake up, go to school, come home, practice cello, do homework, and go to bed." When we drove Jenny home that day, she signaled to us her acute awareness that the route to her home involved driving through the much fancier parts of town before arriving at her more modest neighborhood.

Jenny many times let us know that most of her high school friends were White, but she also made clear that she had little to do with the "popular" White girls—the "really snobbish ones who are rich . . . and with a different boyfriend every two days." We inferred that most of the Korean Americans at her high school attended the much larger Korean churches in the area and were from wealthier families. When Grace shadowed Jenny at her high school one day (with permission of Jenny, her parents, and school administrators and teachers), she was struck by Jenny's nearly all-day-long praise of her classmates, commenting most of all on their beauty and intelligence. About one group of White girls, for example, Jenny said to Grace, "They're so cute. Many guys like them." At lunch, much in keeping with her having told us of her largely White social circle, Jenny sat in the cafeteria room that was largely White; when Grace asked about why there were so few Asians eating lunch, Jenny showed her the other cafeteria, where two big tables were filled with students whom Grace assumed were mostly Korean. (It is possible that a number of those Korean students might have been recently arrived ESL students like Jun-Ho, whom we will meet later.) Grace also asked Jenny about the small number of Asian Americans in all her classes and learned that "most of the Korean Americans are in the AP classes."

In spite of Jenny's sophisticated reading of the social scene at her high school, which was clearly shaped by class and race, Jenny insisted at the time that race did not matter at all in her friendship circles: "When I look at a Korean and a White person, I don't see the difference . . . besides the hair color, eye color . . . you know. . . . But, I don't know. I just hang out with White kids." Yet, as we observed Jenny across different rather do in the company of friends. Grace had joined the mother and daughter for the outing. Grace and Jenny, who had been doing a one-on-one interview, met up with Mrs. Park at an upscale department store's lingerie department where her mother was shopping. About her mother's quite immediate, unabashed openness about private things, Jenny queried in Korean, "Is it OK to talk about that in front of Grace?" Mrs. Park said, "Yes," and the conversation about the front-hook bra that Mrs. Park was looking for that day continued. Mother and daughter bantered over bras and underwear, including Jenny's musings about undergarments that she imagined her father would like and her own casual query to her mother as to whether she too could purchase a front-hook bra. If this was the sort of mother-daughter intimacy that Mrs. Park and Jenny considered "White" (imagining that White mothers and daughters would typically talk like this), the conversation at the thong underwear display took a different turn. In this ever-more-intimate conversation, Jenny drew a racial line around certain lingerie that "Koreans would never buy." "Who would wear those?" Jenny asked her mother, to which Mrs. Park clarified, "Thongs?" and in turn Jenny added that her friends call them "G-strings" and that most of her friends wore them. Jenny added that the mother of one of her close White friends had even asked Jenny if she owned one. Although her friends had told her they were comfortable, Jenny could not imagine wearing them herself. She added that thong underwear would not work for "Korean" women who do not use tampons because, as far as Korean women are concerned, tampon usage would be tantamount to losing one's virginity. A bit later in the shopping excursion, while Mrs. Park was in the dressing room, Grace and Jenny were looking at fancy lingerie, and to Grace's "My sister would totally wear these [scanty lingerie]," Jenny quickly said, "I guess she's very White, right?" to which Grace answered, "Yeah, my sister is pretty Americanized." Jenny told Grace that Korean women are "too vulnerable" for such fare; Grace was not entirely sure what Jenny meant by "vulnerable," but we surmised Jenny had meant to signal that Korean women are more chaste or modest.

While Jenny held onto the notion of herself as a more modest "Korean" girl with respect to lingerie, she and Mrs. Park embraced "American" openness when it came to talks about sex. Tellingly, at one point during one of our weekly research team meetings, Grace warned the team that her fieldnotes were about to turn "R-rated." For Mrs. Park, open conversation about sexual intimacy with then-adolescent Jenny spoke most profoundly to her ideals about mother-daughter emotional intimacy. That she and Jenny spoke about these intimate/sexual matters was a great source of pride. Also clear was that this intimacy signaled the distinctive (from other Koreans, and particularly Korean Christians) ways in which Mrs. Park was parenting, American-style. Mrs. Park pushed herself to be open, even as she headed into uncharted and somewhat nervous-making territory. She gave an example from watching the film *Something's Gotta Give* with Jenny, who asked her why the female protagonist took scissors to her shirt when she was making out with Jack Nicholson's character. Mrs. Park told us that she said to Jenny, "They're in a hurry." While she did feel a bit embarrassed to have to put this into words, she explained that she did so because she wanted Jenny to likewise feel comfortable to be able to tell her *everything*. Mrs. Park was quite certain that Jenny too was proud of this very intimacy, as she related, "[Jenny] says there are not that many kids who talk with their moms about it, and she is very proud of our relationship. She gets very detailed. There is so much I learned from her." As a devoted Christian woman, Mrs. Park's "liberal" ideas about sex talk with Jenny, and even about sex, distinguished her from the Korean immigrant women in her social circle. She told us a story about the time she and Jenny spoke about premarital sex:

> This one time [Jenny] received "purity education" at church and she wore a ring home, which meant she was keeping herself pure for God. She came home and asked me about having premarital sex and took off the ring, saying that she was not confident that she could keep her virginity until marriage. So I said, "[Jenny], I don't think you need to do that [i.e., remain a virgin until marriage]." But when I told my friend about this, she got so upset. She is unmarried and a very conservative Christian. She said that God emphasized purity and asked me how I could possibly say those things to my daughter. I had never really thought about this issue seriously before and I'm not so sexually liberal myself, having only ever slept with my husband. But, I don't think it's right to impose on [Jenny] that she keep her virginity without letting her think about it on her

own. . . . My friend told me that God allows sex only in marriage, but I've never seen that in Bible. So I told her that and she said it's there in various chapters and that it's a cardinal Christian principle. But I still don't agree with her. If [Jenny] enjoys sex and loves someone and she is honest and sincere in the moment and willingly makes a decision, then I don't think she has to wait until marriage. Of course, she would have to take responsibility for her decision. And my friend got very upset. On my way home that day I gave it some thought. I haven't resolved it yet. When [Jenny] took off the ring I told her that it's OK but that she'd have to be mature enough to make the right decision, mature enough not to do it for fun or merely out of curiosity.

In this account, we can see that Mrs. Park held her ground about the virtues of mother-daughter openness and intimacy. This story speaks to Mrs. Park's liberal inclinations in two ways: first, in her openness to premarital sex, and second, in the intimate conversation itself. In much the way that Mrs. Park could take note of her differences from the ethnic fold, so too could Jenny thus appreciate her mother in the landscape of "Korean" (vs. White American) parents.

There was yet another ethnically inflected matter that same afternoon at the mall that reflected Mrs. Park's concern that her immigrant daughter be comfortable in her body—this following a chance encounter with a slender and pretty Korean American girl the family knew. Mrs. Park was worried about Jenny's self-esteem and body image. Jenny, Mrs. Park surmised, typical of many teens, was concerned about her appearance. (To our eyes, Jenny was a healthy, attractive, and normal-weight teen girl.) When Jenny spotted earrings that she described as "pretty, like a princess's earrings," Mrs. Park was quick to offer, "You'd look like a princess if you wore them."

In the final minutes of the shopping outing, walking past the ring section, Jenny held up a ring and laughingly said, "Mom, will you marry me?" Mrs. Park also laughed and replied, "I'm already married." What struck our team was that Jenny and her mother were equally invested in the idea of being close—even as that closeness was strained by some difficult moments over the course of our time with the Park family. We are interested in the way in which these sorts of family ideas and identities—the stories families tell one another, in this case about intimacy—contribute to "making family work" amidst the quite natural strains of the teen years and of immigrant life.

"Happy and Healthy Childhood": Korean/American Parenting

Once, when we asked her directly about her parenting style, Mrs. Park quickly answered that she did not want to raise her children in an "American way." She then, however, added in English, "whatever that means . . ." This afterthought works aptly to remind us that ethnic or racial parenting is indeed a pretty slippery concept, hard to pin down. Most important for Mrs. Park was that she raise "healthy" children. Her ideals included children who can relate easily to others and who can be free. Mrs. Park thinks of herself as having been raised as a traditional Korean woman to please others, with little sense of her own likes or desires. Best about the American system, she described, is the value placed on individuals, individual integrity, and uniqueness. She described a "universal" standard according to which people are judged in the United States, which she contrasted with South Korea's relation-centered society where "who you are and who you know" matter so much. She spoke about her friends in South Korea following standards imposed by society, not their own, and was dismissive of their maniacal focus on beauty and wealth. (Mrs. Park might have been somewhat disappointed to know that her interest in raising healthy and carefree children aside, Jenny often described herself as a pleaser, much like her mother.)

While Mrs. Park strove to raise Jenny in what she viewed as the American way, she knew full well that Jenny was not unaffected by Korean ways. For example, Mrs. Park surmised that the fact that Jenny fretted about whether she was thin or pretty enough was a "Korean" problem that Jenny picked up because of their visits to South Korea and the South Korean soap operas they viewed together. "After all, we are Korean," she mused. Mrs. Park noted, "[Jenny] has picked up a Korean standard of beauty and tends to think that she is somehow substandard. It is all very *unhealthy*." It was in this context that Mrs. Park aspired to a "healthy American" childhood for Jenny, and to that end an intimate and open relationship with Jenny. She worked hard to praise Jenny's appearance, letting her know how nice she looked every morning at the breakfast table. Infuriating for Mrs. Park were her husband and Korean kin who could not stop themselves from commenting on Jenny's weight.

Although Mrs. Park also cared about a happy and healthy childhood for her younger son, Matthew (who, at the time of our first meeting, was eight years old), her touch was much lighter there. About Matthew, she said,

> [He] is so cute but I only kiss him. I don't do anything for him. I don't take him around with me for lessons or to teach him something. I don't monitor whether or not he does his homework. Last time he was below 30 percent on one of his exams but it didn't bother me so much. I just want him to be healthy and happy. That's about it.

But, for Jenny she told us, "I think I value intimacy above all. These days I feel that I want to do anything that is best for her." She continued, "I want to give my best to her, and when there is something nice I think of her first. I don't know why. Maybe is it because she is the first child?" She went on to say that this means their talking about intimate matters, "very private" things. "Intimacy" here seems to mean a number of things: not only mother-daughter friendship and openness but also the level of her investment in Jenny.

As years went by, we wondered if the differences in the nature and intensity of Mrs. Park's investment toward Jenny versus her younger brother had waned, as we were struck by Mrs. Park's rather nonchalant attitude toward her son's achievement. When we checked in with Jenny at the time of her graduation from the music conservatory, she had very clear thoughts about the differences between her own and her brother's upbringing. She described her mother still thinking about Matthew—by then seventeen and waiting for college admission decisions—as the "baby" in the family: "She loves us both equally but she loves us differently." Part of that difference was her mother's considerably lesser interest in Matthew's future career. Jenny spoke of her envy that Matthew "has no idea what he wants to do [i.e., with his life]. . . . I am jealous of that, that he can choose, that he still doesn't know." Jenny, in other words, never had the luxury of being left on her own to figure things out. Another part of that difference—and of the intimacy—was that Mrs. Park had always confided in Jenny. While Mrs. Park had characterized Jenny as "adult-like" even as a young child, her brother had enjoyed the luxury of remaining a little kid. Ironically, even though Mrs. Park had ideal images of her American parenting allowing for a "happy, healthy" and "carefree" childhood for both her children, Jenny had felt anything but carefree throughout her teen and emerging adult years.

Jenny on "White" Parenting

Jenny echoed her mother's ideas about her parents' distinctive parenting, and while "White" is a slippery reference, it did manage to encapsulate some of what she considered to be her family's difference. In a conversation with Grace about her Korean American friends, Jenny began to talk about the shared way in which her friends' families were different from hers. Some of the praise that Jenny lavished on her mother seemed to suggest that Jenny felt that her mother was not so different from her White friends' moms. This mattered to Jenny, who was blunt that "I like White parents better than Korean parents." She continued:

> I don't know why. White parents are more outgoing. Korean parents are more asking questions stuff, but White parents are more telling, you know. . . . "Today I went to . . . uh . . . [the] shopping mall," [laughs] "and . . . I met this really cute guy." [chuckles] Even the mothers always say that and then um . . . it's . . . White parents are . . . they're very youthful. I have more fun with White parents.

"More fun" went to the heart of the (comparative) matter. When Grace asked, "So you like talking to your White friends' parents and interacting with them and you have fun?" Jenny responded,

> Yeah. Yeah. See, one of my friends, we carpool because we live right next to each other. . . . Her mom is so much fun. Her mom is always late to school and I'm always late to school and I'm going to be, probably going to get to a really bad college because of that . . . but it's not my fault [chuckles]. But she's so much fun. She's so much fun . . . I love going to their home . . . [T]hey're all so much fun. They always have stuff to talk about and they're really funny.

Jenny drew a keen distinction between the ways in which she inter-acted with her Korean American friends' parents and the ways in which she interacted with White parents: she felt so much more at ease con-fiding about personal matters with White parents, while with Korean parents she would speak about things like her youth orchestra.

> It's really different actually. I'm very honest to the White parents. I tell them who I like. I tell them . . . uh . . . a lot of personal stuff. But . . . to Korean parents . . . [pause] I just joke around. Uh . . . I'm not saying I'm not honest. I don't lie or anything. I just don't open up or share anything. I might share the little details but . . . no, no . . . no details . . . just say just little common things, you know . . . um . . . "oh I went to MYA [youth orchestra] today" and then we would start a conversation about MYA but then . . . to . . . in front of White parents I'd say, "Oh I like this boy" . . . then I would open up . . . [I]t's a lot more personal.

When Grace asked what it was about White parents that put Jenny at ease and made her "open up," she offered, "White parents are youth-ful." Somewhat confused as to what Jenny was implying about her own mother's parenting, Grace inquired further about how Jenny saw her mother in relation to the "White, youthful" parents, and Jenny con-firmed that her relationship with her mother was in fact much the same youthful one:

> Um . . . my parents . . . are like White parents I'd say. My mom . . . she's intelligent. She is funny [chuckles], God, she's funny, but uh . . . my Dad . . . um . . . you can say he's intelligent in his own way [laughs] . . . um . . . he can be funny . . . I think . . . [chuckles] and the thing is . . . what I love about him is when he dances . . . it's so funny. He has this little dance that he does. So embarrassing but so funny. . . . They're youthful. My parents are youthful.

In naming her parents as "youthful" like White parents, Jenny appeared to be gesturing to her family's mode of being Korean American, which was quite distinctive.

However, the lines of distinction were often quite slippery. Grace once asked Jenny about her two closest Korean American friends' rela-tionships with their mothers, and it turned out that her friends too were quite close with their mothers, but Jenny nonetheless held her ground that hers was a greater intimacy. She insisted,

> Our relationship is so similar, you know. But . . . I have to say, I think, *I'm more open. I mean, I tell my mom everything.* And it's not even funny. Um . . . but when it comes to . . . uh. . . . [pause] I'm not sure . . . but when it comes to really personal stuff then they don't tell their parents.

In this way, the Korean/American contrast, in which Jenny was so invested, frayed a bit even during the course of Grace and Jenny's conversation. In her valiant effort to organize her thoughts, Jenny offered that while Korean parents run the gamut, "White parents seem the same: they all seem . . . funny, open . . . and very intelligent" and that her parents were more like White parents.

We have seen how both Jenny and her mother were invested in their intimacy, which seemed to include both enlightened American parenting and sometimes ethnic uniqueness. But we have also seen that ethnic parenting is hard to pin down, that the neat binary often stops making sense in the thick of or over the course of a conversation. These are contrasts that are hard to moor, even in the largely happy accounts of sex and shopping. We will see, however, that it was Jenny's music and her mother's musical parenting that really gave these apparently tidy contrasts a run for their money. As we will elaborate when we turn next to Mrs. Park's musical regime, we surmise that when it comes to musical matters, Jenny probably would not have been thinking about her mother's parenting as "White" or "American." We listened to the apparent contradiction—not just within singular conversations but also over the course of our family ethnography contacts with the Parks—between, on the one hand, Jenny's suggestion that her relationship with her mother was distinctively non-Korean in their intimacy, and, on the other hand, her daily life being anchored in the enormous discipline dictated by her cello practice (unlike her White friends' more breezy lives). We refer to such contradiction not to undermine the intimacy between Jenny and her mother but to speak to the nuances and the inevitable inconsistencies in the fabric of familial life that are overlooked if we only characterize families by striving to quantify their "Korean" and "American" identifications and styles of parenting.

Orchestrating a Musical Life

While it was very easy to glean how central Jenny's cello was to the Park family, we appreciate that it meant different things for various family members. We think of Jenny's cello as the elephant in the room, always at issue even if not directly mentioned in the conversation. Here we take up what Jenny's cello meant, as it were, for her mother, father, and, of course, Jenny.

For Jenny, the cello was perhaps the source of her greatest joy and her greatest anguish; it seemed to speak to everything that she both loved and hated about her family. Besides intimacy, Jenny considered her family distinctive, again within her ethnic circle, for putting little pressure on her to succeed academically. (This narrative is reminiscent of that of the Koh family, where the parents did not pressure their teens toward academic achievement; they too marked this as unusual among Korean American families.) At the same time, she figured that the pressure her mother exerted on Jenny to achieve musically was a match to the academic pressure faced by her ethnic peers' parents: "So I get equal pressure as the kid who's pressured into studying." She continued:

> Well, I watch a lot of [Korean] dramas. . . . Korean parents seem very . . .
> uh . . . strict and . . . school work . . . very . . . uh . . . a kid has to be talented
> in something. They push them so hard. My mom pushes me but not that
> hard. . . . When I look at White parents, they . . . help, instead of push, you
> know. Korean parents . . . well, what I see . . . they're like, "OK, get an A on
> this test but I'm not going to help you at all." White parents will go, "Do
> your best on this and I'll help you." So, my parents are kind of like that.
> I'm not saying that all Korean parents are like that. But from my point of
> view, most of them are like that.

In this way (and years before Amy Chua's book on tiger mothers made the news with her extreme parenting, especially around classical music practice), Jenny had named her mother's investment in Jenny's musical achievements as very "Korean." And while Jenny held a dream of becoming a veterinarian in the future, she also seemed resigned to follow the path set forth by her mother.

"Entrance to the World of Musicians": Mrs. Park

Jenny's music stood, it seems, for many things in Mrs. Park's "America": she first and foremost thought about it as a joyous way for an immigrant to find her way, which for Mrs. Park spoke both to her own immigrant life and to her imagined future for Jenny. Above all, music was an arena that Mrs. Park could manage, whereas she—with her imperfect English—felt entirely unequipped to get involved with Jenny's schooling. To some extent it also spoke to Mr. and Mrs. Park's sense that in America, the family can help Jenny pursue her musical talent and worry less about the academic rat race, whereas the academic pursuits would have come at the cost of music had they raised her in South Korea. Jenny's music then took on tell-tale significance in the immigrant crucible.[1]

Mrs. Park's musical desires for Jenny were inextricable from both her own life and her sense of Jenny's future as a daughter of immigrants. For Mrs. Park, a church pianist and piano teacher who originally came to the United States to attend a well-regarded conservatory in the Midwest, music was the centerpiece of her entire life. Mrs. Park had been raised by her own mother to "glorify God through [one's] talent," and indeed she grew up with an idea of herself as a church pianist. It was, she told us, only at the piano that she was truly comfortable in church. Different, she imagined, from the sad situation of the over "80 percent of immigrants who do what they do because they have no other choice," hers was a happy situation in which she could make a living doing what she loved. It was this happy immigrant life that Mrs. Park worked to model for Jenny as she attempted to orchestrate the necessary steps to get her there. "So I want [Jenny] to have this kind of a life unless she really has no talent or despises music." And she continued, "With every chance I get, I tell [Jenny] that I am very happy with my life."

With this confidence in life as a professional musician and in her assessment of Jenny's suitability for it, Mrs. Park attempted to carry out a mostly subtle yet strategic campaign to manage Jenny's "entrance into the world of musicians." She described how she was guiding Jenny to want the very things for her future that Mrs. Park had in mind. She described securing well-regarded cello teachers, sending Jenny to music camps and orchestras, and "getting her ready for one competition after another . . . in a way that [Jenny] wouldn't notice." But she quickly admitted, "I am sure that she knows [what I am trying to do]." And at various moments, she was even forthright about the considerable pressure she was imposing on Jenny and about the rigorous musical regimen that characterized their daily lives. Yet, comparing herself to her own mother, she said, "I swore to myself that I would never push my kid in music as hard as she pushed me," and she felt proud that as a musician herself she was managing her daughter much more strategically, with effective tactics. She also spoke wistfully about the reality that in her own life nothing had been her "choice": not her faith, her college major, or "even" her marriage.

While committed to the promised happiness of a musical future for Jenny, Mrs. Park also thought of music as engendering desirable traits and experiences (particularly self-discipline) that would secure a bright future for Jenny, even if a career in music did not work out. Not surprisingly, Mrs. Park had very clear ideas about her own piano teaching. She aimed to foster self-discipline by "letting [students] do something they *don't want to do.*" She described training students to make a commitment and stick to it. Music thus offered, Mrs. Park stressed, an arena in which "effort is rewarded" and in which people can count on "the taste of the fruits of their labor." She described having engaged Jenny very directly on this point, such as when they listened together to a recording that included Jenny's solo and she asked Jenny, "How did you feel at the sound of applause?"

There is, then, a part of Mrs. Park that was willing to "push" Jenny, even as she confessed to wishing that Jenny possessed the same intense desire and passion for music that she did so as to make parental "pushing" unnecessary. Mrs. Park once told us of a time when she knew that Jenny had felt pressured and pushed back. Mrs. Park and Jenny had attended a local symphony in which a Korean American girl (who also played in the same youth orchestra as Jenny) was performing a solo. The girl had begun playing at a much younger age than Jenny (indeed, Mrs. Park regretted not having had Jenny start her cello lessons earlier in her life) and gave a stellar performance ("Younger musicians who are musical usually lack technique, but she was great in both"). As they walked out of the hall, a White woman approached Mrs. Park to ask if the performer was her daughter. Jenny quipped, "She wishes!" Mrs. Park conceded that Jenny must have been put off by Mrs. Park's unabashed praise of the Korean American prodigy. She told us that from time to time, she was honest with Jenny that it was a great deal of pressure for Jenny to have a mother like her—and that she once told Jenny to go ahead and quit: "I've shown you my happy life and I know what it takes [i.e., to achieve this] and that's why I push you; if you don't want to do it, then don't do it—quit anytime." However, when Jenny responded with, "Is it really OK with you if I quit?" Mrs. Park was not, in all honesty, able to answer affirmatively. When we asked her bluntly, "Are you OK with Jenny feeling so pressured?" she replied, "Kids can't do anything without pressure. It's positive pressure." "What else," she asked rhetorically, "can a parent do but discover what your child is made of—their talents—and educate them accordingly?" When it came to Jenny, Mrs. Park's "discovery" was fine-grained: the cello was, she determined, the instrument that was best suited for Jenny and hence she had earlier switched her from the violin ("there is a right instrument for every person," she said).

For many of the parents and children in this book, "South Korean" childhoods or parenting loomed as roads not taken. Mrs. Park spoke of *ch'imaparam* (치맛바람—"skirt wind") mothering to refer to the well-known aggressive educational zeal of the South Korean middle-class mother, which she would have probably administered to her children had she raised them in South Korea.[2] In Korea, she imagined that she would have been a force to be reckoned with at her children's schools, "one of" those mothers who aggregate in groups of women to gather tips about how to best launch their children. "So," she mused laughingly, "it's such a relief that I'm here." But she quickly admitted that when it comes to music, she is different from American parents and by way of an example spoke of the zeal behind having driven quite a distance that Saturday evening for the 8:00 p.m. concert in which the Korean American cello prodigy had played. Mrs. Park was quite honest with us about her grand designs to send Jenny not to college but to a conservatory, perhaps even the same one she had attended when she first came to the United States (all of which did come to pass). Although she was aware of Jenny's dream to become a veterinarian, Mrs. Park was confident that, with time, such a dream would easily fall by the wayside and that Jenny would happily embrace the life of a professional musician.

Mrs. Park described music as the double-edged sword between her and Jenny: on the one hand, her musical expertise had established her as the authority in the relationship; on the other hand, it was their "common ground" and what they shared that deepened their relationship. "Very deep," yes, but it certainly was also fraught with considerable tension due to the possibility that Jenny's rejection of a music career could wreak havoc on their mother-daughter relationship.

"America Is So Good to Kids": Mr. Park

Mr. Park was forthright, especially as he confided to Jin-Heon: it was his wife's piano teaching wages that constituted the lion's share of their household income. He described his wife's musical skill with a saying, "she dug a well," meaning that her early investment in music training had continued to bring in an income. In contrast to his patient and broad-minded wife, he described his own "God-given narrowness," which he also thought about as the fate of men. As the only son of a wealthy South Korean family, he admitted to having grown up coddled and to having little ability to persevere. After completing his MBA degree, he worked for a U.S. branch of a major Korean corporation that helped him secure a green card. He then switched to a major American consumer goods corporation, which sent him to South Korea to export and market the American company's upscale coffee to Korea. Although he lived and worked in Korea for nearly three years, returning to see his family in Chicagoland every three months or so, the venture ultimately failed and he returned to the States. By the time we first met Mr. Park, his work life as an immigrant had become a patchwork of menial part-time jobs, and his biggest goal was to gain status and stability as a full-time UPS driver. He shared that his (quite wealthy) parents had told him that they expected nothing of him—their highly educated son—and that he needed to compensate for their love only by "doing what he loves independently." And as Jin-Heon tagged along once on Mr. Park's UPS delivery shift, Mr. Park regaled him with his having figured out how to make his delivery route as efficient as possible.

Mr. Park fully supported his wife's musical strategy for Jenny. He praised his wife's knack at identifying children's talent and told Grace that he envied those who study psychology and "can understand personality and predict what a person might succeed at in the future." He admired the discipline of a musical life and the "no waste" tight schedule that his wife had engineered for Jenny. And like Mrs. Park, he spoke of the particularity of their musical strategy in its U.S. context. "America is good to kids," Mr. Park once said, continuing with, "If I were in South Korea I would be fiercely pushing my kids to study hard. But here, studying alone doesn't do it." And he went on to introduce instances of friends' children who had done well in high school but had not fared well getting into colleges. On the one hand, "America is good to kids" seemed to imply a contrast between South Korea, with its enormous academic pressure, and the possibility of a carefree U.S. childhood. On the other hand, however, "studying alone doesn't do it" suggested a very different U.S. reality in which a child needs to nurture talents *in addition to* academic accomplishments. These American images were, we think, quite unresolved in fact, and Mr. Park seemed less assured of an eventually successful music career for Jenny, even as he was supportive of Jenny's (and his wife's) pursuit.

"Mom, You Still Have a Long Way to Go!": Jenny

Consonant with the way in which Mrs. Park described her subtle and sophisticated orchestration of Jenny's musical life, Jenny did sometimes comment on the fact that she was being swept along. She once reflected on her participation in an upcoming Midwestern Young Artists (MYA) trip to Portugal and Spain and in music summer camp the year before in this way: "I didn't even know about it and then one day my Mom just said I was going . . . just like she had suddenly told me I was going to camp." Sometimes, it seemed as if Jenny was at peace casting herself to the winds of her mother's plans, but there were times when Jenny did register her dissatisfaction. She told Grace that on the eve of music camp she really did not want to go and even thought to protest—"I thought about causing some kind of trouble when I got there, just talking back to the teacher, not smoking or anything radical like that, so that they might send me home." But camp turned out to be great fun, and she especially cherished a budding friendship with a talented White boy who had impressed her as a truly great cellist.

Even if Jenny did not protest loudly as she was swept along a musical path, she was very forthright about the emotional difficulties of her musical life. Once Jenny told Grace about feeling sad, usually at night. "Honestly," she said, "it's often about the cello," and she continued:

I practice at night and my mom and I would get into a fight; I would say, "I don't want to; I only want to practice an hour and thirty minutes" and she'd go, "Practice two hours!" and I'd get upset, really upset. And then I think . . . you know . . . "Oh she doesn't care," you know, because I have homework too and she just wants me to simply . . . [T]hat's what I thought, but now I know she doesn't think that . . . [S]he doesn't mean it that way. . . . Oh, I don't know. It's just . . . it's night usually when I get sad.

We sensed that Jenny's vague language reflected the way in which she wrestled with her mother's pressure on the one hand, and on the other hand her keen awareness of her mother's loving investment. We cannot help but wonder at her unspoken thoughts: Her mother "wants her to simply . . ." *what*? Her mother "doesn't think . . ." *what*? And her mother "doesn't mean . . ." *what* in *what* way? We understand that it is with this internal voice that Jenny navigated her mother's musical management, probably making some sort of peace at the time by recognizing her mother's sincere commitment and deep-seated belief in Jenny's musical future. Here, though, we can also remember Jenny's remark that even as her parents were different from other Korean immigrant parents and did not pressure her academically, hers was an "equal pressure."

It should come as no surprise that musical occasions were often tense for Jenny and her mother. Grace got a feeling for this when she accompanied Mrs. Park and Jenny to one of Jenny's auditions to continue as a member of a youth orchestra. While waiting for the audition, Jenny admitted to being nervous, and Mrs. Park tried to reassure her not to be, but Mrs. Park also quipped, with Jenny's Korean American school friend standing by, "Your [cello] case is all scratched up! You should have taken better care of it." Grace could not make out what Jenny said next, but moments later Mrs. Park said to Jenny, with obvious irritation, "You do it. I'm tired of this." Jenny quickly shot back, "You still have a *long way* to go." While we cannot be sure of the exact thing that the mother and the daughter were quibbling about in this instance, we took Jenny to be saying, "Mom, this music stuff is your thing and if you're tired *now* let me remind you that you still have a *long way* to go [i.e., in guiding my musical career]." Another telling tidbit Grace observed that day found Jenny standing and holding her cello bow in front of a sliding bathroom door. Mrs. Park repeatedly cautioned, "Get out of the way! Be careful."

With an obvious attitude, Jenny snapped, "It's fine!" as if to communicate to her mother, "Your precious bow won't get broken!" That audition day, Grace noted in her fieldnotes that "Mrs. Park constantly monitored Jenny's behavior in public and tried to discipline her." When Mrs. Park saw Jenny chatting with her school friend, she turned to Grace to say, "I should have told her not to bring [her]—they keep chatting" (and presumably distracting Jenny from focusing on the audition). These sorts of small moments seemed to signify the larger tension ever present in their relationship.

As Jenny's turn to perform in front of the judges approached, the air between Jenny and her mother grew only more strained. Jenny turned to her mother to consult about which of her two pieces to lead with, and Mrs. Park offered a definitive opinion, adding that Jenny should remember to play one part louder. "OK!" said Jenny, miffed, and walked off. Mrs. Park looked at Grace and said, "She hates listening to me . . ." As it turns out, Jenny was not very happy with her audition that day and announced after her playing, "I must've been really good last year [i.e., to have gotten accepted]. I screwed up this year." Calmly Mrs. Park replied, "You played well without any major mistakes." Grace was struck by Mrs. Park's teacher-like calm, quite a different mode from Mrs. Park, the mother, who had shared with us her considerable concerns about Jenny's self-esteem. As they left the audition site, Mrs. Park asked Jenny whether she wanted to ride home with her or with Grace. When Jenny could not decide, Mrs. Park told her to go ahead and ride with Grace. We can only surmise that, by then, Mrs. Park might have imagined Jenny enjoying herself more with Grace and even perhaps that she opted for the easier passage home for herself as well. When Grace let Jenny know that she had recorded some of her performance, she was eager to see it, but when she watched the clip she offered a steady stream of self-criticism and was quick to tell Grace, "Don't show it to my mom because she'll just say what was bad." Grace was not surprised that Jenny fell asleep in the car while her friend stared out the window the whole ride back. It had clearly been an emotionally exhausting day.

When, at age twenty-two, Jenny told us that her unremitting performance anxiety had sullied her resolve to pursue a professional music career, we were not surprised. By then, she had graduated from the conservatory (her mother's alma mater) and was holding multiple part-time jobs while living at home. One of her three jobs was teaching Sunday school at the same church where her mother worked as the piano accompanist: even teaching Bible study made her nervous, and she described nervously practicing delivering Bible lessons in front of the mirror. We were reminded of how the younger teen Jenny had really known herself: "My Mom really loves music. I love appreciating music, but when it comes to playing, I have incredible stage anxiety. I just don't like to play for other people. I can appreciate [music] as a hobby."

Jenny's Crisis: "I Need a Listener, Not a Counselor"

"The most rebellious thing I've ever done," Jenny told us as a teen, was insisting to her parents that she wanted a pet dog. "They told me 'no,' and I told then 'I'm gonna.' I said, 'No matter what I'm gonna' [get a dog] because, you know, I need a pet or I'm going to go crazy." From both Jenny and Mrs. Park, we learned about a moment when Jenny had become so despondent that she had threatened suicide; this moment in turn led to Jenny getting a pet dog. By the time we heard about it, both of them gave the moment a light touch as if it had been fleeting and not very serious after all. We came to think that Jenny and Mrs. Park were similarly invested in making light of this craggy spot in Jenny's teen years. And we also had determined that Jenny had not been, nor was she at any point during our contact with her, at a serious risk for suicide.[3] Both Jenny and Mrs. Park agreed that Bella, the dog that Jenny was finally allowed to get after this episode, had made a large difference in smoothing over this impasse in what had, up until then, been a mostly happy childhood.

Mrs. Park recalled that Jenny first mentioned suicide in the context of not wanting to go to music camp. Jenny had, Mrs. Park recalled, purchased a jar of aspirin, telling her mother that she would use the pills to make a palliative paste for her acne. Advised by a Korean American friend that she should tell her mother, she told her mother of a stomachache from having taken six pills. Purportedly Jenny told Mrs. Park that she was lonely and felt that no one loved her. Mrs. Park spoke of crying then, shocked that in spite of their close relationship, Jenny could have felt unloved. Mrs. Park thought to seek the counsel of appropriate experts at a local university but then thought the better of it, figuring that these thoughts were after all commonplace for teen girls and that calling attention to the matter would probably only make things worse. A Korean adage said it perfectly for Mrs. Park: "If you scratch an itch, it only makes it worse." She described Jenny's "moody, oh so moody" days before getting Bella and admitted that she was "worried about her," but she described "the whole suicide thing" as having passed by quickly. She declared that "after Bella she [was] *always happy.*"

Even as Mrs. Park made light of emotional difficulties in Jenny's teen years, she was keenly aware of her own emotional vulnerability and that "like me, [Jenny] is very sentimental." For the most part she described her own sentimentalism and tendencies to get teary and nostalgic as but a matter of melancholic temperament and a mood that she sometimes reveled in, for example, when listening to music alone. Interestingly, she once described her own attachment to a sort of morose nostalgia as being at odds with Christianity for being unproductive and for being the stuff of self-hatred. Once she spoke of her adult self as not unlike a sentimental teen. As we mentioned above, Jenny described her own need to always put on a happy face as something she modeled after her mother, or perhaps as a vulnerability that the two shared.

From Jenny, Grace understood that there was much more to the story of Bella. Jenny described having wanted a dog for her entire life, and having been again and again denied by her parents even as she met one condition after another that they had posed for getting a pet dog. When we spoke with Jenny at twenty-two about her career change, she told us humorously that the second word she had spoken as an infant had been "dog, not dad" (a comment on both her love of animals and perhaps in passing a remark about her father as well). She admitted that with her talk of suicide, she had used the dog as a bit of a threat: "[H]ere I come saying, 'I don't want to live anymore. . . .' It's kind of like saying that I want a dog [and] if you don't get me a dog then I don't want to live." As a teen, Jenny had also admitted to Grace that she had used the threat of suicide as one of her tactics to persuade her parents to let her get a dog. She recalled the conversation:

Um . . . this is exactly what, well not word for word, but this is really what I said, "I might die tomorrow in a car accident or someone might shoot me you know, so if you want me to live my life to the fullest just buy me a dog and then you'll be satisfied." Well, how I said it was, she had promised me to get me a dog before I died [laughs] and then she said, "What if I [i.e., Mrs. Park] die first?" . . . and then I went, "You know people die from car accidents, from murder, from you know . . ." and then she asked me, "Are you threatening me?" *And I guess in a way I was threatening her.* . . . And then I went, "What if I killed myself, you know," well, I didn't say that. I didn't say *that* [what if I killed myself], but um . . . what if I did something like that, or something like that. And she knew I was joking. This was when I was really young [chuckles]. . . . But then I really didn't want to talk to her about my problems of not wanting to live because I thought she'd take it the wrong way saying that I'm threatening her to get me a dog. I don't want her to feel that way. I just want her to listen.

Although Jenny, like her mother, made light of this past suicide talk, there was indeed a larger conversation about teen suicide that had unfolded in her community that year. One of Jenny's close friends had moved out of state but was open to Jenny and other friends that she was entertaining thoughts of suicide. When friends at school and Jenny were discussing the girl who had moved away, Jenny reported that they all looked at Jenny to say, "What about you?" Jenny figured that classmates turned to her because "we have the same personality: being a happy person on the outside but a lot more may be going on inside." On another occasion when a friend confronted Jenny, "You never show us your real feelings," Jenny told her, "Well that's just the way I am [chuckles] and *since my Mom's always like that* [i.e., acting as if she is happy] *to me.*" Jenny had quite a bit to say about her own investment in *seeming* happy and drew a connection to trust: she found it difficult to trust people enough to confide in them.

I don't want people to [pauses], I mean I like the way people think about me as a happy person. I don't, it's not that I want them to think, I don't want them to think that I'm a cry baby . . . it's not that. Just [pauses] I guess the main reason honestly is because if I tell someone I know it will be passed on and everybody will find out. And I don't like the idea of that. . . . I know people tell people. It's just a habit. I'm not very good with trusting people, but . . .

That same year that Jenny had "threatened" suicide, there was also a school classmate who died by suicide. While the classmate's suicide had been a huge shock to Jenny, it also made her aware of how far she really was from truly suicidal thoughts:

Oh. It's not that, I never thought I wanted to kill myself. But I thought I don't want to live [chuckles] you know. So um . . . well actually, I'm too . . . Yeah, it's too scary to think I could kill myself [laughs], it's really scary. I'm too scared about that idea. And um . . . I just, I wouldn't be able to do it [chuckles] and it's just a scary thought and I think about the people around me and there are so much more to live for, you know. I mean there's a lot of things, I mean there's a lot of people, a lot of dreams and a lot of goals, why just throw it all away just because of a couple problems, you know. There's more good stuff than bad stuff to it. And this kid was one of the popular kids and it was just such a big shock. It's really sad. So, so many people cried and threw banners up for him and people were singing "Amazing Grace: and uh, he was, ahh [sighs], it was just horrible.

Reflecting on the early ninth-grade time when she thought about not wanting to live, Jenny spoke of "the usual stuff": "So much pressure—school work, cello . . ." When the friend who had moved away asked Jenny if she was suicidal, Jenny described having answered, "No, I'm not. I mean, like people with, who had the same level of pressure, stress as me, they would be . . . but I'm just not like that." With this purported answer, Jenny at once minimized her hardship but also gave voice to the considerable stress in her life at that time.

Bella the dog was, Jenny maintained, the answer to all her woes. Bella would "listen": Jenny did not need to put on a happy face for the dog, and she could trust the dog. For starters, the dog had cured her of TV addiction; she gave her constant companionship and kept her busy taking care of the dog. Above all, though, was that Bella offered a set of ears for times when Jenny felt sad:

I just need someone to talk to when I'm sad because I don't want to call my friends and you know start acting like a baby. I mean, I don't think people who you know call me and go "oh I'm sad," I don't think they are baby but I'm just not that kind of a person. I don't call people when I'm sad or I just, how can I say this. I just like to stay alone by myself but at the same time I want to tell someone my problems.

Jenny struck a humorous note, too, as she spoke of the dutiful way in which Bella "just listens" without talking back:

When I talk to her, she just sits there and just looks at me and it seems like she's listening [chuckles] but I know she can't understand a thing. [With friends though] they're usually the one talking and saying, "It's OK, everybody has hard times" . . . but then [Bella] can't talk back [laughs] you know.

Bella seemed to give both Jenny and her mother a way to both recall tough times and make light of them: if a puppy could be the salve, the problems must not have been so dire after all. We were impressed that Jenny seemed to understand exactly that her mother did not want to entertain any outright conversation about suicide or dark thoughts. Bella's silent attentiveness aside, though, it was clear that Jenny did want someone who could really listen. At her saddest, for example, she described "playing [the cello] really hard—you know so my parents know I'm mad," screaming into her pillow, and playing music really loud.

When I was talking to her [i.e., Mrs. Park], I was saying, "I don't want to live anymore." . . . She didn't want to talk to me about it. . . . Like, she found that I wasn't [truly suicidal], and she listened but not exactly. She didn't know exactly what my problem was but she knew the surface of it, you know. A little bit of it, but not the exact problem, but she knew what led to it, you know, the cello especially. So she told me if I wanted to quit the cello I can. *But I can't* [laughs].

Mrs. Park appeared to have known that cello was the reason Jenny was upset. And yet, rather than engage Jenny in deep conversation about suicide, Mrs. Park's solution was first to give Jenny the apparent choice of quitting cello. When that proved to be a difficult choice for Jenny, Mrs. Park relented and allowed Jenny to get a pet dog. Years later, when recounting the episode, Jenny mused maturely, "I just wanted my Mom to listen. But yeah, I understand. It's way too hard for a mom to handle that."

Coda: Managing Consensus, Continued

It was quite clear that Jenny was still making considerable efforts to "make family work," and probably her parents were as well. With her decision to pursue a nonmusic career, Jenny had to reconcile her new independent path with her orchestrated life, in which her mother was such an actor. Jenny—who had been able, even amidst turbulent teen years, to describe a harmonious family life and a unique mother-daughter friendship—continued to smooth out the rough patches with her family, at least those pertaining to her mother.

We spoke with Jenny soon after she had graduated from the same conservatory that her mother had attended, and soon after she had decided not to pursue a professional career in music. That summer, Jenny was enjoying an exhilarating musical stretch—a sort of last hurrah of her musical career—at a prestigious summer music festival. Even as she knew that there were seventeen college-level science and math courses between her and an application to veterinary school, she was excited and optimistic. However, six months later when we caught up with her, she was living at home with her parents and managing three part-time jobs, and the thought of taking science courses had grown a bit distant. Jenny reported that some of her private cello lessons with Korean American high school students she taught were scheduled as late as midnight, and we could not imagine how she was managing. Her father had suggested that Jenny contribute to her brother's college education fund. Indeed, this was, Jenny described, the lowest point in her family's economic history, coming off years of her father not working; and to make matters worse, her mother was suffering from arthritis, a frightening condition for a musician and music teacher. Jenny was still madly in love with her boyfriend, whom she had met at the conservatory, a musical whiz who was headed for a professional career in music. She had agreed with both her boyfriend and her mother that it was best that they both first get settled into their careers before marrying. But when would that be, if Jenny had to first take years' worth of science courses before even applying for admission to a veterinary school? Yet, Jenny seemed to be at peace with her situation.

Even over a year later, in a conversation with Sumie when it was becoming clear that Jenny's dreams of becoming a veterinarian might be deferred, she still expressed no ill will toward her mother. Interestingly, for Jenny it was her father who seemed to figure as a negative role model. Jenny was, in the face of his persistent failures to provide for the family, determined to work hard and become financially solvent. And with the financial realities sinking in, particularly as Jenny's income from working as a receptionist in a medical office and as a cello teacher was helping to finance her brother's college education and her wealthy grandfather had passed away, Jenny had changed her career goal. Now, instead of pursuing veterinary school, she was studying toward a nursing degree. She surmised that it might take her until she was thirty before she was working professionally as a nurse, but she seemed at peace with this pathway and told Sumie that her mother was very supportive of her decision.

Jenny was not wallowing in immigrant pity, and in fact expressed no resentment about the family financial responsibilities that she was shouldering. In her conversation with Sumie, Jenny instead sounded grateful for the past contributions of her grandparents and her parents to her musical education, and she felt that it was her turn to contribute to the family's economic well-being. And she made no reference to wealthier peers from high school days or the conservatory. Of course, this does not mean that Jenny had not made some of these calculations. While it was indeed her pre-professional musical training that was making for Jenny's probably considerable supplementary income, she did not call attention to the ethnic contours of her musical training's value within her community nor to its origin as the only asset that her immigrant mother could imagine passing down. In her young adulthood, Jenny was reconciling with her immigrant circumstances and their implications as she faced the challenges of switching gears. Jenny made clear that summer right after she decided to quit music—Nancy asked explicitly—that she harbored no resentment toward her mother. In fact, Jenny spoke of being grateful that she had been able to decide to change course. She was still working on making her family work.

6

Eric

The Long Diagnosis

The Shin family is the only family in our study with a son, Eric, who—at the time of our initial ethnographic engagement and still a decade later—did not proceed to college (or to a conservatory, as in Jenny's case). In fact, whether Eric would graduate on time from high school, given his frequent truancy and various misdemeanors, was a real question for the family at the time. They were also the only family in which a parent (Mr. Shin) had immigrated to the United States prior to his adulthood, in 1974. They emerge as a family that, by necessity, was compelled to think hard about what had happened to derail Eric from an expected pathway toward college and about their own immigrant lives in relation to those developments. They also come to life as a family that has made considerable efforts to come to terms with Eric's nonnormative path: Korean American adulthood without a college degree. Yet, as with the other families featured in this book, race—and how it mattered—was a considerable part of these reflections, both for their own lives and for Eric's.

Eric and his younger sister, Christine, do not figure into this chapter as much as we would have liked them to: they were not always enthusiastic participants in the family ethnography. For Eric's part, we can surmise that tense relations with his parents during his adolescence made the thought of speaking with our team unappealing at best; that said, he was always entirely polite. For her part, Christine was all too aware of her older brother's rocky road and seemed focused on forging her own smoother way toward college and a career; Hyeyoung's conversations with her proceeded apace but did not seem to build easily to something more comfortable.

That all was not well for the Shins made for a veritable torrent of reflections to which we bore witness. Over the years, Mr. and Mrs. Shin's thinking ranged from the personal to the structural: together, the parents ruminated over many of their own parenting decisions and practices that may have contributed to Eric's meandering path toward adulthood. Mr. and Mrs. Shin also deliberated endlessly about both the ethnic and the larger American community that they felt had not served them so very well. We hope that the reader will at once appreciate that their circumstances made for reflections that strike more painful notes than those of many of the other parents in this book, while also observing that the fault lines of their often quite anguished reflections are ones that are, in fact, not so very different from those of the other families who managed more mundane struggles.

Throughout the years, our research team heard the parents' reflections about how much "Korean" parenting was too much or too little and what it took for their children to carve out a life in "America." Whereas other families in this book could make more casual references to what "Korean" and "American" stood for, Mr. and Mrs. Shin had to mull over these matters with considerable pain.

The Eye of the Storm

The Problems with Our Survey

The Shins, like the Kohs, were a family that put themselves on our map to be studied. Our relationship with them began with the parent survey that we administered at their Korean Protestant church in the north suburbs of Chicago. As she turned in her completed survey to the research team members, Mrs. Shin also let the graduate researchers know that the survey had not managed to capture the situation of the likes of *her* family. She thought that we should have asked about the experience of childrearing in greater depth. Mrs. Shin put it bluntly to Hyeyoung, saying, "You don't have a child, do you?" and continuing, "So you probably don't understand what parents go through to raise kids in this country." When Hyeyoung asked her to elaborate, Mrs. Shin suggested, for example, that when asking about conflicts between parents and teens, we should have been more specific (such as conflicts over serving Korean versus American food, which is quite different from conflicts over values). And she added that the survey had not allowed her to register her frustration at the difficulty of finding resources that document "what other parents in similar situations go through." The team was quick to let her know that the ethnographic phase of our project was designed to do just that: to document the complexity of people's family lives. As was the case with our initial contact with Ben's family, and Doug's as well, this first encounter would prove remarkably foretelling of what we would learn about this family in the years to come. (In fact, well into the first year of our ethnographic engagement, Mrs. Shin told us outright that she and her family had agreed to participate in our study both to set the record straight and to perhaps ease the suffering of other Korean immigrant families.)

When, days later, Hyeyoung called Mrs. Shin at the dry cleaner she then owned and ran, Mrs. Shin again mentioned her unhappiness with the survey questions. "It was not the length that bothered me," she noted, "but that it was limited in addressing a *different* experience." She explained to Hyeyoung that she felt particularly bad when she compared herself and the Korean community more generally with Jewish people and the Jewish community—a comparison that probably came to mind because her family resided in Elk Forest, a northern suburb of Chicago with a notable Jewish presence that she described as a very "Jewish town." Two years later, over a quiet dinner with us in their impeccable suburban home, Mrs. Shin would wistfully describe her perception of the well-resourced Jewish community, with an infrastructure that provided Jewish children with "just what they needed." Mr. and Mrs. Shin were frank in their opinion that not all was well with their Korean American community, least of all with their own son, Eric.

With hindsight, we appreciate that the Shins' mention of their "different experience" was foremost a matter of their considerable difficulties with Eric. With the same hindsight, we can also reflect on Mrs. Shin's quick mention of Jews and their better community resources: a resounding issue for the Shins was their sense of isolation and a feeling that there was no ethnic community to which they could entrust the complexity and perhaps the "differences" of *their* family life. But let us turn back the clock to Eric's problematic high school days, when we first encountered him and his family.

"How Could He Have Done That?"

We start with a particularly memorable story. About six months into our ethnographic observations with the family, Mrs. Shin had agreed to meet Hyeyoung after a Sunday church service. When they met up, Mrs. Shin asked her to wait while she served sandwiches and drinks to the children—the church members apparently took turns on various tasks and this day was apparently her turn. While Mrs. Shin stood in front of the gym serving, Hyeyoung thought to look for Eric. She spotted him chatting with some girls but worried that she might be intruding if she were to approach him. Just as she was wavering as to what to do, Mrs. Shin called out to Eric. It appeared to Hyeyoung that Mrs. Shin was scolding Eric and what she could make out was, "Why didn't you answer your phone? Where were you? And what were you doing?" Hyeyoung took note that Eric remained calm and told his mother that he would meet up with a friend after church. As they parted, Mrs. Shin said firmly in Korean, "Be home by five!" Eric answered in English, "I'll try, we'll see," and she repeated herself in Korean, "by five!" As Mrs. Shin and Hyeyoung walked out to the church parking lot, Mrs. Shin said, "Eric is giving us so much trouble these days. *It's a war-zone with him.*" As they drove, Mrs. Shin began a detailed accounting of the events from the preceding summer.

The story went that Eric had been caught stealing his classmate's wallet from a backpack at school. Eric had insisted that it had all been a joke and that after taking it, he had in fact given it to a friend who ended up spending the money. Mr. and Mrs. Shin asked Eric to call the boy from whom he had stolen; Eric claimed he had tried but could not reach him. At their wits' end and learning that the incident had been reported to the police, the Shins reached out to the boy's parents, learned of the amount in question (forty dollars), and took Eric to the boy's house for a personal apology late one evening: the Shins apologized to the parents (the boy was not home), but Mrs. Shin reported that Eric had said *nothing*. By this point in the telling, Mrs. Shin was becoming visibly emotional:

He's my son, but I just don't understand how he could have done that. Is it that there is something wrong with him ethically? Or . . . how could he have done something so wrong and not apologize to the bitter end? . . . And even though I am his parent, I could barely bring myself to show my face to that boy's parents.

Mrs. Shin added that the victim's mother said she had remembered Eric as a "good student" in middle school, and it was clear that the boy's mother too seemed to be wondering, "What happened?" By this point in the story Mrs. Shin and Hyeyoung had arrived at an American-style restaurant—interestingly, a restaurant near the church but not frequented by church people—and when Hyeyoung asked whether she could record the conversation, Mrs. Shin replied, "From the start I said I would help, so if I'm going to help I have to go through with it." A four-hour conversation ensued.

As it turns out, the victim's father scolded Eric that evening in exactly the way that Mrs. Shin would have liked to herself. The victim's family eventually dropped the charges; Mrs. Shin speculated that they may have done so because they remembered Eric as a good kid in middle school and because the Shin family appeared at their door to apologize. For Mrs. Shin the incident had been "the greatest humiliation of my life." The Shins grounded Eric and took away many of his privileges. It was, however, Eric's nearly blasé response to it all—a response that she could not fathom—that made her recall this incident with irony: "[A]t that time, it was *me* who suffered the most."

Although the fallout from Eric's theft was, at the time, what felt most devastating to Mrs. Shin, we had been hearing about her struggles with Eric from the start of our ethnographic contacts. Six months earlier when Hyeyoung had first met with Mrs. Shin, after a long discussion about some of the indignities of running a dry cleaning business, Mrs. Shin turned the conversation to Eric. It all began in seventh grade, she told Hyeyoung. The teacher called Mrs. Shin to say that there were missing homework and missing parent signatures. Eric promised his parents then that it would never happen again, but in retrospect, this episode was only the beginning. Soon thereafter they learned that Eric had begun skipping school. She recalled a meeting with the teacher to try to resolve Eric's truancy, but the problem only got worse, with many fights and poor grades to follow. By this point in that conversation, Mrs. Shin observed that the Korean music in the restaurant was "depressing" and suggested moving to Starbuck's. Over coffee, she told Hyeyoung another story signaling Eric's trouble. After a family trip to Mexico, they found Mexican cigarettes and condoms in his wallet. Mrs. Shin asked her husband to speak with Eric, but the conversation did not go well and Eric began staying out late at night.

Over the next eighteen months of the family ethnography, the Shins would return to these and other episodes from Eric's teenage years again and again. The litany was long, but the details were repetitive: Eric's transgressions, attempted interventions at school and at home, promises that would be quickly forgotten, and then another transgression.

"Where Do I Draw the Line?"

It was clear that managing Eric's behavior had become a daily headache and heartache for Mrs. Shin. Again and again, Mrs. Shin asked, "Where do I draw the line? It's not as if you can lock up a big kid like this [at home]." This was all the more complicated because Eric recruited his parents to cover for his failings. There were, for example, several incidents in which Eric had asked his parents to lie to the school for him: once when he was exhausted from staying out all night and wanted to skip the morning classes; another time because he was not ready for an exam and asked his parents to call him in sick. Both times, further lies had ensued. "We knew he was heading in the wrong direction, but what were we to do?" she told Hyeyoung.

The calculations were messy and many considerations muddied the picture, whether it was their own frustrations with Eric's school or their inevitable concerns about Eric's general well-being. Tellingly, in the very first discussion with Hyeyoung about Eric's school problems and a recent face-to-face meeting with a teacher to discuss Eric, Mrs. Shin (although fully aware of Eric's transgressions) was dismayed at the teacher's punitive approach and wondered whether racism was at play. Then there was the fact that Eric said things to his parents that stymied them as they contemplated what to do: he spoke, for example, of his own loneliness and of having few people to confide in. Mr. and Mrs. Shin could not help but worry about his mental health in the midst of the trouble he was causing. Even as Mrs. Shin was keenly aware of her own vulnerability to Eric's often manipulative manner with her, worries about Eric's mental health and loneliness nonetheless struck a chord, sometimes resonating with her own immigrant experiences.

Enormously frustrating for the Shins was that, through it all, Eric seemed quite impervious to discipline. The systems of reward and punishment that the Shins knew would work for most children simply did not seem to register with Eric. For hours, Mrs. Shin reviewed the vicious cycles of reprimanding, punishing, worrying, and finally comforting—"We knew that it was, after all, important to somehow show him that we *still* loved him"—and the near despair as the patterns repeated themselves. "Never mind the betrayal, I really have absolutely no idea what to do with him. Truthfully, I'm frightened." She detailed the cycle of lies upon lies and admitted that there had been times when she had to stop herself from saying, "Whenever you open your mouth you lie. No wonder you have no friends." But, then again, at another point she described being torn. "[I]t is sad that I know I can't trust him 100 percent," she said, but "at the same time, [I want] to believe him . . . and in any case, I can't ask him every time to verify that what he has just told me is true." And adding another layer of complexity, she second-guessed herself: "He is the age at which you want to hide things from your parents. That's the age at which *to some extent you have to lie.*" But, just the same, she was still confused: "So where do I draw the line? What lies do I accept?" Further, she worried that were she to corner him about each and every lie, Eric's "personality might be ruined."

Hyeyoung had witnessed these sorts of machinations in the making even during her first visit with the whole family. She observed a tense exchange as to whether the teens could go out in the evening. At one point in the conversation, Mr. Shin had put his foot down, "No one leaves this house!" Later, he capitulated that Eric might go out but would need to be home by 11:00 p.m.—it seemed that he had given in because Eric would be driving his sister and another girl as well. As the teens left that night, Mrs. Shin said to Hyeyoung, "From time to time we need to give them the satisfaction of deceiving us."

Struggling to Graduate

It was very clear that at the height of Eric's difficulties at high school, it was not a foregone conclusion that he would graduate from high school, let alone go on to college. Mrs. Shin described just how often her husband talked to her about Eric not making it to college and how piercingly painful his words had often been for her. She told us that Mr. Shin had said, "If that kid even graduates from high school, it will be 'thank you' [in English]." And she continued, "Can you imagine as a mother how painful it was to hear those words? I was in such pain and so angry that I couldn't even answer him. [I told him] 'Are you really his father? How can you say such crazy things?'" For her own part, Mrs. Shin had this to say:

> I want [Eric] to have a comfortable job, a comfortable life. Of course, if it's a professional job, all the better. So I guess that's why we worry about a future that hasn't even happened yet. With these grades, what will he be able to do? But in the U.S. at least you don't starve. I guess he'll end up being able to graduate from "high school" [in English]. I'm thinking that he'll end up going to a "community college" [in English].

Once, Mrs. Shin admitted to Hyeyoung, "I just wish that when problems arose there was someone who could have given me the answers!" She shared that once Christine had asked her, "Why aren't you stricter with Eric? How come you don't punish him more?" to which she had answered, "In the long run, is it punishment or patience that would get him back on track?" Mrs. Shin described talking with her husband after yet another scuffle with Eric and their wondering together, "How did it come to this?" Hyeyoung and many members of our research team heard and saw the agonizing ways in which Mrs. Shin tried to factor in Eric's psychological makeup, racialized immigrant experience, and adolescent development as she attempted to navigate the challenges of dealing with his ceaseless maneuverings.

The Long Diagnosis

"Mine Is a Stern Face": Immigrant Masculinity

In many encounters over the years with us, Mr. and Mrs. Shin ventured a number of psychological theories about Eric. What troubled Mrs. Shin was her sense of her son's fragility in the face of her husband's macho style, which, in his words, was his "gambler's confidence," his "winning hand." Eric had been a sickly, asthmatic child who required constant attention and many doctors' visits, and she recalled having to go pick up Eric from school frequently for even minor cuts and scrapes. Eric's delicacy was, she described, a sore spot for her husband, who would have preferred a rough-and-tumble type of a son; boys should be "sturdy," he once told us. Eric was a careful child, "the kind of kid who would go to pains to match up his socks," unlike his tomboy sister, "who grabbed any which sock and would be dressed in an instant." Mr. Shin would scream, "What's a boy doing taking so much time to do *that*?" While her husband did understand that Eric was a bit of a "pitiable child," Mrs. Shin sensed that for her husband Eric was a disappointing first-born, and she surmised that Mr. Shin's disappointment perhaps accounted for the corporal punishment he had meted out to young Eric. She said, "It broke my heart, so I would just snatch Eric away from him and scream to Eric, 'Why did you do that? Just tell dad you're sorry!'"

Understanding the great divide in character between the two, Mrs. Shin wondered whether Eric had perhaps suffered from what he had experienced at his father's hands. She once described how her husband yelled at the then five-year-old Eric to "stop coughing! If you keep coughing we're going home." She protested, "How can you tell a coughing child to stop?" Mrs. Shin thought of her husband's manner as entirely consistent with that of "the men in his family, who can't express their emotions in an appropriate fashion." In Jin-Heon's earliest encounter with the family (Jin-Heon, our sole male graduate researcher, was often called upon to interview the fathers in our family ethnography in order to put them at ease), Mr. Shin himself was honest about his own parenting mishaps. Not unlike his wife, Mr. Shin described the patriarchal ("Korean") culture of his family and particularly of his own father, who was also an eldest son. Taking after his father, he described his own cold demeanor, which had once scared a niece and sent her crying: "My friends have told me that although I am small, mine is a stern face."

Indeed, a significant part of Mrs. Shin's analysis of Eric concerned his constitution—his physical and emotional delicacy. If only she and her husband might have, she mused, "let Eric be." Once she described Eric's "fate": "If only I could have better understood his character, well, it makes no difference now, but maybe we could have raised him with less resistance."

Even the Doctor Is Confounded

In addition to Mr. and Mrs. Shin's own deep reflections on Eric's psychological makeup, we learned that the parents had also consulted with a co-ethnic psychologist whose thoughts and words—and change of heart—both guided and echoed the parents' parenting calculations. When Eric's challenges began, the parents sought the help of Dr. Suh, a family friend and fellow church member who was also a psychologist. It seemed that some of the consultation arrangements had been informal (e.g., family dinners joined by Dr. Suh), whereas others had been more therapy-like sessions. Mr. Shin described Dr. Suh as someone he respected deeply, and indeed Dr. Suh figured across many of the accounts as another voice in the room, wondering both how "things had come to this" and where they might be headed. That said, Mrs. Shin once told us that she wondered whether it had been a problem that Dr. Suh was in fact a drinking buddy of Mr. Shin's.

Mrs. Shin's struggles as to where to draw the line in responding to and disciplining Eric appeared very much to have formed in dialogue with Dr. Suh, who had a great deal to say about the delicate act of teen parenting. He told the Shins not to stress about Eric's academic performance, telling them, "Eric is facing a tunnel that he needs to pass through alone. We, parents, just have to wait." Mrs. Shin acknowledged that the doctor was right but admitted to finding the wait pretty challenging. He encouraged them meanwhile to be loving and supportive parents. In the light of this interaction, we can appreciate that some of her travails about where to draw the line were born of her interest in providing the love and support the doctor had prescribed. Also hard for Mrs. Shin was Dr. Suh's prescription that parents should never disagree in front of their children. We can only imagine how vexing this advice was for Mrs. Shin given her sometimes misgivings about her husband's disciplining methods.

However, Dr. Suh's advice was not entirely consistent over time. In later years, some of Dr. Suh's messages changed, advocating instead for a tough love approach so that Eric might not become "too dependent." And even later, Dr. Suh would intervene at a critical moment when he diagnosed Eric's biggest problem as his having lost all confidence in his own future. Dr. Suh would even arrange a part-time job for Eric, hoping that it would open up a new path for him. In this way, as a family friend and a psychologist, Dr. Suh seemed to have been drawn into the Shin family's dilemma over how to best parent a troubled Korean American teen and to ponder along with the Shins on their evolving "diagnosis" and strategies. As a co-ethnic and a family friend, the doctor seemed to have no obvious cultural or clinical solution to offer the distressed family.

The Teenagers

In contrast to the agonizing tales of various parenting challenges that Mr. and Mrs. Shin shared across occasions, our team's meetings with Eric and Christine had left us wanting. When we first met Eric and his younger sister, Christine, as teenagers (ages sixteen and fourteen, respectively), they both struck us as quite ordinary teens. They were both also somewhat shy and reluctant to reveal much of themselves to Hyeyoung despite her considerable efforts to draw them out. For example, upon learning that the family had owned a Maltese dog some years earlier (that had died of an illness) and that Christine had been quite fond of her pet dog, Hyeyoung traveled with her own Maltese puppy (making the three-hundred-plus-mile round-trip drive from Champaign to the Shins' Chicago suburban home) to one of her early visits with Christine. Aside from a momentary excitement at seeing Hyeyoung's puppy, Christine did not very easily engage with Hyeyoung or other members of our research team.

Notwithstanding keeping Hyeyoung at arm's length, Christine did reveal as a young teen that she did not feel especially close to her parents. (This lack of closeness with parents, Christine felt, was pretty normative among her friendship circle, made up entirely of Korean American teens.) Mr. and Mrs. Shin appeared to be vigilant about Christine's friendships, constantly assessing which friend might exert a good or bad influence on her. Christine did not feel resentful about their protective stance and understood that their strictness was their effort to protect her from going down the same troubled path that Eric was traveling. Christine had remembered a period of constant and intense fighting between Eric and her parents, which she reported to have ended about a year or two before our initial contact with the family, and the stress that the family discord had exacted on everyone, including her. She had been scared enough by how upset and angry Eric's behavior had made her parents, especially her father, and she had resolved to behave well. At the same time, she had felt caught between her loyalty to her parents and her loyalty to her brother. In one instance, she recalled Eric confiding in her that he planned to run away from home. She had given her cell phone to Eric to take with him because the parents had taken his away as a punishment for some misdeed, but she then had to answer to her parents' inquiries as to why she had given her phone to Eric.

From time to time over the subsequent years, we would get small glimpses of Christine as the daughter who rarely strayed from the role of a well-behaved younger sister. We surmised that Christine herself may have felt the implicit obligation to avoid adding to her parents' stresses. Her uneventful adolescence, her college attendance and graduation from a well-regarded liberal arts college in a neighboring state, and an eventual career path as a naturalist for a state park system provided solace and pride to her parents.

On the other hand, while Eric's reputation as the troubled son preceded our meeting with him, he at age sixteen struck our research team members as an unassuming, if somewhat bored and unambitious, teenager. Hyeyoung noted, for example, in her conversations with Eric that he did not try to strike a "macho" pose and readily acknowledged to her that a recent horror movie he had seen with his buddies had spooked him. He also admitted to Hyeyoung, "I kind of got messed up in high school" and had gotten into various fights in and out of school. In the instance where he and another student were caught fighting and were suspended for three days from school (and subsequently grounded for two weeks by his parents), Eric felt that his parents had not really listened to his side of the story but also that his own behavior had been "stupid."

Eric had said that he did not do well at school (and when pressed, he revealed that he had a "B average"). Whereas a B average in and of itself did not strike us as a particularly poor showing, we understood that within his family circle, his middling school grades, combined with constant misbehavior, were sources of distress. In a somewhat poignant note, Eric told Hyeyoung a story about his older male cousin, who was his role model. This cousin had graduated from the same high school as Eric and had a reputation as an intimidating figure because of his associations with Korean "gang bangers." In one instance, Eric had a run-in with a large group of White high school classmates who accused Eric of giving them a dirty look. Eric, sensing trouble, called his "legendary" cousin for help. His cousin arrived some twenty minutes later with a posse of his Korean American friends and scared away the White group, which impressed Eric. Eric said that his parents liked this cousin because he was successful—the cousin had done well academically in high school even though he was not a "good boy," had gone on to attend a Big Ten university, and was well on his way to a prestigious law school. The story of this "legendary" cousin struck a sour note in that same evening, as Hyeyoung and Eric joined the family for dinner and the topic of Hyeyoung's attendance at the University of Illinois came up. Mrs. Shin mentioned that perhaps Eric could attend the University of Illinois, and Eric retorted that it was unlikely that his poor grades would qualify him for admission. Eric was quite clear, even as a sixteen-year-old, that he was already derailed from the expected Korean American pathway toward "attending a good university and becoming a doctor" (Eric's shorthand for what he understood to be the desirable second-generation Korean American emerging adulthood).

In a casual afternoon outing that started with a lunch at a hamburger place and then went on to a few games at a pool hall with Hyeyoung and Brian (a Korean American male undergraduate research assistant who had grown up in a town neighboring Eric's), Eric revealed that he was interested in becoming either an architect or a chef. Eric had some thoughts about applying to a different Big Ten school that was reputed to have less competitive admission than the University of Illinois. Eric had listened intently to Brian's tales of his high school experience and applying to colleges. We had felt hopeful, then, about Eric's prospects for his transition from a high school "bad boy" to a more engaged college student, even as our research team's ensuing conversations with his parents suggested that his journey toward emerging adulthood was a bumpy one.

Our ethnographic encounters with Eric and Christine, alas, did not provide fresh insights into their perspectives. We surmised that Christine's "strategy" in response to the struggles between Eric and the parents was to cast a thin shadow—that is, to do her best not to add to the family distress. Eric, on the other hand, seemed rudderless. For the most part, he appeared disinterested in accommodating to his parents' efforts to right his course. And surely, it was this apparent lack of empathy toward his parents' efforts to help him that frustrated Mr. and Mrs. Shin the most. It was only years later that we saw some movements on Eric's part to be more "Korean" in ways that he knew pleased his father (e.g., showing respect to his elder relatives, being kind when his father fell ill) and to accede to his parents' plans to carve out a career path for him.

Parents' Immigrant Trials

As with many of the parents in this book, Mr. and Mrs. Shin were outspoken about many of the indignities of life for immigrants as racial minorities in the United States. As we have seen in our discussions of the Kohs, the Chungs, and the Parks, race was an intergenerational equation for this family as well, as parents calibrated their children's second-generation challenges in dialogue with their own immigrant paths.

"I Am Not 1.5": Mr. Shin and Race in America

The sense we had from Mr. Shin was of parenting for survival in a less than benevolent America. He was proud of his hard-earned wisdom; we could sense that he meant to offer his children the notes from the trenches—even as he once admitted to Jin-Heon, "My parenting was all wrong. I was too strict." Although Mr. Shin had immigrated as an adolescent, he was insistent that he was not a "1.5-generation" immigrant, meaning that his had been no easier a path than that of the other adult Korean immigrants in his midst. Indeed, having come as a high school student in the 1970s, Mr. Shin counts as one of the earlier post-1965 immigrants—most Korean immigrants would arrive in later decades—and it is not surprising that he would suggest his affinity with first-generation immigrants. If anything, Mr. Shin seemed to want to stress that his problems in the United States had been even greater while "*their* problem is only being, you know, being a stranger in this country." He continued that people like him had language problems that were in some ways harder than those of adult immigrants, who are "expected" to have those problems. It seemed that Mr. Shin foremost wanted to deflect any easy teleology that adjustment is smoother for those who immigrate before adulthood. Moreover, he rejected any facile notion that integration into American life becomes easier for American-born children of immigrants. He explained, "And my kids, [their challenges] will be somewhat less than mine, but they are still going to go through the same problems that I've gone through."

In this light, it is not surprising that Mr. Shin's thinking about raising "American" children was ambivalent. Although he figured that it was inevitable that immigrant children raised in the United States would become "American," he was not eager for his own children to become "99 percent American." He stressed that Korean Americans needed to become a particular kind of American who is "raised to compete in this world." In this vein, Mr. Shin was also keen to observe over several conversations that Eric was "becoming one of us [Koreans]," which for him seemed to speak of a particular moral fiber.

Many of Mr. Shin's seasoned thoughts about Eric had been honed across his own employment biography. For a total of twenty-three years, he worked for a large American corporation. He said he even used to call himself "Mr. [name of the corporation]" until he lost his job in 2003. Once, early in his corporate career, he "gambled"—Mr. Shin prided himself on being a gambler—leaving the company to strike out on his own in California. The business failed, he lost all his assets, returned to Chicago, moved the family to Newport Crossings (the well-known barebones apartment complex in the area where, it turned out, the Hyun family in chapter 7 resided at the time of our ethnography), and hung his head low to ask for his old job back. As to eventually losing his corporate job, he claimed that he had long seen the writing on the wall: "I knew this was coming, knew it all along" and "I knew exactly what I had to do." He had in fact bought a dry cleaning shop, which Mrs. Shin ran, on the eve of being laid off.

Mr. Shin peppered this employment biography with accounts of his own careful and objective assessments of the situation, enlivened as well with a dose of bravado. In an early meeting with Jin-Heon, for example, he described having once made a list of his own strengths and weaknesses as he plotted his future. Even his marriage was testimony to his firm character; he decided nearly immediately upon being introduced to his future wife that he wanted to marry her. And as the gambler that he prided himself on being, he proposed to her with a confident statement: "I think I have a winning hand."

His winning hand aside, it was "this [American] life" that had been giving him trouble and would, he surmised, continue to do so in his children's lives. Mr. Shin had a tidy list of his challenges as an immigrant: language, race ("I don't want to call it racism, you know, but the different race is one thing"), and culture. Language and culture, he explained, are part and parcel: not being able to "get" American jokes even as he could follow them word by word. It was the "heart" of the matter that was somehow lost on him, he told us: "different from the way of touching our heart. That's what I meant by the cultural differences." And as the years wore on, Mr. Shin said he had watched his own social circle become exclusively Korean as he aged. He knew well and liked his former White coworkers and used to spend time with them, but there was an inevitable ethnic narrowing of social ties all around. By the end of our ethnographic encounter, most of Mr. and Mrs. Shin's social circle consisted of Mr. Shin's Korean American friends from high school and college.

Noting that his American-born children were still marked as being different from mainstream America—and again running against any talk of easy assimilation—Mr. Shin figured that it would be the "third, fourth, or fifth generation [who will be] similar to them [i.e., Americans]." What then was Mr. Shin's toolkit for managing this unforgiving and powerful U.S. society? He described to us that he had foremost tried to "protect the kids . . . rather than, you know, let nature take [its course]." Although family matters had not gone as he had hoped, he had prided himself on having given his children a set of "bullet points": "Ok, you do what you want to do, you do what you want to do, but don't forget: *These* are the principles." He spoke of children's primary job as getting good grades so that they can pursue something "they love to do." Mr. Shin explained that, to him, the necessity of having good grades had everything to do with being an immigrant of color: "For being a minority, you have to have knowledge." On another occasion, he explained his resolve to Jin-Heon this way: "I'm alone in the United States. Friendship is rare in the U.S. A person's foundation in American society is education. A person's degree is really important." He did, though, regret that he had been so hard on Eric: "Honestly," he put it to Jin-Heon, "sometimes I punished [my son] just because I was emotionally in a bad way myself." In the same way that Mrs. Shin wavered over where to draw the line, we found Mr. Shin struggling over what—after all—mattered: functional immigrant values or a more flexible approach to parenting.

Mrs. Shin: "It's a Sad Story"

Much like the case of Mr. Shin, it was clear from our conversations with Mrs. Shin that in her mind Eric's problems were intimately tied to her own struggles as an adult newcomer to the United States. Immigrant America was not easy, and neither was immigrant parenting. In one of our many conversations with Mrs. Shin about Eric, she mused, "I'm an easy figure for him," thinking about all the ways he took advantage of her. Then she paused and continued, "I can't help but feel sorry for him. Our being Korean and his growing up in the U.S.; there is no question, it has been hard for him."

Having married into a Korean American family who had left Korea in the 1970s and having initially lived with her husband and her in-laws, Mrs. Shin had found herself in a household that was more traditional than she could have ever imagined. Her husband's family was one "that still did [Confucian] ancestral services!" She arrived in the United States in 1986 but told us that it was not until after living in the States for seven years that she was reconciled to staying for good. It was in fact a trip home to South Korea and the stark realization that she no longer fit in there ("I saw that it would have taken much more than seven years to readjust there") that cemented her reality: she would live out her days and eventually be buried on U.S. soil. "Now when I pass a cemetery, I just think, OK, I'll find a better spot, prettier than that one," she joked to indicate that she had accommodated to her American destiny.

Early in her marriage, through a referral by a relative of her husband's contact, Mrs. Shin became a local "star" as an announcer on Chicagoland's premier Korean radio program, and later as a part-time TV anchor. She was thus a working mother in the early years of her children's lives and relied on co-ethnic babysitters. It was the challenges of childcare, however, that led her to eventually quit her job, the last straw being the winter when it was "so cold that the oranges froze in Florida." When she later returned to work, she worked in the family's dry cleaning shop that Mr. Shin had opened as a cautionary measure on the brink of losing his corporate job. When we last saw the family, she was busily—and with considerable panache—running a nail salon.

Although at the nail salon it was apparent that Mrs. Shin had become quite comfortable speaking English, for years it had been her Achilles heel. For Mrs. Shin her lack of comfort with English had often figured as the protagonist in her tales of immigrant woe. Told that as a radio announcer she would be an emissary of the station, Mrs. Shin spent her early years entirely swept up in the Korean-speaking community. Mrs. Shin was always dressed impeccably when we met, so this employment history came as no surprise to the members of our research team. In retrospect, Mrs. Shin thought of this early chapter in her immigrant life (where she had been immersed in ethnic media) as having prevented her from taking the time to learn American ways and to make progress in English. The toll was, in her eyes, a heavy one. College educated, she simply could not bear the indignities of her faltering English in public. Several times she described Christine's attempts to draw her mother out into their neighborhood playground and her own pathetic retreats to her home, which she justified by protesting that "Korean cooking takes so much time so I need to leave now." Little Christine, she described, "literally pulled my arms, begging that I socialize [with other neighborhood mothers]" on the playground and on the streets. She described being nervous "to even step out of the house" for fear a neighbor would approach her and engage her in a conversation in English. Her pained accounts resonate with those of many of the parents in this book. Like them, she also described the anguish of strained conversation with her children: that she could not relay her innermost thoughts, especially to her younger daughter, was not, she stressed, "a hard story" but a "*sad story . . . sad.*"

But the issues were larger than English alone. Mrs. Shin was keenly aware of the cultural and racial divides that her children faced as immigrant Americans of color. She had a great deal to say about observing her children becoming racially self-conscious in elementary school, and in turn about the process through which her children came to have nearly exclusive Korean American social circles—spurred in part by the many Korean immigrant families that had been moving into their neighborhood over the course of their childhood. It all began in grades three to five, she told us, and cemented in middle school. She described it as a process by which they came to see themselves as "different." She was initially shocked, for example, when a young Christine told her that it would be better to not put out *kimchi* when her non-Korean friends came over, worried that they would find the smell distasteful.

Her halting English communication skills were also very much a factor in the long saga of Eric's tortured relationship to school: the many
phone calls from the school as to his whereabouts, the visits to the
school, and so on. Indeed, the parents of troubled children are called
upon to verbalize much more to the schools than those of children who
are making their way without problems. She described literally sleep-
less nights if she knew that the next day would require English—even
arranging a play date was terrifying. She did eventually make more
formal efforts to learn English, but the sense we gleaned from her was
that her efforts were "too little, too late." Perhaps clearest of all, across
our conversations, were regrets about having decided early on that their
home would be an exclusively Korean-language household. However,
their decision was tested time and again with every linguistic challenge
that she and her children faced. For example, Mrs. Shin recalled being
startled when Eric did not answer to his English name when the kindergarten teacher approached him. Until then Eric had been a fan of
Korean-language children's television programs and the parents had
prided themselves on his perfect Korean. However, in the aftermath of
the small but jarring incident with his kindergarten teacher, Mrs. Shin
started having Eric watch English television and eventually withdrew
both children from the Korean Saturday language school. The Shins
seemed to wonder whether an English-language household would have
bridged some of the divides, but we sensed that they were not entirely
convinced of this either.

In a later conversation with Mrs. Shin some years into the family ethnography, at a point when we could sense that the eye of the storm had
finally passed, she mused that it was in fact because of Eric's problems
that she had begun to "speak out" in English, to hold her head high even
with her still-partial command of the language. In the calm of reflection,
as she had to contend with Eric's present and future, which were somehow "good enough," so too was her English.

Isolated in the Ethnic Enclave

A sticking point for the Shins that emerged even within our earliest encounter with this family was the Korean "community," to which
they decidedly felt they could not turn in their times of need. Mr. and

Mrs. Shin detailed a complicated relationship to their suburban Korean Protestant church that included times of retreat as well as of return to the fold. But both Mr. and Mrs. Shin had had periods in which they were closer to the church. There had been, for example, the time when the church approached Mr. Shin about teaching Sunday school in the English youth ministry, with the logic that as a 1.5-generation immigrant, his English was better than that of other Korean immigrant adults. Mr. Shin in fact said yes, hoping that this might bring Eric closer to the church. After some time, though, Mr. Shin quit. In the midst of Eric's troubles, he reckoned he had little authority to be meddling in the lives of other teens with his own ship in such disrepair. And over time, Mr. and Mrs. Shin had come to think of their Korean church as a rather inhospitable space that did not allow them to talk about Eric without feeling vulnerable to censure and gossip.

Mr. Shin once asked Hyeyoung a somewhat rhetorical question, "What comes to mind when you think about Koreans?" and then answered himself: "[T]hey are intelligent and good at making money but very mean." He continued that they are interested in their own success but not in that of the community. As for many Korean immigrants, it was the church that epitomized the best and the worst of Koreans for Mr. Shin. For example, Mr. Shin was very disgruntled about his church's search for a new youth minister that considered only newly arrived pastors from South Korea. He took this to mean that the interests of the youths were not paramount, as the American-born teens were unlikely to warm to a Korean-born and -trained minister, and that instead the Korean church elders cared more about making sure it would be someone *they* could control. When Mr. Shin spoke with Jin-Heon about the matter, he admitted that his was a difficult constitution (in keeping with his "stern face"), and that he had no ability to stomach anything to which he objected.

There had been other incidents with the church—for example, a Bible study group that they hosted at their home at which the group members seemed to run off early to another event—that somehow all added up to a feeling of "not being able to break in" to the social circle at the church. Mrs. Shin wondered if her husband having immigrated earlier might have made other people feel less comfortable with them, perceiving him as somehow "more Americanized." She told Hyeyoung that her husband also felt ill at ease going drinking with church members, given the church's official stance against smoking and drinking.

There was also the time that Mrs. Shin joined an intensive summer evangelism program. She described having found joy there and having repented on her own arrogance for having ever judged the ways of other people's children. But she also described the limits of the fellowship. The talk among the fellow program participants ran from "great weather today" to "what a nice sermon" to what people had for dinner the night before, or maybe to someone's husband having been out too late drinking, and all the bragging about their children's grades and study habits. In this milieu, perhaps most importantly for Mrs. Shin, "I still wouldn't be able to tell them: 'Oh, my child stole a wallet today.'" Mrs. Shin had even bravely confided to the pastor about Eric and asked for his help in requiring him to do mandatory community service. However, the pastor ended up letting Eric off the hook by reporting more hours of service than Eric actually did. Mr. and Mrs. Shin found this act by the pastor to be unhelpful and inappropriate. Most hurtful to the Shins was their sense that the church did not seem to welcome Eric: there was an instance of a church carpool excluding Eric, which confirmed their sense of some communal reproach to the family.

Over the course of the time when we compiled this family's ethnography, the Shins periodically spoke of searching for another Korean church, but it felt to them that the other local Korean churches would provide no better support to the family. Thus, it did not come as a surprise to Nancy and Sumie when we learned that by the time Eric and Christine had reached their twenties, the Shins were no longer attending church. The Korean church they had belonged to had broken apart about two years earlier over fights about church leadership. The Shins told us an absurd story of the tense relations between the members, one faction wearing badges to worship services that proclaimed "I love my pastor" and the other faction wearing no badges. The Shins did not fit into either faction. When they started getting e-mails from both factions with conflicting stories, they decided that they could have God in their lives without attending that church. They tried going to other Korean churches but felt as though they were sitting in "someone else's seat" and never found a comfortable spiritual home.

Coming to Terms: Different Futures

The process of the parents coming to peace with Eric really was about reconciliation of values: if degrees and academic achievement were not the pathways toward Eric's adulthood, the Shins had to shift their measures of success. Through the language of his suffering and acting out, it was clear that Eric had demanded a different yardstick.

Eric Is Korean after All

Even amidst Eric's various challenges, Mr. Shin took pride and comfort in the "Korean" young man that Eric was becoming. Although "Korean" here is a flexible signifier, we understood it to refer to moral fiber. In our meeting with Mr. Shin after Eric had graduated from high school, Mr. Shin shared glimmers of evidence (he was, he told us, "studying Eric") that somehow Eric had indeed digested some of his "bullet points" about life in America but also that now "letting him be" might be the best course of (non)action. If Eric was fundamentally okay, their task now was to let the cards fall as they might. As for imagining what they might have done differently with him—a nearly impossible mental task—they might, he seemed to hint, have suffered less if they had trusted those foundations earlier.

For Mr. Shin, that Eric was "okay" after all was, to some extent, a "Korean" story. Mr. Shin reflected that they had in fact known all along that Eric's "humanity" was "Korean." He admitted that while the family was thrust into the midst of all the troubles, he had questioned Eric's essence, but as the years wore on, he found reasons to believe that Eric had the "grace" of a Korean. Mr. Shin often described, for example, Eric's respect for elders, which struck us as a lifeline for the parents in the eye of the storm. Eric had been loving to his maternal grandfather, who traveled all the way from South Korea for his favorite grandchild's high school graduation; Eric had shown them that he was a responsible worker (he had meanwhile put in a stint at family's dry cleaning storefront); and a summer trip to Korea had confirmed his respectful ways with family elders.

In the context of that conversation, Mr. Shin admitted that he had always wanted his children to be raised "the Korean way," although he paused to acknowledge that he might offend some of the research team members with his firm belief in the moral superiority of the Korean way ("I know that Nancy is American"). He told us that he would have refused the prospect of raising an "American" child. "Even though [Eric] resisted all the time, he became *one of us*," he reassured himself. This sort of a reference to "being Korean" is not what the psychological literature on acculturation and acculturation gap envisions, as the essence of being Korean to this family is much more than preferences for food, entertainment, the company you keep, or even cultural values. For a family that struggled to navigate the rocky racial landscape, having wavered to and fro between how to be a certain kind of American, Eric's Korean essence signified what mattered the most to the parents—his humanity.

A Different Course: "I Will Support Him All the Way"

When we met with Mr. and Mrs. Shin about a year after the period we describe as the "eye of the storm," Eric had graduated from high school and was working part-time and enrolled in a community college part-time. It had turned out that there had been a realistic danger of Eric not graduating from high school, and Mr. Shin had personally negotiated with the high school principal to allow Eric to graduate. With that drama behind him, the Shins appreciated that they had come a long way from the point when they had thought that not graduating from high school was tantamount to death for a Korean family. Mr. Shin laughed as he then spelled it out for us, "d-e-a-t-h." They also described a recent evening out to celebrate Mrs. Shin's birthday at which Eric had joked, "Mom, you must be bored without the daily call from the Dean! He called you every day, didn't he?" and she replied, "I'm sure he still has my number." Of course, none of this is to say that the journey had now come to make sense. The Shins were still, it struck us, squarely in the middle of trying to stay afloat.

At that time, Eric was "on course," albeit a very different one from the course they had initially imagined, the course from which Eric had been so aggressively diverging for many years. As we were enjoying some delicious take-out food, Mrs. Shin poetically described how on one of her drives to work she had noticed a fragile blossom on an otherwise barren tree and had thought of Eric, that Eric too would somehow flourish, even in the midst of all the trouble, the barren landscape of his life. Mrs. Shin went on to offer yet another story about trees and used religious metaphors to affirm acceptance of Eric above all.

> As long as he is healthy, I am fine with whatever he decides to do. So what if he doesn't become that "apple tree" [in English] I had wanted him to become; if he was destined to become a "grape tree" [in English], and I'm just puffing away that it is grapes, not apples, what is the use? It would be nothing but my own ignorance. Once I figured that out, even if there was a "moment" [in English] in which I got angry, I could laugh and still speak with him. "Ah today's another day this young man hasn't come home!" "I wonder when he'll come?" "Like Jesus, Jesus" [in English], who knows when he'll come? So, who knows if Eric will come home today? Who knows if my Jesus will come home today? So, I can smile about it.

All this is to say that the wisdom of hindsight—Eric had, after all the trouble, managed to graduate from high school—had Mrs. Shin reflecting on the battle zone that had consumed their last few years, wondering how she and her husband might have played the hand differently. However, we had observed that even in the eye of the storm, the Shins described their resolve to make peace with Eric's predicament and to let things run their course. Eric thus emerged as a son who both "needed to just let it be" and needed to be very delicately coaxed along: a difficult balancing act for his parents, never assured of where and when to draw the line. Yet, convinced of the essence of Eric's character, Mr. Shin was resolved to support him "all the way," whatever that might be. Yes, Eric might finish the community college course he was taking, and someday Eric might find his way to a four-year college, but the Shins seemed at peace. Mr. Shin shared, "He may be a late starter, but he may not be one of those [who never get "on track"]. But I still have to support him. And I *want* to support him, until whenever the time comes, and you know, if he doesn't go to college, I will still support him. It's OK to not go to college."

Mr. Shin was guardedly optimistic that his family nonetheless was not so very badly off, after all. Repeating the expression "*kûredo*" (which, in Korean, means "although," "nonetheless," or "in any case") four times, he had this to say:

> It wasn't that I came when I was young because I wanted to, but *in any case* it was that I followed my parents and didn't know any English. I somehow graduated from school, and *although* it was a pretty flimsy school, I did make it through college and got a job in American society, and I started a business, and although they were small but in our own way, we had our dreams, and we had plans for our future; and *in any case* our kids are kind, and our married life, well we've lived together for eighteen years without separating, so *in any case* that makes us pretty good [i.e., as immigrant families go].

When Nancy and Jin-Heon visited with Mr. and Mrs. Shin a few years later, Mr. Shin looked noticeably thin, and he revealed that he had indeed been quite ill. He let us know about the stomach cancer that he caught early, and while he thought he was going to recover fine, he was definitely trying to not let himself get too stressed about things and particularly about Eric. Mrs. Shin, too, had been ill with some gastrointestinal troubles, and she had even gone to South Korea to get a diagnosis and a treatment. The sense was that they had had so much heartache about Eric for so many years that they were simply trying to live with Eric differently—caringly but with more distance. During this visit, Eric was home and appeared twice; a tall, gangly, acne-ridden emerging adult with a sock hat, very quiet and shy. He was about to start exams at a community college he was attending. While he lived with his parents, it was clear that Eric and his parents led pretty separate lives. At the time, Christine was away at college, attending a solid four-year private liberal arts college in a neighboring state, majoring in environmental science.

Mr. Shin seemed to be somewhat pleased that he and Eric had been getting along of late. Mr. Shin had been a member of the Korean hiking club for four years. Eric had joined Mr. Shin on a recent trip to Yosemite with the club because Mrs. Shin was unavailable due to the business. Nancy and Jin-Heon noticed that a camping photo of father and son was prominently displayed in their home—clearly Mr. Shin was very happy about it. Eric had been a big help on the hiking trip because Mr. Shin was still recovering from his illness at the time. The father described how good it felt to be hiking and that when he looked out at the beautiful views he did not think about anything that troubled him. However, "the moment you head home it all comes back to you," sighed Mr. Shin. This moment for the family was one of hope but uncertainty about Eric's future.

Coda: Still an Uncertain Course

Yet another few years later, we caught up with Mr. and Mrs. Shin. In the intervening years, Eric, it turned out, had had a string of unsuccessful stints at dead-end jobs that he kept quitting, along with multiple attempts to go back to community college without ever getting a degree. He then managed to land an AmeriCorps (a national service organization) position as a post-disaster construction worker on the East Coast, yet even this opportunity Eric did not manage to complete. Eric had met another Korean American young woman from Colorado at the AmeriCorps stint, and through this relationship had an epiphany about what he wanted to do—become a teacher. Yet this turn in the story was another red herring, as Eric came home to try to get into a four-year college but because of his poor academic record, he was unsuccessful. Eric was put into a remedial class at the local community college but did not persist and decided once and for all that the academic path was not to be. The story that the father told was that Eric had not been able to persist and complete anything. He was backed into a corner.

Mr. Shin made a point to note that there are actually many "Erics" out there. Eric's social circle at the time was comprised of other Korean American young men in their twenties who were in and out of community colleges, working a string of dead-end part-time jobs, and not especially hopeful about their futures. True, many Korean American peers from his high school (including his sister, Christine) had gone to college, left the area for a professional job, and never came back, but there were many who were left behind in the middle-class suburbs with no good prospects. In their younger days, Eric and his downtrodden buddies used to just drink and hang out, but now they seemed to talk mostly about their futures and how to plan for some semblance of a stable life; becoming business owners seemed like the only possible option because obtaining a four-year college degree was a fading possibility for all of them. The Shins insisted that half of the Korean American young people they knew fell into this group but that the local Korean community—which the family had long felt jilted by—refused to recognize that reality. The family's acceptance aside, there were real repercussions for Eric for not having a college degree. As mentioned earlier, he had met a Korean American young woman in AmeriCorps and had dated her long distance after he had left AmeriCorps. The relationship had progressed to the point of his going to Colorado to meet her parents. However, his girlfriend's parents did not approve of the daughter's relationship because Eric had no higher education or a real job prospect, and they stopped dating.

Mr. and Mrs. Shin told us that after they closed the dry cleaning store, Mrs. Shin had managed a nail salon in the city of Chicago for many years. An opportunity then arose to sell the nail salon, and they decided to retire. However, with Christine's college debt still a factor and Eric without an educational prospect, they had recently come out of retirement and had bought a small nail salon in an affluent suburb of Chicago (coincidentally in Lakeside Park, where the Kohs had owned their first dry cleaning business). Their reentry into the workplace was a deliberate move to provide on-the-job training for Eric in small business ownership. Eric had acceded to this plan and had been working alongside his parents at the nail salon.

We were invited to visit the salon, and our visit confirmed that Eric in fact looked like a young salon owner in training, third in command after his parents. The upscale salon located on a main street shopping district in this wealthy suburb was decorated tastefully with beautiful nature photography taken by Christine, who by then had graduated from college and was working for the state parks. The salon was bright, pleasant, and customer friendly. It appeared to us, at last, that Eric was accommodating to his parents' new strategy for him to make a living without a college degree. Eric's job—if not quite a career yet—was a family project by dint of his parents' ability as small business owners to rescue Eric and to provide a pathway for him.

For the Chungs and the Parks, the inevitable bumps of adolescence and emerging adulthood seem to have ironed themselves out; these families had somehow settled into quite consensual ideas about how to make their families work in immigrant America. Because Eric's parents did not have the luxury of enjoying Eric's settled present, our team was cognizant of their still quite unsettled thoughts about immigrant parenting. We listened in as they sometimes took up competing diagnoses and prescriptions for Eric's past shortcomings and future prospects. Undoubtedly, the dilemmas of the Shin family are not unique, but they simply came into plainer sight because the path toward emerging adulthood for Eric was accompanied by much anguish and turmoil *and* because the parents bravely wanted the story of their struggles told. While other parents could only make passing reference to the delicate balance between "Korean" and "American" parenting, Eric's parents had to ruminate, plan, and eventually roll up their sleeves to make their family work. Eric, in turn, seemed at last to also be reciprocating to make his life work as well as theirs.

7

Jun-Ho

Emigration, on Balance

Having immigrated to the United States in 2003 and having been in the country just shy of two years when we first met them, the Hyuns were the most recently immigrated family we followed. Mr. and Mrs. Hyun had two sons: Jun-Ho was fifteen when we met him, and his younger brother, Min-Su, was fourteen. They were also the only family whose longevity in the United States was still uncertain, as they were constantly weighing whether to stay in the United States or return to South Korea. The boys, who were already in their teens (or nearly a teen, in Min-Su's case) when the family relocated, were truly immigrants in their own right, and they at various points came into conflict with their second-generation Korean American peers as well as Korean peers who had immigrated at a much younger age. When it came to this family, the notion of "strategy" seemed overblown: not because the family did not have ideas about how they might act with one or another goal in mind, but because they really felt they could not count on one or another future. While the Hyuns, like all the families in this book, had thoughts about race, language, and identity, Jun-Ho—whom we began to follow in his sophomore year of high school—emerged as the teen most dogged by the challenges of negotiating a social landscape populated by other recently immigrated Koreans and Korean Americans. This becomes perhaps most palpable in the account when Euna shadowed Jun-Ho at his high school for a day; we will later zoom in on that day in some detail because the moments she observed offer a window on the trials of new immigrants tenuously making their way within an academically rigorous suburban high school that was itself adjusting to a new influx of Korean- and Spanish-speaking students as well as second-generation Korean American students.

As with many of the families featured in this book, the story of Jun-Ho's recruitment to our study revealed something about the family struggle. It is not surprising that it was not a trivial matter for this family—truly in the middle of immigrant adjustment—to agree to participate in our ethnographic study. We met Jun-Ho when we surveyed a small group of Korean students recently immigrated and enrolled in the English as Second Language (ESL) program at Valley Creek West High School (the same school that Jenny attended). Of the twenty-one students who completed the survey (they were offered the choice of completing an English or a Korean version of the survey and all chose Korean), Jun-Ho was one of a dozen or so who indicated their interest in joining the ethnographic phase of the study. Tellingly, he was one of the very few from this group who was living with both parents; some were living with only one parent (while the other parent had stayed behind in Korea) while other students were boarding with a relative or a family acquaintance whose home was in the school district. However, when Euna contacted Mrs. Hyun, she was forthright that she could not join: monthly interviews, she told Euna, would just be "too much." Jun-Ho, on the other hand, was eager to participate and told Euna that he had "lots to say" (and he did). He immediately let her know, as if to prove that he was ethnography-worthy, that "these days there are lots of bad things I can tell you about," such as (in response to her query) one of his good friends' recent diagnosis with leukemia.

Even as the research team realized that this family might not work out for the family ethnography, given Mrs. Hyun's initial hesitation, Euna decided to meet with Jun-Ho (with his parents' permission). This turned out to be a wise decision because not only did Mrs. Hyun decide to join in on Euna's first visit with Jun-Ho, but Mrs. Hyun ended up nearly taking over the encounter. In fact, Mrs. Hyun's eagerness to tell her side of the story was so intense that when Jun-Ho heard his mother start to drone on about him, he rudely interjected, "Get out of here." From then on, the family ethnography was off and running, with the family tensions front and center.

Indeed, the tension between Jun-Ho and his mother that Euna observed that first day persisted throughout much of our encounter with the Hyun family during Jun-Ho's high school years. Even as Mrs. Hyun had initially balked at the idea of participating in a research study, we could quickly see that she was considering possible advantages of her family having contacts with university researchers.[1] The first evening that Euna visited, she joked with Jun-Ho, "Do you think you are good enough to get into the U of I?" and then advised, "You'd better study hard to go to the U of I," to which he snapped, "I know that!" This small moment encapsulated for us the dynamics of the Hyun family, which often felt a little like a tug of war between Mrs. Hyun's persistent and intense pursuit of the immigrant dream for herself and her family and the rest of her family's resistance, which was sometimes equally fierce but at other times showed them giving in little by little.

Settling down Tentatively

Early Study Abroad Redux

The Hyun family's migration story resists easy classification. Of the five families featured in this book, theirs is the most obvious case of "education migration" because Mr. and Mrs. Hyun told us they immigrated to improve the educational and career opportunities for their school-age children whereas all other Korean parents in our ethnography immigrated to the United States before they had children. However, this family's case also diverged from a typical South Korean early study abroad (ESA),[2] where a student is sent abroad to a boarding school or to a home stay, or in many cases accompanied only by the mother while the father remains to work in South Korea. The intent of the Korean ESA is to allow Korean student to attend schools in English-speaking locales in a quest for cultural immersion and English-language mastery so as to gain advantage in the competitive Korean economy. Certainly, with two middle-school-aged boys, the Hyun family's immigration was timed rather late for English mastery. Moreover, Mrs. Hyun's brother in Minnesota sponsored her and the boys, allowing the family—who, except for Mr. Hyun, arrived initially on short-term tourist visas—to be on course for a permanent residency in the United States. At the same time, the Hyuns retained their apartment in a suburb of Seoul and had not in fact closed the door on their own return to South Korea, or even that of their children. (They explained that they were renting in Newport Crossings because they could not afford to purchase a home outright in this affluent suburb while still maintaining a mortgage in Seoul. They also had not decided whether their move to the United States was a permanent or a temporary one.) Yet, ostensibly, the family immigrated together in order to improve the educational outcome for the boys. If this family was indeed engaging in ESA, it was certainly a rather unplanned one, done on the fly with uncertain duration for all concerned. With cases like theirs, we appreciate the porous boundary between family immigration and ESA from Korea.

It had turned out that Mrs. Hyun's brother had invited them to the United States immediately after the International Monetary Fund (IMF) crisis of 1997, when economic opportunities in South Korea seemed to be rapidly diminishing. Mr. Hyun recalled saying to his wife, "Are you crazy?!" at the initial idea of emigration. Mrs. Hyun added that the educational and corporate policies of the South Korean president, Roh Moo-Hyun (a progressive who served between 2003 and 2008), had put her and her husband on edge, what with the costs of education and the economic squeeze of the dwindling middle class. In that context, Mrs. Hyun could easily understand why other Korean parents were rushing to send their children abroad: "These days there are tons of unemployed Seoul National University graduates," and she continued that it was the bilingual capacities that would appeal to South Korean companies. Her sentiments and rationale for wanting her children to acquire English-language education as a form of a social capital are entirely consistent with the "English fever" (Park 2009) that was sweeping South Korea at the time.

In an era of escalating ESA, theirs was a case of choosing emigration because the option of sending just their middle-school-age sons abroad was unaffordable for them, as it would have involved the expenses of maintaining a Korean household (typically by the father, with or without the mother) while also paying for the overseas expenses for the child (with or without one parent) to live abroad for multiple years. As Mrs. Hyun put it, "South Korean parents with money had already started sending their children abroad two years [prior to the IMF crisis]." Mr. and Mrs. Hyun had briefly considered sending just their two sons abroad but had decided that doing so would bankrupt the family. Over time, as Mr. Hyun warmed to the idea of emigration, his own birth family protested the idea of their eldest son moving to America.

This protestation makes great sense in contemporary South Korea, as it is often the wives of first-born sons who most desire to emigrate so as to escape from the particular familial burdens shouldered by the so-called first daughter-in-law (where they are expected to care for their husbands' aging parents). It took three years for Mr. and Mrs. Hyun to finally decide to seize the opportunity to emigrate to the United States—though they only shared the news of the impending move with the boys two months before the departure date. "Stop studying Chinese, we are emigrating to the U.S." was how Jun-Ho characterized the manner by which he learned that they were moving to America. Jun-Ho and his brother were old enough that they had mature reflections on the logic and wisdom of the decision; and they were knowledgeable enough about South Korea to really be able to imagine their might-have-been lives there. When we spoke with Jun-Ho at age sixteen, it did not surprise us that he was still in touch with his peers in South Korea and that he could easily compare his life in the United States with those of his friends who remained in Korea.

Mr. Hyun's rationale about the emigration underscored more than just economic feasibility. Foremost it was about wanting to show his sons a "wider world," but he also described the family emigration as an option that was superior to ESA. To some extent Mrs. Hyun echoed her husband, once commenting that sending children abroad unaccompanied is like "throwing them away," then adding further that it "ruins their character."[3] As she pointed out, even children who emigrate *with* their parents were vulnerable. Mr. Hyun brought up the case of his former boss in South Korea whose troubled daughter had been sent away for ESA. Mrs. Hyun was certain that the girl's early study abroad outcome would come to naught: "A troublemaker there is a troublemaker here." Mrs. Hyun offered her assessment that those families were engaging in naïve thinking: "[I]f you don't have to look [their troubled children] in the eye, then things are OK." But Mr. Hyun made a point of adding, "But what do they have to worry about? They're rich!" In consideration of the family finances and well-being, they decided to emigrate wholesale as a family to seek out new opportunities for the children and for the parents as well.

A cautionary tale had taken place in Newport Crossings that would certainly feed Mr. Hyun's suggestion of the importance of an intact family emigration. Around the same time that we were engaged in family ethnography with the Hyuns, there had emerged some rumors within Korean immigrant communities about the recent murder of a teen Korean girl in the same apartment complex in which the Hyuns lived. (The rumor had even reached downstate to the Korean immigrant community in Champaign-Urbana.) One version of the story had it that she was an ESA student who had been murdered by the guardian to whom the girl's family had entrusted their daughter.[4] As it turns out, Jun-Ho knew the girl who had been killed (although not well) and told us that, in fact, it was a story of things going awry when the Korean girl's mother remarried: the girl's poor relationship with her stepfather was so obvious that Jun-Ho reported having even asked her about it. Although Jun-Ho acted rather nonchalant when Jin-Heon asked, we imagine that a tragedy so close to home within his Korean ESL circle must have been a jarring reminder of the precariousness of life as an immigrant high school student.

Having come to the United States against the wishes of her in-laws, Mrs. Hyun was clear that the only way to vindicate the family's decision to uproot themselves from South Korea would be the boys' success in America. Very aware that the boys were later immigrants, Mrs. Hyun once told Euna of her hope that the boys might choose careers that were technical and less reliant on spoken English. Mrs. Hyun repeatedly reassured Euna that she thought of herself not as pressuring the boys but merely as sharing her opinion about desirable outcomes. Our encounters with Jun-Ho suggested otherwise. It was clear that Jun-Ho registered his mother's sentiments that his academic performance *was* the crux of the matter. We observed and heard about study-related matters big and small. On the small end of the spectrum were asides like this one from Mrs. Hyun: "If the kids don't study I hold a refrigerator strike—I simply stop stocking it!" Mrs. Hyun shared with Euna the story of a Korean immigrant mother who had been so hard on her daughter that a neighbor intervened, but eventually the girl came to so appreciate her mother's method that the girl vowed to raise her children in exactly the same way. Mrs. Hyun drew this lesson from the tale: "There is no one way to raise a kid, and a certain amount of stress, pressure, and anxiety is character building."

Whereas creating a better educational opportunity for the boys was the ostensible reason for the family immigration, Mrs. Hyun once shared a detail that was not a part of the more public family discourse. She told Euna that if Jun-Ho had been a better student in South Korea, the family would not have thought to emigrate. As we got to know the Hyun family further, their stories of emigration revealed—beneath the initial story, which sounded much like those of other immigrant families, of seeking better educational opportunities for the children—that there were complex layers of motivations that were in play.

School Calculations

The Hyuns did not mince words about Newport Crossings, their apartment complex. Mrs. Hyun even called it "a slum" and a "frightening neighborhood." Readers may recall that Nancy and Grace had walked around the apartment complex in the early phase of Chicagoland ethnography to get a sense of the "Korean ghetto" that various informants had mentioned. And while another Korean resident there had acknowledged that it was a transitional place for many new immigrants, our team's impressions of the complex from our repeated visits never matched the sense of danger and decrepitude suggested by words like "slum" and "ghetto." If anything, it was the contrast between the complex's rather nondescript, unadorned, and slightly worn aspect and the more spacious and well-kept single-family homes in the surrounding area that may have contributed to the shared consensus among the Korean American community about their low assessment of this apartment complex.

What was indisputable about the Hyun family's residential choice was that they were renting in this apartment complex because of the school system. The apartment complex was located in an unincorporated area of the county, and while they could attend the nearby public schools that were highly regarded, there were a number of public services, such as a library card, that they had to purchase. The Hyuns spoke of the Chicago suburban school zones by imaging their Seoul analog, figuring that Jun-Ho's American high school was like a school south of the Kang River in the Apgujeong ward (an affluent neighborhood in the Gangnam District). But when they elaborated the gist of their calculations, speaking unguardedly as immigrants not quite aware of the dangers of race talk, they gave a frank assessment of American education: they told us that an index of the quality of the school district was that there were no Blacks and many Jews. At hearing such a frankly racist remark by his mother, Jun-Ho tried to derail the discussion by interrupting his mother to say that his school was not, in fact, the best school and that there were other suburban schools with better college admissions outcomes.

Quite undeterred, Mrs. Hyun told Euna on another occasion about having taken Jun-Ho downtown for his driver's license, where "the run-down Black neighborhood" with its decrepit buildings and broken-down cars made her feel like she was in the "shadow of darkness." She offered how suddenly grateful she felt for her suburban neighborhood. Jun-Ho also surprised us in one conversation with his knowledge of just how much money it would take to purchase a more standard single-family home in the neighborhoods in the school district. At the time, the family told us, fully half of their income was needed for paying rent at the apartment complex. In fact, the parents were thinking that, if they were to stay in the United States, they would purchase a home after the boys graduated from high school (we surmised that the calculation aligned with the point when the public school district would no longer matter), perhaps in a neighborhood closer to a local college should the boys end up there.

The Strains of Family Immigration

Family Bickering

Like many of the other families, the Hyun family too had its share of banal conflicts between the parents and the teens. In one interview, we learned (in a rather matter-of-fact way) that the week before, Jun-Ho had been so angry with his mother that he had left for a night and had slept in the family car in the parking lot. The account of his quite restrained "runaway" incident was somewhat humorously told, even though it had been quite a recent event when our research team heard about it. Indeed, Jun-Ho himself chuckled at many points in the telling. As to why he had "run away," he told Euna, "I just got mad, nothing big. Just being stressed at school . . . [R]emember I told you that one B, 89.3 [I received in the English as a Second Language class]? Well my parents said something about it at home . . . something about my not studying and going out all the time." Jun-Ho, those days, happened to be learning how to drive, and he admitted that he thought of driving off with the family car. But then he thought better of this plan: "[O]n second thought, I only have a permit and if I get caught, I would be in deep trouble." In the end, all he did was drive as far as to the entrance of the apartment complex and park the car there to spend a night, and he laughed recalling how cold it had been sleeping in the car.

Jun-Ho was less light-hearted in telling us, however, that after turning on the engine and running a heater in the car at 4:00 a.m., he woke up feeling suffocated and had only realized later how dangerous it could have been to have slept in a car with the engine running. He laughed while telling us that he made sure to return home that day in time to meet his 3:00 p.m. tutor. Euna had known from the family that the tutor was scheduled to come at 1:00 p.m. that day, so she asked Jun-Ho how it was that he returned at 3:00 instead. Jun-Ho admitted that he had actually returned home in time for the 1:00 appointment but learned that the tutoring time had been changed. To pass the time, he went out again, first to a game center and later to a karaoke place with one of his Korean school friends. Reflecting on the incident, Jun-Ho mused, "Fighting doesn't solve anything for us." This somewhat humorous event aside, we will see below that there were, in fact, many ongoing and bitter fights between Jun-Ho and his parents.

Jun-Ho was quite matter-of-fact about family tension: it was natural, and family ties were, after all, intimate affairs. His own explanations for the constant conflict included the notion that he was a teenager in puberty (which he himself thought he was entering late) and that his was an immigrant family, and for that matter family fighting was to be expected in any normal family. He also put it this way: "My mom mostly chides my dad for not chiding me, [but my dad] figures 'what would that [accomplish]?' All that after my dad comes home so exhausted anyway." Often Jun-Ho laughed while speaking about the conflicts. As for the more proximal causes of conflict, such as his going out with his friends, staying out too late, not calling his mother when he was out ("Honestly speaking, I could call, but I just don't . . . [It is] too much of a pain [to call]"), they indeed sounded like the stuff of typical teenage behavior.

When Haeyoon (an undergraduate researcher) asked Jun-Ho how he and his parents resolved things after a fight, Jun-Ho replied, "It's just. . . . we're a family, so it's just, it just, slowly it undoes itself." He mentioned that actually he felt a bit bad for his parents when they fought, but added, "What can I do about it?" He described the typical process through which the tension resolves itself: "There'll be a whole day of fighting. A day will pass and then it will get better. And then things get better." He poetically added, "[I]n any case my dad gives me a ride to school the next morning." Thus, notwithstanding the moments of bitter strain (once, the parents even reserved an airline ticket and threatened to send him back to South Korea, which was ironic, as Jun-Ho told us that actually he had been wanting to return to Korea), the Hyun family did indeed seem to be working hard to accommodate each other under the stress of emigration. Euna, in fact, had ample opportunity to observe the family together, and it helped that their quarters—a modest apartment—were small. Furthermore, the apartment was often packed to the gills with computer equipment that seemed to have something to do with Mr. Hyun's employment; indeed, the already-limited floor plan was pinched as we sat among boxes and monitors. Considerable family drama happened right before our eyes.

On the Decision to Emigrate

We were struck by the extent of the Hyun family's day-to-day reflection, both individually and collectively, about their family's decision to emigrate; clearly it was still raw. Mr. Hyun once summed up his own thoughts this way: "[E]migration isn't easy. If you don't know how to give up some of your own stuff . . . [you couldn't do it]." He also added, "[There's] no use regretting it . . . but there are times when I feel so agitated." On one visit to the family, Euna found all family members in the living room responding to her questions about the family's immigration history. In that conversation, Mr. Hyun was defending what he saw as clear virtues of the United States even as he sometimes questioned their immigration decision. "It's good, it certainly is good," he mused, as if to convince himself. He went to considerable pains to give some examples, but one or another family member weighed in to object to nearly all of them with either their opinion or contrary information. For example, when he praised the fact that there had been English translation services at the airport when they first arrived, Mrs. Hyun remarked that the United States would no longer be issuing work visas. Similarly, when he told the family that he had been impressed that he had not been asked his age or gender on a recent job application form for employment as a computer programmer at a nursing home, Jun-Ho offered skeptically, "Actually, Dad, you probably did need to write down your age."

These sorts of conversations often tacked uncomfortably close to family fault lines, such as with the conversation that ensued when Mr. Hyun told Euna that although he did not regret it, there was no question that South Korea—"where, without going straight home from work, there are all sorts of places [for a man] to go"—is more fun for men. Rather provocatively, he added that "people say that women prefer the U.S." Mrs. Hyun, in a contrarian manner that we all became very familiar with, broke in: "What woman would say that? We're here only for our kids!" Perhaps trying to cut the mounting tension in the conversation, but also holding his ground, Mr. Hyun came back (if a bit tongue in cheek) with, "People say that the U.S. is a good place to tame a man." Indeed, in what may be quite a typical story of South Korean immigrant families, Mr. Hyun both began attending church in the United States and also began focusing his attention more on the family and childrearing in a way that he had not done in South Korea. On another occasion, when Mrs. Hyun mentioned their family having become more "family oriented" in the United States, Mr. Hyun rebutted, chortling, "Nonetheless, I want to be back in South Korea."

If the United States—as we heard from both Mr. and Mrs. Hyun—is ideal for neither mothers nor fathers, it was, then, the children for whom it had to make good sense. Jun-Ho, for his part, had his own thoughts about the matter; he echoed his father in describing South Korea as "much more fun" and offering "much more to do." He reminisced, for example, about his all-night escapades during exam time in South Korea. However, he also knew that he was already too behind academically to return to South Korean public schools and that he was stuck here in the United States for the time being. At the same time, Jun-Ho and his brother seemed less sanguine about what their prospects really were in the United States than the parents were. Mrs. Hyun once spoke about the possibility of Jun-Ho attending the University of Illinois at Urbana-Champaign or DePaul, but Min-Su broke in, "[M]y older brother can't get into those places!" Mrs. Hyun retorted angrily, "Why are you saying he can't go?" With this exchange, we sensed the daily tension in the Hyun household, as they were each beginning to realize their distance from the achievement of their American dream, which included an easier time mastering English and a smoother pathway toward admission to a reputable university.

English Wars: What It Takes

For Mrs. Hyun, the key to establishing her family in a path toward success in the United States was mastering the English language, and she was quite vocal and demonstrative to this effect. A particularly memorable episode with the family involved Euna's second visit with the family. As the conversation proceeded, it was Mr. Hyun—whom Euna had met for the first time that day—who did most of the talking. In the tight quarters of the apartment, Mrs. Hyun grew more and more agitated with everything her husband was saying as the nearly five-hour-long conversation between him and Euna continued. Mrs. Hyun made her objections plain: at one point, she turned her back on the whole conversation, took out a pencil, notepad, electronic dictionary, and an English-language dictionary and began jotting things down. When Euna asked what she was doing, she retorted, "[W]hat do we accomplish with all this [i.e., talk]? I'd rather at least study some vocabulary." As Euna continued to converse with Mr. Hyun, Mrs. Hyun interrupted by getting Euna's attention and asking her, "So how do you pronounce 'comb'?" Even with her nose in her books, several times she interjected that her husband was off-point, that he was repeating himself, or that he was not answering Euna's question. Towards the end of Euna's conversation with her husband, Mrs. Hyun was nearly exasperated: "You seem to have lots to say today, why don't you just answer the question!" "Are you telling me to shut up?" was Mr. Hyun's heated reply. Euna was not surprised at Mr. Hyun's irritation, having marveled throughout that he had managed to keep his cool despite the nearly continuous run of his wife's cutting remarks.

In the meantime, Jun-Ho had been watching the then-popular South Korean television serial drama *Love Story in Harvard* (a romance between South Korean international law and medical students at Harvard). Even as he was using headphones to watch the drama on the computer, it was quite clear that he was also catching most of the conversation. At one point Mr. Hyun admitted how much he loved Korean dramas and that he would love to watch more of them but also that he restrained himself because of his wife's disapproval. Min-Su added to the tension with his appeal for some computer time. Mrs. Hyun gave him permission and asked for a deposit; this was how Euna learned how the Hyun brothers "rented" computer time from the parents. Later, Jun-Ho said this about his mother: "That's how she is; there are always calculations, always strings attached." Once, he told us matter-of-factly that "[h]onestly speaking, I don't really like talking to [my mother] because no matter the conversation it all leads to her pleading that I study more. . . . So I just get mad and then just end the conversation." He also bemoaned that she seemed to have become more fanatical in the United States. "To tell you the truth, she is a real pain." Once, we wondered aloud what it was that his mother wanted, especially given that Jun-Ho was actually performing quite well at school. Jun-Ho explained the impossibility of the situation:

> But from my Mom's perspective, "those are the grades that of course you need to get. You've come here for study abroad." . . . There is a great deal she wants from me. And then I'm the first son, and my dad was the first too, so the first son of a first son [must excel].

Even as Mrs. Hyun herself was going to great lengths to work on her own English (both during and beyond family visits), she revealed some contradictions and ambivalence in her assessments of the importance of English. Mr. Hyun had been talking about the fact that his coworkers had been blaming their own mistakes on Mr. Hyun's English. Although he had meant to tell Euna about the indignities of being an English learner, for instance when it had taken three visits to the auto shop to negotiate a tune-up, Mrs. Hyun weighed in that English should not really matter "if you are determined to feed your family and not be intimidated by Americans." She continued, "English isn't a valid excuse, saying 'I couldn't do this or that because of English'" and gave the example of a very successful restaurant owner who had little command of English. Mr. Hyun continued to recount his English indignities: for example, his American coworkers joked that his English was "all nouns, no verbs." Mr. Hyun was also indignant at the intolerance of customers who said,

"You can't speak English" when he answered the phone at his workplace. He told Euna that he sometimes answered, "Yes, I can't speak English so you'd better call again tomorrow." Notwithstanding Mr. Hyun's tales of woe surrounding his English skills, Mrs. Hyun was determined to make her point that it is a person's attitude more than English alone that matters, and she gave the counterexample of some prestigious South Korean college graduates with good English skills who had not been able to succeed in the United States. Even Min-Su protested his mother's logic, asking, "But Mom, how would you know?" And in yet another conversation about English, the family debated as to whether oral skills alone were enough. The boys weighed in strongly against their father's comment that grammar does not matter at all. Mr. Hyun was persisting with examples when Mrs. Hyun weighed in: "Don't waste our time with your useless talk, just answer [Euna's] question!" For this family, but especially for Mrs. Hyun, mastery of the English language was a touchy subject and also the foremost barrier to their imagined futures in the United States.

Mrs. Hyun's "Bigger Stage"

Mrs. Hyun's views of emigration become very vivid through her discussions of her own work desires and reflections, and of her special family situation as a recent immigrant with nearly grown children. The manner in which she told her side of the story, with a semi-tragic mixture of bravado and profound disappointment—and always in the company of her sons—impressed us as her way of expressing her own frustrations as a recent immigrant parent whose family immigration "project" was not quite turning out, so far, the way she had imagined. In the previous chapter, we bore witness to Mr. and Mrs. Shin's pained ruminations about immigration's effect on the family as they struggled to make sense of their son Eric's bumpy road to adulthood. Here, Mrs. Hyun seemed at pains to convince herself and her family that uprooting the family with two teen sons from Seoul to suburban America, where no one in the family felt good about their English-language skills, was still the right decision. Her rumination seemed driven not so much by the American schooling going badly for her sons—though Jun-Ho and Min-Su were quite vocal about their unhappiness—but by her own struggles.

A number of family squabbles played out over the course of our encounter with the Hyun family, including quarrels about Mrs. Hyun's on-again, off-again employment. The discussion touched on her ideas both about ideal integration into American society and about proper parental roles. As we will describe, Jun-Ho took issue with both lines of his mother's thinking, which often resulted in tense or distressing mother-son exchanges. From the start, Mrs. Hyun made her own personal suffering and sacrifice very clear. "Choked" and "as if in prison" were the ways she described how she felt about being stuck at home (i.e., not working). Although she had been employed in South Korea, she told us that she had decided to stay at home in the United States in order to "save my family" by providing her boys with "safety and security." She maintained that she and the family became generally "happier emotionally" than they had been in South Korea, even though she took pains to detail her own discontent.

Four months into our encounter with the family, Mrs. Hyun secured a job at a Korean dry cleaner shop, to some extent for the money but as much for the chance to work on her English. She aspired to someday be able to work at the counter, but even her largely behind-the-scenes work had afforded her some experiences that she relished, such as learning that there are numerous ways to greet Americans and slowly losing some of her fear of navigating life in the United States. But there had also been the day when the owner had stepped out and Mrs. Hyun found herself speechless at the counter, deciding only later what she could have said to the customer; nonetheless, stories like this one, even as it was about her inability to communicate with English speakers, clearly excited in her a sense of the possibilities for her own future. Her eyes sparkled as she talked about this menial, low-wage job and the world that it was nonetheless opening to her. Euna could hardly believe that this was the same woman who had appeared a bundle of frustrations and resentments at their first meeting. At the cleaners, Mrs. Hyun saw herself "plunged in the American scene" while helping her family out financially. Such initial excitement at her first employment in America, however, soon gave way to disappointment. The back-breaking labor was not easy, and six weeks into the job, she had already reduced her hours from eight to five hours per day. She was determined, though, to stick it out: "[I]f I can't manage this I will be left behind." Having "sacrificed" two years at home with the boys, she was confident that they could now manage without her.

It became clear to us during this period that the family had begun to tire of her accounts of the new job. On one visit, Jun-Ho, at the computer nearby, interrupted suddenly when he heard his mother begin to speak to Euna about likening her work struggles to those of Joseph in the Bible. Jun-Ho quipped to his mother, "So you're saying that I sold you [into slavery]? Wow, how ridiculous you sound!" Undeterred, Mrs. Hyun related that like her, Joseph had worked at a subservient job but later triumphed. "God won't hold me back in this [hardship]. He will bring me happiness." And she continued her celebratory tone, almost as if to prod her family about their lack of appreciation for her having sacrificed her work life in the family's first two years in the United States: "Working is so much more productive, a hundred times better than staying at home," she said. "Thank you God for giving me work." She even told Euna of her own ambition to become a successful global player, perhaps in Christian ministry or international education, once she mastered the English language.

As it turned out, Mrs. Hyun did not last a year on that job. First there was her own sheer exhaustion: the days when she literally felt like crawling home. But there was something else as well, namely, what she perceived as her family's total lack of support for her efforts and their instead belittling her paltry wages. Feeling grossly underappreciated, she quit. She surmised that daughters might have appreciated her efforts but that sons were callous. Mothers of sons, she told us, are destined to develop a harsh voice and become brash. (A decade later we found her working at a Korean-owned beauty supply shop, although Jun-Ho would insist that her English had not improved.)

Indeed, as is already apparent, we did witness her sons' considerable derision, enough so that some of us felt ill at ease as the mother and the sons bickered continuously during our ethnographic visits. Euna could not help feeling awkward about how polite Jun-Ho was to her by comparison. For example, Euna visited shortly after Mrs. Hyun quit her dry cleaning job to find her chiding Jun-Ho, "You have a guest who has arrived. How can you just go on watching TV? Get over here!" Speaking about the job, Mrs. Hyun defended, "It isn't as if I was saving for myself, it was for the family, but they didn't seem to appreciate that," at which point Jun-Ho interrupted angrily, "Don't talk like that!" Later in the same visit, Mrs. Hyun brought up the topic again and told Euna just how sad, lonely, and frustrated it made her that the boys helped so little and were so unappreciative. It was clear that she was out on a limb raising the issue *again*. And indeed Jun-Ho *again* retorted, "Why do you say this kind of stuff? It makes me crazy. Don't say that stuff," and then retreated quickly back to his earphones. Even as her sons hardly seemed to be appreciating their hovering mother, for her part she explained her quitting as timed with the boys' summer break. And even as her own course seemed to be wavering, Mrs. Hyun was trying hard to convince herself and her sons that her devotion to the family at the expense of her own work life would, one day, bear fruit.

Jun-Ho's Path to Adulthood

Social Wars: The Ethnic Un/Fold

When we once asked Jun-Ho what the family's immigration had been like, he answered with two words: "like hell." Prior to arriving in the United States, he had imagined that it would be much easier to learn English and to integrate into American life. "But it wasn't like that. . . . Somehow I thought I would just immediately learn English." He remarked that if only he could have learned earlier about his parents' plans to move to the United States, he might have prepared better. He observed that most of the other recently arrived South Korean students at his school were much better at English upon arrival and were placed in more advanced English classes, much to his frustration. "But it was my parents' deal, so what was I to do?" After being in the ESL program for two years at his present high school, Jun-Ho was starting to realize that it would not be so easy to get into an American college. He had used to think about attending college in California, but now even a local four-year college seemed out of reach for him.

Jun-Ho let us know that most of his friends were also recently immigrated South Koreans—the so-called FOBs ("fresh-off-the-boats") he told us—and he was closest with those who were a couple of years his senior (*sûnbae*—선배). He told us that most of them were born in the United States but had spent long stretches in South Korea; thus they spoke a mix of Korean and English, with a preference for Korean. His older friends mostly had cars and were savvy about where to go out and have fun. He laughed while telling Euna and his younger brother about the "bad stuff" these friends taught him, but he refused to elaborate. (For starters, they all smoked, but Jun-Ho did not.) He stressed that these were guys who had a feeling for Korean *chôngsô* (sentiment). Above all, what drew Jun-Ho to them was his feeling that they were the "only people who pay any attention to me." However, as the year drew to a close, Jun-Ho became increasingly disillusioned about his own prospects in comparison to those of his peers. It seemed to him that his Korean friends (who were seniors at his high school) goofed off and were generally lacking in seriousness; they could afford this attitude because they had already gained acceptances to prestigious American colleges while he was left to struggle at school.

A point that united Jun-Ho and other recently immigrated Korean students was that they all had little interest in hanging out with second-generation, U.S.-born Korean American students at their school. Jun-Ho reported feeling belittled by the "Twinkies" (yellow on the outside, white on the inside) who looked down on him as if to say, "You can't speak English so why do you even try?" And to boot, those Korean Americans who were bilingual did not add "*hyông*" (the proper Korean address for an older male) when calling his name in Korean, surely a sign of disrespect. He once described the "Twinkies" who had their big English-language youth ministry and their own building at a local Korean American church, while the same church hosted a small and less well resourced ministry for Korean-speaking youths like him. (As angry as this made him, Jun-Ho did not want to stop attending the church. He told Euna that he felt better and that his worries lifted when he attended Sunday church services. Sadly, as soon as the service was over, he would feel the return of all his struggles.) Some months later when Euna, Nancy, and Jin-Heon went out to dinner with Jun-Ho and Min-Su, Jun-Ho was more sanguine about the intra-ethnic fighting. He was confident that the Twinkies' prejudices against recent immigrants like him would not matter by the time he got to college.

ESL Battles

Six months into our encounter with the family, we obtained permission from both Jun-Ho and his high school principal for Euna to shadow Jun-Ho for a day at Valley Creek West High School. (This is the same principal featured in our ethnography of Chicagoland Korean America in chapter 2; he had also granted permission for Grace to shadow Jenny, featured in chapter 5, who attended the same high school.) The day gave Euna a clear sense not only of Jun-Ho's day-to-day routine at school but more generally of the Korean and Korean American scene at the school. It was clear that recently immigrated Korean students were not going unnoticed at the school and that not all of the notice was so favorable. Euna sat in on two ESL classes that were populated not just by Korean- but also by many Spanish-speaking students, the first taught by a twenty-something Korean American woman who struck Euna as "perky." The teacher had brought breakfast foods for an end-of-year celebration and presented each student with a personal commendation. Jun-Ho had been standing, showing little interest and mostly chatting with Korean senior buddies. When one student suggested to the teacher that it might be fun to let them guess who each of the commendations was for, Jun-Ho perked up and suggested, "How about extra credit if we guess right?" Jun-Ho's commendation from the teacher came second: "This is a student who really enjoys arguing. I really enjoy my conversations with him. I predict that he will become a lawyer." Euna felt that this tribute was not as favorable as those for many of the other students that followed. Jun-Ho himself told Euna that he did not understand whether this was a praiseworthy award or had been meant as an indirect message about his weakness, and he went to the teacher to ask. Despite the teacher's insistence that she meant for the commendation to be positive, Jun-Ho remained unconvinced.

Later in the day, in his second ESL class, this time with a non-Korean teacher, events unfolded that spoke to some of the struggles that Jun-Ho had shared with our team. The class began with a quiz that Jun-Ho finished very quickly; Euna noticed that while the teacher took the time to ask some of the other early finishers if they had checked their work, she said nothing to Jun-Ho. The students were then put in groups to work together on a worksheet. Jun-Ho immediately asked her if he could be moved to another group, a request that was quickly denied by the teacher. (The teacher explained to Euna that Joe [Jun-Ho's English name] wanted to work with one of his Korean buddies and that she thought it was better for that to not happen.) Jun-Ho approached the teacher again to switch to a different group, which prompted the teacher to walk over and ask Jun-Ho openly, "What is the problem here?" Jun-Ho told her that the other members of the group did not want to work with him because he had not prepared his answers and that they were already nearly done. The teacher insisted that he stay with the group and prepare his answers, which Jun-Ho did for a while but eventually returned to his own seat early while the others continued to work. When one of the group members brought a sheet to him, he just tossed it. Jun-Ho's classroom behavior that day landed him in detention. The teacher took Euna aside to convey that Jun-Ho's behavior that day was not unusual but added, "I don't know him personally."

Jun-Ho left the ESL classroom in a huff, thwarted in his efforts to explain himself to the teacher. He seemed deeply angry and told Euna that other students in that class ignored Koreans. Euna was somewhat shocked by what had transpired and surmised that she had witnessed both Jun-Ho's tribalism and his sense of inferiority. During the lunch period his Korean friends, as if to support Jun-Ho's anger, described to Euna what they felt was the school's racism. They also mentioned not liking the "Twinkies" (that is, assimilated Korean Americans) who were seated at the next table. The recently immigrated Korean students told Euna that they had no desire to be called Korean American. At the same time, they acknowledged that having so many recently arrived Korean students like them created a bit of a dilemma both for the school and for themselves, as they tended to not learn English as a result of their social circle being limited to other Korean-speaking recent arrivals.[5]

In discussing the small-group incident later with Euna and his family, Jun-Ho explained that while he had been working, his groupmates had been goofing off (although this is not exactly what Euna had observed). As for what had pushed him into detention, he admitted that as he exited the class that day he had hurled profanity at his classmate. He first told Euna the first letters, "m" and "f," and then, demurring no further, he went ahead and whispered the word to her. It turned out that as he spoke, his mother was hearing the story for the first time. Euna noted that Mrs. Hyun was surprisingly blasé about Jun-Ho's behavior and the subsequent detention except to share that she was surprised that Jun-Ho would let his anger get the better of him. Jun-Ho's irritability and volatility were, by this point, hardly a surprise to the parents who had weathered, as we have seen, their own indignities.

Because Jun-Ho's biology teacher did not give permission to have an ethnographer observe her class, Euna was able to spend some time with Ms. Pak, the Korean American school liaison whom we had met earlier. She gave Euna a tour of the school and then they sat on a school bench and chatted. Euna was surprised at the pains Ms. Pak took to distinguish herself from recent immigrants like Jun-Ho. Ms. Pak explained that the first wave of immigrants was typically well prepared academically, was wealthy, and had hailed from the professional class in South Korea. The second wave (whom she was dealing with at the school) was typically neither well prepared nor very academically driven, and sometimes (just as was the case for Jun-Ho) the students only knew weeks in advance that they were emigrating to the United States. This particular narrative from the school staff who viewed recent Korean immigrant students like Jun-Ho as "problematic" underscored what Euna learned about Jun-Ho's frustrations at his school. Jun-Ho had complained to Euna that the school guidance counselor would not let him enroll in an honors class, telling him that he did not know enough about how the honors classes worked at the school. Jun-Ho imagined that the unvoiced real reason was his lack of English fluency: "But what can I do? I am a person from a foreign country . . . an immigrant from another country."

On Balance

One year later, Jin-Heon and we met Jun-Ho for dinner as he was approaching his final year in high school. By this time, he was visibly less frustrated at his own situation. Even as Jun-Ho was still not entirely sure about his exact pathway toward a brighter future in the United States, he balked when we asked if he still held on to the possibility of returning to South Korea for college. As we talked about the sagging economy and the difficult employment prospects for young people in the United

States, he was steadfast that the United States compared favorably: "After all," he told us, "for South Korea, Seoul is it, but in the U.S., if it doesn't work out in Chicago, there's another city, and another one after that—so you'll be able to make it somewhere!" It seemed to us that during his junior year in high school in the months that we had not seen him, he had "signed on" to building a life in the United States. He even spoke appreciatively of his parents' sacrifices that brought him to this country and his resolve to pursue college and a career here.

We were all struck by the way Jun-Ho had come to terms with his parents' immigration decision. (When asked how he had come to this conclusion, Jun-Ho shared that his church pastor in the Korean-language youth ministry encouraged him and his peers to be more appreciative of their parents.)[6] As if to underscore his new outlook, he told us that he had lost touch with most of his friends he had left behind in South Korea, and as a matter of fact, he was not as much into all things "Korean" these days—including Korean food, Korean dramas, and such. Only a year earlier, he had been dead set against applying to the University of Illinois and decidedly not interested in a medical career, but on this occasion, we found him quite enamored with the possibility of attending Illinois (perhaps the Chicago campus, if he could not get into the flagship campus downstate) and willing to accommodate his parents by entertaining medical training even if he planned to never practice (he told Jin-Heon that he hated the sight of blood).

And even though he was a bit discouraged to find himself doing little else but studying for yet another retake of the ACT that summer after his junior year (he told us he had not done well in the previous ACT attempts), and even though many of his school friends had gone back to South Korea for the summer (where he imagined them having fun), he knew that his test preparation was but a fraction of what he would have been doing as a South Korean high school senior. At the same time, he was keenly aware that his parents in fact understood little about American colleges. While other parents were taking their children on campus visits and touring campuses with them, his parents could not understand the prospect of taking time and money to visit a campus where admission was not secured. Jun-Ho was, for all intents and purposes, on his own to navigate his own educational pathway in America.

A Detour toward a Career in America

When Nancy spoke with Jun-Ho over the phone nearly a decade after his family's arrival in the United States, he took it as a matter of course that the early years had been hard times: "Of course we all struggled at first—with English, with communication. We all felt so isolated," he continued, "but we have all found a way to enjoy and live here." We could not have predicted, however, that the pathway toward an American adulthood that Jun-Ho had decided to take involved enlisting in the U.S. Army. Having enrolled in the local (Chicago) campus of the University of Illinois, Jun-Ho decided to pursue a career in medicine after all and began to strategize about how he would realize this career aspiration. He told Nancy that he researched various options on his own and found out about the G.I. Bill, which might help him finance his education, so he e-mailed an army recruiter who responded immediately and invited him to have lunch. He withdrew from the university in the fall of his sophomore year and enlisted for a four-year stint in the military.

Nancy asked him how he felt about serving in the U.S. military, and he responded, "It's hard to explain but I'm proud to be in the U.S. Army. I'm happy to serve." He acknowledged that his parents were shocked by his decision. His mother had worried about his safety, and she had also felt it would be a waste of time. In fact, she did not understand why he wanted to be financially independent, as she was willing and able to support his college education. Jun-Ho said that his father came around to supporting him and was even happy about Jun-Ho's choice. Jun-Ho explained, "[My father] served on the Korean military and he knows that it really makes you grow up, get an experience, grow up and get mature." (Jun-Ho had kept in touch with one friend in South Korea who served in the military, with whom he compared notes about their military stints. Jun-Ho concluded, "We get treated better in the U.S. Army.")

Jun-Ho enlisted as a combat medic within an infantry unit and served one tour in Iraq and one tour in Afghanistan. He said that he loved working with patients and wanted to continue to pursue a career in medicine: "That is my plan." He told Nancy that he planned to pursue a physician's assistant degree if he was not able to get into a medical school. At the time that Nancy talked to him, Jun-Ho was nearing the end of his military service and was stationed at an army base in Fort

Riley, Kansas. He had met other Koreans in the U.S. military at the base (who had been recruited as Korean-English translators), and he had met other Koreans who were in nearby Jackson City, where there was a Korean restaurant on account of the many Korean women who had married American soldiers during the Korean War. Jun-Ho had even met a girlfriend at a local Korean church in Manhattan, Kansas, where she was doing some kind of an internship at Kansas State University.

Throughout this conversation, Nancy was struck by a near total transformation, as Jun-Ho himself said, "I have changed a lot . . . more mature, really grew up. If I see people I haven't seen in a while they say they can't even recognize me." Jun-Ho did note that he did not keep in touch with his Korean high school classmates who had gone on to college. He told Nancy,

> I didn't want to talk to them anymore. I felt like we are so different. I feel like they are living their lives [that are] dull, careless. I don't want to be that kind of a person any more. . . . [A] few of them are irresponsible. They party all the time. I used to be like that.

He told Nancy that part of the reason his old Korean ESL friends acted like that was that they were immigrants (implying that, of course, an immigrant is a difficult thing to be), but he added that second-generation Korean Americans were also living their lives similarly. When Nancy pressed him about his own decision to live life more seriously and meaningfully, Jun-Ho reflected that he was able to do so because he had figured out what he wanted to do with his life.

Nancy remarked that his parents must be proud of him, and Jun-Ho replied that he hoped they were proud of him but that they knew little of his life in the military. By this time, his younger brother, Min-Su, was a rising senior at the University of Illinois at Chicago, and his parents had bought a single-family house in a squarely middle-class suburb just north of the Chicago city limits. The parents still had not sold their apartment in South Korea, and it was still possible that they might eventually return (but not for at least the next ten years). His father was still working in the IT field, and his mother was not working at the time. Jun-Ho added that his mother was doing "much better" than when we had first met her—a clear acknowledgment that she had been having a hard time back then. As for Jun-Ho and his brother, it was clear that they planned to live in the United States permanently.

Coda: Becoming American

We met with Jun-Ho one last time, nearly eight months after his return to civilian—and college student—life. Encouraged by a physician with whom he had worked closely as a medic in the U.S. Army, Jun-Ho was back at the University of Illinois at Chicago and studying toward medical school admission, though he was thinking of studying for both the MCAT and the GRE so that he could apply to both medical schools and physician assistant programs.

On the day we met up, Jun-Ho was wearing a pair of tight, tapered khaki pants, stylish and colorful Docksiders, and a blue shirt embellished with faux leather accents. His hair had brown highlights, and he hardly looked like a recent army veteran. He told us that he continued to feel a sense of camaraderie and loyalty to the troop and the fellow medics with whom he had served, and he had kept in touch with them via social media—though those connections were starting to fade somewhat. He shared that he had obtained American citizenship while he was in the service and felt quite patriotic. Clearly, it meant something to him to be an American citizen, and he revealed that he felt emotional when he heard the national anthem. He also admitted, a little apologetically, that he did not feel at all patriotic to South Korea even upon hearing the Korean national anthem. In this way, Jun-Ho—who had been our study's most recently immigrated Korean youth—had transformed into a fiercely American emerging adult.

It appeared as well that his parents had undergone some changes. By then they had sold their main apartment in South Korea (although it emerged during the conversation that they actually owned two other properties there as well). His mother was working full-time again, this time as a cashier in a beauty supply shop catering to African Americans in the south side of Chicago (there are a number of Korean-immigrant-owned beauty supply shops in Chicago's south side). Jun-Ho said that Mrs. Hyun now wanted to own her own beauty supply store, but he was skeptical that she could manage owning a store given her poor English-language skills. (He was frank in his assessment that her English skills had not improved in all the years that she had been in the United States.) All the same, Jun-Ho had told his mother that he would try to help her one day each week if she ever did become a shop owner. As for his father, he had also recently become a naturalized American citizen. Jun-Ho thought his father, who used to be more "traditional," had also become more helpful to his mother by helping with the dishes. Jun-Ho attributed his father's transformation to their church, where the importance of being more family oriented was a central message. His younger brother had graduated from the University of Illinois in computer science and was working in an IT job for a local Korean company. After all the family bickering and tugging and pulling we had witnessed in this family's early years, many of the hopes that Mrs. Hyun had held for her family's immigration project—for her sons to make their way up the American education and career ladders and for her family to become closer—appeared to be bearing fruit.

Conclusion

When we began our collaborative, interdisciplinary, mixed-method research on Korean American immigrant parents and teens, we could not have imagined that the work would eventually end up as a decade-plus longitudinal portrait of Korean American families in transition from their children's adolescence into their emerging adulthood. Of course, it was not by design that the process was so drawn out. The intervening years had two monumental personal events that extended the life of this collaborative project: first, Sumie's move from the University of Illinois to New York University—and the ensuing long-distance collaboration between two busy professors who were parenting our respective children from preteen years well into late adolescence while tending to a myriad of our own respective research projects and administrative duties; and second, Nancy's illness and untimely passing. The first of these events was in some ways a blessing in disguise, as the sheer fact of our slow but steady progress on the manuscript gave us opportunities to continue to check in with our five Korean American families. It was through these follow-up conversations and visits with the Korean immigrant parents and their now emerging-adult children that we were able to tell fuller stories of their lives—replete with the surprising twists and turns of the emerging adults' career path decisions and the parents' quiet appreciation of, and even pride in, the progress their family had made on their American journey. Nancy's illness added urgency to our writing. And, truly, Nancy continued to write, edit, and comment on our manuscript until her health failed her altogether. So how do we even begin to sum up a work that spanned a decade-plus of our career and friendship as well as those of five Korean American families who opened their doors and hearts to us?

What Is Korean? What Is American?

Let us return to the origin of the project and trace several discoveries about Korean American families. First, we began our collaborative project with the question that lingered from our campus survey with Korean American college students at the University of Illinois campus. As we have seen (and further detail in the appendix), we found that Korean American college students' individual well-being was not directly connected to their assessment of their family dysfunction, despite their assessment of their families as not functioning all that well, and despite the interviews revealing considerable family hardship. Moreover, we were intrigued that the Korean American college students we interviewed seemed to be deploying "redemption" narratives to make sense of the hardships of their immigrant childhoods and their parents. In our Chicagoland study, we saw similar parallels with Korean American parents and teens. The families we followed were not necessarily beholden to the hegemonic ideals of the "normal American" family. Although some of the Korean parents and teens (such as Jenny and her mother, and Mr. Chung) sometimes spoke glowingly of American families at large or of specific White American families they knew, other parents and teens (most notably Mr. and Mrs. Koh and Doug) leveled criticism at or pointed out difficulties with various segments of White America. For recent immigrants like the Hyuns, White Americans did not especially figure in their lives or in their discussion. That is, rather than holding a singular gloss of the "normal (White) American" family as the ideal against which they measured their lives, we found both the parents and the teens struggling to make sense of what it meant to be a healthy Korean American family.

We must note, however, that while Korean American parents and teens seemed to hold variously complex and nuanced (and sometimes inconsistent) notions of all things "American" and "Korean," many immigrant parents were all too comfortable trading in racial stereotypes of Blacks, Latinos, and Jews—with their children often bristling at such frankly racist talk—even as they themselves felt humiliated by discrimination and racism in the United States. That the immigrant Korean parents were so un-self-conscious about trafficking in racist stereotypes against other minorities in the United States is, actually, unsurprising.

Korean immigrants have often been cast by the media as a party to urban racial conflict with African Americans (most notably, the Flatbush [Brooklyn, New York] boycott of Korean grocers by Black activists in 1990[1] and the Los Angeles riots in 1993 following the Rodney King verdict).[2] The Chicagoland Korean American community has not been rocked by racial conflict with other communities of color to the same extent as the coastal cities, although such racial tensions between Korean merchants and African American clientele have been documented in Chicagoland as well.[3] Korean immigrant parents in Chicagoland were certainly not immune to the racialized (and racist) narratives about various communities of color in their midst, even while their primary concern with respect to raising their children to be happy and healthy Korean Americans was in relation to middle-class White America.

Chicagoland Korean America

Our findings about Korean American families are, inevitably, tied to the particulars of the time and place and community. The decade (2004–2014) in which we collected the bulk of our family ethnography data saw Chicagoland (and Illinois) decline in prominence within the national Korean American scene, with coastal Korean American communities (Los Angeles, New York/New Jersey, Virginia) and those in southern locales (Texas and Georgia) growing at a much faster rate than Korean American communities in Illinois.[4] And even during our presurvey ethnography of Chicagoland Korean America, some of our informants hinted that Chicagoland Korean America was considered more "old-fashioned" and conservative than the coastal Korean American communities. Coming into this somewhat stagnant ethnic community scene was an influx of new Korean immigrants, in the form of early study abroad (ESA) students and their parents.

The Korean ESA phenomenon, which we had dubbed a veritable "education exodus" from South Korea,[5] saw tens of thousands of precollege Korean students go abroad, sometimes alone but often accompanied by their mothers, to obtain a Western education and English-language mastery. The number grew exponentially in the early aughts, peaked in 2006, then declined steadily thereafter. (The social science literature on Korean families took note of this phenomenon and produced volumes of scholarship on this topic.)[6] Although we did not realize it at the time, the first two years of our family ethnography coincided with the period of notable uptick in the number of Korean ESA students and families. And, the rise in the presence of recently immigrated students was duly noted by social workers and school administrators in the north suburbs of Chicago. Most notably, Jun-Ho (as a part of this Korean ESA wave) and Jenny (a second-generation Korean American) occupied nonoverlapping spaces within the same Valley Creek West High School and regarded each other, figuratively and quite literally, as sitting apart in the school cafeteria, quite sure that they did not have much in common despite their shared Korean heritage. Yet, both Jun-Ho (who lived in the low-rent apartment complex dubbed the "Korean ghetto" in the unincorporated area of the suburbs) and Jenny (who lived in a lower-priced townhouse within the town limits of affluent Valley Vista) both felt alienated from the center of gravity of the Korean American community.

 counternarratives

In fact, all five families had a complicated relationship to their coethnic network, which was revealed most acutely through their relationship with their church communities. The families had different feelings about their Korean churches, with some more critical than others (e.g., Mr. and Mrs. Shin feeling marginalized), some feeling ambivalent about their family's religiosity (e.g., Mr. Chung's concern about Esther's religious fervor), some finding work and meaning through church (e.g., Jenny's mother as church pianist), and some even coming to appreciate their immigrant parents through their faith (e.g., Jun-Ho growing from bitter to appreciative of his parents' decision to immigrate, at the encouragement of his minister). Their complicated feelings about church notwithstanding, they all at least had sufficient financial security to be able to attend church in ways that some very low-income, working-class Korean Americans cannot.[7] Yet, none of the five families in our study revealed an easy sense of belonging within the ethnic fold. To us, these data points speak to the notion that a tight-knit and inclusive Korean American community might be more myth than reality.

What Mattered the Most

Our findings provide further counternarratives to other "myths" about Asian American families. Scholarly writings as well as news and opinion in the media about Asian American families abound with certain discourse (e.g., "tiger mother," "model minorities") about Asian American families that signals America's unease with immigrant parents and students. For example, Amy Chua's 2011 book, *Battle Hymn of the Tiger Mother*, and the 2007 Virginia Tech massacre committed by an ethnic Korean college student were two cultural events that put Asian Americans at the center of national attention. Yet, at the time that many Asian American parents and college students were actively debating the "perils" of immigrant parenting and immigrant adaptation alongside (seemingly) everyone else, we found very few explicit references to these narratives in the everyday talk of Korean American parents and teens. (The only exception was Mrs. Koh, who referred to the Virginia Tech incident to argue for her sons' local high school to establish a Korean PTA so that she could advocate for greater socioemotional support services for Korean American boys.) In the hundreds of conversations—short and long—our research team had with our Korean American informants over the years, there were remarkably few self-referential remarks about how Koreans and Korean Americans might be viewed within America. Admittedly, these key moments that consumed the attention of Asian America at large (and scholars of Asian America like us) occurred in the phase of our family ethnography where we were having only annual or semiannual contacts with the families. However, we also think it is telling that, when it came to matters of making their own families work, these national headlines appeared to be mere background noise to the more immediate concerns of immigrant families.

Of course, this is not to say that our Korean American families were not subject to racial stereotyping. Although we heard remarkably little talk from the families about Korean Americans (and Asian Americans, more generally) being perceived as the model minority, some of the teens (Ben, Esther, and Doug most explicitly) did talk of being racialized by their peers in high school. Most of the Korean American teens in our study were not academic superstars, and except for Esther (who had applied to Stanford), none of the Korean American students in this study even aimed to attend Ivy League universities or other such elite private colleges. Their academic aims—to attend four-year state universities—were more modest than many media portraits of Korean American (and other East Asian American) high-achieving families would have one believe, although these outcomes are entirely in line with the sorts of colleges attended by the bulk of Korean American students in the United States. And at the time we concluded our ethnography, none of the emerging adults were headed for the kinds of professional careers that take center stage in Asian American success stories (e.g., doctors, lawyers, engineers). Here, we must take heed of Mr. Shin's words to us (at what turned out to be Nancy's last ethnographic trip to Chicagoland)—that there are many, many "Erics" (underachieving second-generation Korean American emerging adults) out there whose stories are untold and unheard. Our ethnography data provided an in-depth look at one such family's painful struggles to come to terms with the disappointments of an unrealized immigrant family project. We speculate that there are other—and different—experiences of underachieving Asian Americans from whom scholars could draw new insights.

By following the Korean American teens into their emerging adulthood years, we confirmed that what we had observed with Korean American college students in our campus study who were working hard psychologically to make sense of their difficult immigrant childhood had, in fact, been in the making since adolescence. Korean American teens and emerging adults in our study had, in ways small and large, made concessions and accommodations to their immigrant parents and engaged long and hard in making meaning of their racialized existence. In turn, we observed that immigrant Korean parents were also actively participating not only in meaning making and strategizing to help their children grow into healthy Korean American adulthood, but also in accommodating and evolving with their children. Whereas other works about Asian American immigrant families have conveyed these expressions of flexibility and resilience on the part of immigrant parents and children separately, ours is one of the first studies to strive to portray the day-to-day struggles (and squabbles) between Korean American parents and teens that made for both short-term and long-term accommodations to each other's perspectives and failings.

Our final discovery was that, more so than academic and occupational aspirations, the Korean American families we followed were dealing foremost with matters of race and racism, especially in relation to the psychological health of the children. In addition, we underline the fact that for some of the Korean immigrant parents, boosting the self-regard of their American-born daughters and sons necessarily involved contending with gendered ethnic stereotypes and cultural expectations of Korean femininities and masculinities. The parents were keenly aware of the potential damages from gendered ethnic expectations and stereotypes: that Korean and Korean American girls and women are expected to be petite and feminine, or that Korean and Korean American boys are seen as unathletic. Against these forces, the immigrant parents were constantly thinking of what skills, experiences, and personal characteristics in their children needed to be fortified to ensure safe passage from adolescence to emerging adulthood.

Survey as a Starting Point

The psychological scales that we used in our effort to assess individual acculturation and intergenerational acculturation gaps fall short of capturing what is practically meaningful to the immigrant Korean American families. The portraits of Korean American families that emerge through our ethnographies suggest that the families are more functional than surveys might have suggested. Yes, we witnessed moments (especially in the teen years) when many of the families were struggling and squabbling; but the struggles appeared to be productive in that both the parents and the teens were working hard to insist on what was important to them and, in time, to appreciate and accommodate the other. As well, the acculturation measures that are used in the psychological research to test the acculturation gap–distress hypothesis, such as the Vancouver Index of Acculturation we used in our surveys, are crude indices of personal cultural affinities that do not speak well to individual aspirations, motivations, regrets, ambivalences, and other amorphous sentiments wrapped up in references to things "Korean" and "American."

As we struggled with what we could conclude from the quantitative aspect of our study—which, admittedly, was hampered by a rather small sample size and the cross-sectional (one-time only) nature of the data—we were reminded that it was not just we as researchers who quickly realized the limits of our survey. The Korean immigrant parents, too, were not shy in letting us know that the survey had "failed" them by not asking the critical questions that they were contending with—namely, the difficulties of raising Korean American children who were not always thriving. Tellingly, our survey did not include any questionnaires about the parents' and teens' experiences with racism, racial identity, or their sense of the racial terrain in which the families lived and worked. At the time that we designed the survey, our research had been focused primarily on the questions of individual and family mental health and parent-child relationships, as those were the primary themes arising out of the data we had gathered from our University of Illinois campus study student informants. Had we had more resources or wherewithal to design a longitudinal survey (i.e., collecting survey data from the same families at different time points in their transition from adolescence into early adulthood), undoubtedly such data would have been far more revealing. In our case, the survey started an extended conversation within our research team and with the Korean American community about what was "missing" from a study that purported to understand Korean American immigrant parents and their teen children.

Navigating Immigrant America

As we bring our study of Chicagoland Korean American families to a close, how do we answer our subtitle question: How do Korean American teens and their immigrant parents navigate race in America? We find that the family portraits that emerge from the five ethnographic family cases, by and large, speak to the resilience and generous spirit of the families: resilient—because each family had faced its own indignities, uncertainties, and obstacles to a comfortable family existence (and had considered escaping the messy immigrant crucible for a life back in South Korea) yet they persisted; and generous—because despite disappointments and harsh words, the parents and their emerging adult children were willing to persist to make their family work instead of cutting off relations. At our last check-ins with the families, we saw that there continued to be some tensions between the members of some families (e.g., Jenny's disappointment with her father, Mr. and Mrs. Shin's worries about Eric's uncertain future), yet the immigrant parents and their emerging adult children were forging on with largely warm feelings toward one another.

The long-view portraits of immigrant Korean American families that emerged over time in our study stand in contrast to dominant narratives of East Asian American families as either upwardly mobile and full of high achievers or ridden with the emotional scars of an intergenerational gap.[8] Perhaps our work managed to capture divergent family dynamics among Korean American teens and parents because unlike previous studies that were limited to single interviews with each informant or were focused on just one generational cohort (either parent or child), we interviewed and spent time with both parents and children—together and separately— for a significant length of time. We also must acknowledge the fact that we, as University of Illinois professors from downstate, were essentially outsiders to the Chicagoland Korean American community. We cannot know for certain what effect our outsider status—not to mention the rather odd pairing of two middle-aged Jewish female professors: one an Asian immigrant unable to communicate in Korean and the other a White American with an impressive command of the Korean language— had on the data we gathered with Korean Christian families. However, we cannot help but think that perhaps we were privy to frank talk about the realities of Korean American lives that the families had not previously been invited to share. We had the good fortune of personal introductions by Professor Kwang Chung Kim and Mrs. Shin Kim—two trusted elders as well as respected professors and researchers of the community—to many of the church pastors and social agencies, and these introductions got our survey and ethnography project off the ground. Once those doors were opened, the five Korean American families who became our informants shared many stories—and many unguarded moments in their daily lives—with our talented bilingual graduate researchers as well as with us. No doubt, however, it was Nancy—a supremely gifted ethnographer with a generous spirit, a polyglot with a near-native command of the Korean language that delighted immigrant Korean parents, and most of all a consummate scholar with insatiable curiosity—who was the heart and soul behind this work.

The majority of the literature and public discourse concerning Asian American immigrant families has historically centered on the idea of intergenerational cultural conflict (traditional vs. modern; collectivistic vs. individualistic; Asian vs. American). As well, the prevailing discourse about Asian immigrant parents has focused on the idea that they made personal sacrifices by immigrating for the sake of their children's future, which in turn compelled the parents to hold high expectation for their children's academic and career accomplishments. However, our work shows that these are simplified portraits rather than lived reality for many Asian American families. Our examination of the cultural and psychological challenges that Korean Asian American immigrant families face and the strategies they enact to overcome them adds nuance to our understandings of the ways in which contemporary Korean American families navigate immigrant America. As this work has demonstrated, while generational differences between parents and teens certainly existed, they were not a major cause of conflict in the family. Rather, these families struggled to cope with an American society in which they understood themselves to be racial minorities and were subject to racial biases. Thus, the foremost goal in the minds of Korean American parents in our study was to prepare their children for successful adulthood by instilling protective character traits and skills to navigate the demands of a racially diverse society. In addition, we saw that immigrant parents, too, had dreams for their own American careers and lives that had motivated them to immigrate and to stay in the United States. Thus, while acknowledgment of, and gratitude for, immigrant parental sacrifice played a certain role in the maintenance of family relationships, we suggest that it is also important to appreciate how immigrant parents see themselves as achieving personal fulfillment in the United States above and beyond their children's accomplishments. Korean American families are continually making and remaking themselves in response to local, national, and global contexts. We think that these family transformations and reinventions are part and parcel of the ways in which immigrant parents and their children work to maintain their family bonds while striving towards fruitful American lives.

ACKNOWLEDGMENTS

How does one write acknowledgments for a collaborative work—one that spanned over a decade—when the co-author and friend is no longer here? Certainly, Nancy and I had anticipated the necessity of putting down in writing all the thanks we owed to many people who made this book possible, yet she and I never did manage to write these acknowledgments together. Perhaps we knew that this was the last act of putting a book manuscript together, and we were not ready to declare it done. As for me, I admit to anxious avoidance; it felt like writing the acknowledgments out of order might somehow speed the inevitable.

Nancy passed away on January 6, 2016, after a two-year battle with cancer. She and I were still working on the book manuscript at the time of her death. Even a few months before her passing, Nancy had had her trusted assistant, Maria, print out the pages of the book—some chapters long completed but under heavy edits and others still in rough drafts or outlines—and assemble them into a binder. In the materials retrieved from Nancy's home and work offices shortly after her passing, I found her handwritten scribbles (which were always charmingly illegible) on the manuscript in a binder among the pile of papers and folders with a sticky note labeled "Sumie." I preface our acknowledgments with an apology, knowing that I am probably failing to thank some individuals in this space; please know that the acknowledgments would have been much more spirited and inclusive had Nancy written them with me but that our gratitude remains the same.

As for those we must thank, first and foremost, Nancy and I are deeply grateful to the five Korean American families—those whose names appear as pseudonyms—who allowed Nancy, me, and the rest of the research team into their lives. Their participation in this project was truly an act of generosity and courage, as they invited us in at their most vulnerable moments. As a current mother of two teens myself, I am more cognizant than ever that the Korean American teens in our ethnographies had been exceptionally good sports not only to let us into their homes but also to let us follow them to the places they inhabited— their schools, churches, sports games, music performances, and then some—and they patiently answered our questions over a period that stretched into years. That Nancy and I could witness these teens grow into confident emerging adults has been simply incredible. Thank you to those who, as emerging adults, also read earlier drafts of their family ethnography chapters and gave us feedback. The immigrant Korean parents were also amazingly generous with their time. They shared countless meals with us in and out of their homes, let us hang out at their shops, shared opinions about our survey, and told us story after story that revealed their anxieties, worries, steadfastness, and joy of parenting their adolescent children in America. It was not unusual for most of our visits with the parents to last four hours or longer, with moments of laughter and levity as well as tension and sorrow. Thank you for entrusting us with your families' stories.

We also acknowledge the support of over a dozen Korean church pastors and Korean social service agency administrators who allowed our team to collect the survey data at their sites; as well, the principal and the Korean liaison at a suburban high school talked to us at length about their school's efforts to serve the newly arrived Korean students and gave permission to our graduate ethnographers to shadow their teens for ethnographic observation. The late Professor Kwang Chung Kim, Mrs. Shin Kim, and Charse Yun were our valuable local guides to the landmarks and key stakeholders in the Chicagoland Korean American community.

Next, Nancy and I are forever indebted to the graduate researchers— Grace Chung, Hyeyoung Kang, Jin-Heon Jung, and Euna Oh—who went above and beyond their research assistantship duties to connect with the churches and the families for their work on the survey and family ethnography data collection. They drove miles and miles (and took copious fieldnotes about good Korean eateries and shops in Chicagoland) to meet with the families, wrote drafts and drafts of fieldnotes and memos, transcribed and translated the interviews, and contributed valuable ideas to our analyses. They also spearheaded the survey data collection at the churches and the agencies. Three other graduate researchers, Chu Kim-Prieto, Noriel E. Lim, and Shanshan Lan, were instrumental in the design, collection, and analyses of the campus survey that paved the way for the Chicagoland study survey. We truly could not have carried out this work without all of them, and we are so proud of the incredible scholars and psychologists they have become. Undergraduate assistants at the University of Illinois at Urbana-Champaign also helped with the survey data entry and ethnographies. Lisa, Rich, Brian, and Haeyoon are named in the ethnographies, but I know there are other unnamed students who contributed energy, time, and ideas to this project.

We are grateful to the University of Illinois internal grants that made this work possible. One of these was the College of Literature, Arts, and Sciences Faculty Study in the Second Discipline program that first brought Nancy to the Psychology Department to take classes, including one with Sumie, and later allowed Sumie to take anthropology courses, including one with Nancy. We also received generous grants from the University of Illinois Campus Research Board (project title: "Asian American Immigrant/Second Generation Mental Health in Familial Context") and the University of Illinois Critical Research Initiative (project title: "Korean American Mental Health in Its Familial Context," joined by Angela Wiley). The New York University Department of Applied Psychology hosted one of Nancy's visits and allowed us to present our emerging work to the department audience. This project was also supported in part by the Academy of Korean Studies Grant to Nancy, funded by the Korean Government (Ministry of Education) (AKS-2010-DZZ-2101).

Jennifer Hammer at NYU Press was an incredible supporter of this book project long before Nancy and I had much of a "manuscript" to show. Jennifer has been steadfast and patient and utterly amazing. Amy Klopfenstein at NYU Press was also exceptionally helpful to me as I navigated the ins and outs of preparing the manuscript.

Now to the colleagues, friends, and families: Nancy (and I) were truly fortunate to have the capable and devoted administrative support of Kelley Frasier in the University of Illinois Office of the Vice Chancellor for Research (where Nancy served as the Associate Vice Chancellor for Research in Humanities, Arts, and Related Fields). Maria Gillombardo was the "right-hand woman" to Nancy for all her work endeavors. Nancy loved and relied on Kelley and Maria to keep her work life humming along even in the sickest of her days. Nancy's incredible graduate students (Dohye Kim and Jeongsu Shin were the most involved in this project, but there are probably others) provided additional research and commented on manuscript drafts. Sumie's students at New York University (namely Joonhee Kim and Esther Sin) provided valuable translation help. Soo Ah Kwon, Laura Nelson, and Eun Hui Ryo provided insightful feedback on our book proposal. We are indebted to all of the students and colleagues for their support on this project.

I thank my husband, Allen Poteshman, for his unfailing support throughout the life of this project, allowing me to travel as much as I needed for data collection and for writing. He also was a scrupulous editor of the manuscript drafts. My daughters, Abby and Lucy, "grew up" with this project and provided light and inspiration. My family loved Nancy so dearly and always looked forward to her visits to New York for our week-long writing sessions; invariably her visit meant seeing an off-beat movie, visiting a museum, and engaging in invigorating conversations that included everyone in our family. I know Nancy had endless love for her family: Andy Gewirth, Carmen, Simone, and Isaac. I extend my love and gratitude to the Gewirth family for allowing me to spend days and nights in their home on my many writing visits to Urbana (and even once in Seoul, South Korea, while Nancy and the family were on a sabbatical leave there). I hope our families' friendship lasts a lifetime.

As I mentioned earlier, Nancy and I continued to work intermittently on this book manuscript throughout her two-year battle with cancer. There are many people who supported and sustained Nancy throughout the decade-plus of this work but especially in the last few years. Karen Winter-Nelson and Dana Rabin were Nancy's dearest of friends and neighbors; I know they were there for Nancy every single day. Their families (Karen's family: Alex Winter-Nelson and their sons, Tim and Ezra; Dana's family: Craig Koslofsky and their children, Jonah and Evie) provided unwavering friendship and support to Nancy and her family. I am certain Nancy was eternally grateful.

I asked Karen Winter-Nelson and Dana Rabin to help me generate a list of people that we know Nancy would have wanted to thank in these pages. Nancy's family (Rena, Ruthie, Arthur, Minky, Karen, and their partners and children) were her rock of love and support. The following people came from out of town to provide support for Nancy and her family: Keiko Sakamoto; Ann Saphir and Miho Matsugu; Tim

Sonder and Maret Thorpe; Tina Choi; Eve Epstein; Nicole Constable; Noboru Murakami and Akiko Takeyama; Jesook Song; Jiyeon Kang; Cara Seiderman; Kristin Tonn; Letty Naigles; Dan Gewirth; Susan Kumar; Haley Deitch; Elizabeth Schön Vainer; Laura Nelson; Patricia Sandler; Jeryl Abelmann. Janine Berlocher spent many hours teaching yoga to Nancy to help her be more comfortable. Eugenie Massudom was a source of great comfort and strength through the weakest days. Elizabeth Moscoso also provided support for the family. In Champaign-Urbana, the following people provided food or other support that gave Nancy nourishment and warmth and strength: Soo Ah Kwon; Faranak Miraftab; Mary Wraight; Leslie Reagan; Melanie Loots; Gina Hunter; Ramona Curry; Cathy Prendergast; Sharon Irish; Bea Nettles; Sally Mc-Mahan; Frances Harris; Jo Kibbee; Carol Spindel; Kelly Deaton; Anne Adams; Ivana Bodulic; Gisela Sin; Nate Schmitz; Ingrid Melief; Andy Orta; Craig Koslofsky; Alex Winter-Nelson; Helga Varden; Shelley Weinberg; Andrew Megill. Nancy's cadre of graduate students were also her biggest supporters. There are without a doubt many others to whom Nancy felt very grateful for support during this time.

To this list, I add my friends Karen Rudolph and David Donnini—Karen and I have been friends since graduate school and Dave, Allen's friend since college. Karen and Dave and their children, Zachary and Emma, opened their Champaign home to me and provided a comfortable guest room, wonderful meals, and many late-night conversations during my many trips back to Champaign when Nancy and I were writing together. My other Champaign friends—Sylvia Liu, Chifan Cheng, Paddy and Jim Sobeski, Kristin and Brett Feddersen—kept me connected to the life of the community years after my move to New York. My parents-in-law, Norman Poteshman and the late Sharon Poteshman, opened their homes in the Chicago suburbs to me and Nancy on our many ethnography field trips from Champaign. And finally, I am grateful to my immigrant parents, Kenji and Michiko Okazaki, for raising me to be the scholar and the person that I am today.

APPENDIX

The Campus Survey

In order to provide a psychological portrait of Korean American students in relation to other students at the same university from similar middle-class suburban backgrounds, we initially began with the aim of surveying Korean American college students from Chicagoland suburbs and contrasting them to White American peers who had attended high schools from the same suburbs. We added South Asian American college students, also from Chicagoland suburbs, when we realized that it was difficult to parse our preliminary results as reflecting culture/race differences or immigrant/nonimmigrant family differences. Because South Asian Americans, another post-1965 Asian immigrant community, constituted a sizable presence both on campus and in Chicagoland communities, we thought they would make for an apt contrasting group.

Methods

Participants

We surveyed 299 students (131 men and 168 women, mean age = 19.94 years) from three ethnic groups (104 Korean Americans, 102 South Asian Americans, and 93 White Americans) at the University of Illinois. Of the 299 participants, 291 were undergraduate students and eight were graduate students (three Korean Americans, three South Asian Americans, two White Americans). Seventy-three percent of the Korean Americans, 76 percent of the South Asian Americans, and 100 percent of the White Americans were born in the United States.

Procedure

In order to participate, students had to (a) be at least eighteen years of age, (b) have graduated from a Chicago-area high school, (c) identify as Korean American, South Asian American, or White American, and (d) be currently enrolled at the university. They were recruited in one of three ways: through an introductory psychology research subject pool, for which the participants received course credit; through flyers advertising a paid web survey that were distributed at campus libraries, dormitories, ethnic student organization meetings, and Korean-language courses; and through snowball sampling, in which survey participants were asked to refer eligible friends and acquaintances.

Participants were given two dollars for every person they referred who completed the survey. All participants recruited by the latter two methods were paid ten dollars either in cash or a gift certificate for completing the survey. All Korean American subjects were recruited through campus advertising. Of the 102 South Asian Americans, 76 were recruited through flyers and advertisements and 26 were obtained through the referral system. Of the 93 White Americans, 64 were recruited through advertisements and 29 through the psychology subject pool. To minimize potential barriers to participation, the survey portion of the study was conducted online. Potential participants were screened via e-mail or telephone on the basis of the eligibility criteria, and those who met the criteria received an e-mail containing the link and the password to the web survey website. An informed consent form was placed on the first page of the survey so participants could choose to either continue or leave the website.

The quantitative results described below will refer to three questionnaires in particular. The Family Adaptability, Partnership, Growth, Affection, and Resolve scale (family APGAR; Smilkstein, Ashworth, and Montano 1982) is a five-item scale that assesses the level of family satisfaction in five areas (adaptability, partnership, growth, affection, and resolve). We used the twelve-item "General" subscale from the McMaster Family Assessment Device (FAD; Epstein, Baldwin, and Bishop 1983) to assess the overall family functioning, and we used the Center for Epidemiologic Studies Depression Scale (CES-D; Radloff 1977) to assess the participants' depressive symptoms. The survey also contained open-ended questions about their perception of mother's and father's psychological wellness, along with demographic questions about the students' and their families' backgrounds.

Results

Although our primary interest was in understanding how Korean American college students were perceiving their families, and to what extent such assessments about their families were related to their individual mental health, we also wanted to understand the Korean American students' results relative to other students on campus. We thus began by examining the relative levels of family functioning and depression across the three ethnic groups. Table A.1 shows the mean levels of perceived family functioning (as assessed by the family APGAR and FAD measures). Note that these two measures are scored in the opposite direction, in which higher APGAR scores suggest higher satisfaction with family functioning whereas higher FAD scores suggest more negative views of family functioning. On the family APGAR, Korean American students rated their families more negatively on a measure of family functioning (e.g., mutual support, open communication, decision making, getting along). On the FAD, Korean American young adults also reported lower satisfaction with their families (e.g., communication, support and acceptance, expressions of emotions, spending time). In other words, Korean American students seemed to rate their families as functioning less well than South Asian American and White American students. In table A.1, we also show the mean depression score for the three groups, as reported on the CES-D (where higher scores indicate higher levels of distress). Although the Korean American students' mean scores appear slightly higher than those of other ethnic-group students, the differences here are not statistically significant.

Finally, we examined the zero-order correlations between students' depression score (reported on the CES-D scale) and their perceived family functioning (reported on the Family APGAR scale). There were statistically significant, albeit small, correlations between their depression score and their satisfaction with family for South Asian American

TABLE A.1. Means and Standard Deviations of Family and Individual Variables by Ethnicity

	Korean American	South Asian American	White American	$F(2,298)$
FAD-general	2.3[a]	2.1[a]	2.0[b]	12.0*
	(.5)	(.4)	(.4)	
Family APGAR	12.4[a]	13.3[ab]	14.7[b]	6.5*
	(4.9)	(4.4)	(.4)	
CES-D	18.4[a]	17.5[a]	16.7[a]	1.0
	(10.4)	(10.4)	(10.0)	

*p < .01; Means with same letter superscripts within each row signify that they are not significantly different from each other using the Tukey's HSD post-hoc test.

($r = .34$, $p < .05$) and White American students ($r = .34$, $p < .05$), but not for Korean American students ($r = .08$, n.s.). In other words, Korean American students' personal distress did not appear to be associated with how satisfied they were with their families (this, despite their reporting the lowest level of satisfaction with family).

Taken together, these survey results distinguish Korean American students from other ethnic-group students with respect to their relatively negative assessment of their families, yet they also appear to be psychologically well-functioning, and their individual psychological well-being appears decoupled from their distressed families. It was in relation to these findings that we decided to examine Korean American students' immigrant family narratives to understand their perspectives on family and individual mental health.

NOTES

INTRODUCTION

1 Names of all Korean American participants in this study as well as the names of towns and schools have been changed to pseudonyms. For the purpose of this book, the parents in the same family are referred to by the same surname (e.g., Mr. and Mrs. Park) although some of the mothers had kept their maiden surnames following the Korean custom.

2 Emerging adulthood is a concept popularized by the psychologist Jeffrey Jensen Arnett (2000) as the developmental period from the late teens through the midtwenties that is distinct from both adolescence and young adulthood in cultures that allow their young people a prolonged period of independence and role exploration (e.g., through higher education and other training) prior to their entering into adult responsibilities such as marriage and parenthood, full-time work, and independent living.

3 Psychology research on immigrant families is replete with the notion of parent-child conflicts caused by differences in acculturation, or the question of how much immigrants retain heritage culture and how much they take on the culture of their new host nation (e.g., see Juang and Umaña-Taylor 2012). The acculturation gap–distress model in psychology gained widespread acceptance with the work of Jose Szapocznik and colleagues (Szapocznik and Kurtines 1993). In a similar vein, psychological research on Asian American immigrant families has also focused on family conflicts that arise from cultural differences in values between parents and children (e.g., Costigan and Dokis 2006; Hwang 2006; Lee, Choe, Kim, and Ngo 2000) and the effects of such conflicts on children's academic and psychosocial outcomes (E. Kim and Cain 2008; E. Kim 2011; Qin, Chang, Han, and Chee 2012; Wang et al. 2012). Although recent studies with Asian American families as well as Mexican American families have not consistently found evidence to support the acculturation-gap hypothesis (e.g., Kim and Park 2011; Lau et al. 2005; Lim et al. 2008), psychological research and treatment continue to view dysfunctional family relationships primarily through the lens of the acculturation gap (Hwang, Wood, and Fujimoto 2010; Ying 2007).

CHAPTER 1. FAMILY CONTEXT

1 David's case was featured in a much more abbreviated fashion in an earlier article by Kang, Okazaki, Abelmann, Kim-Prieto, and Lan (2010) on how Korean

American college students narrated—and reinterpreted the hardships of—their immigrant childhood.

2 The interviews ranged from one to three hours long, averaging one and a half hours. Participants were given an informed consent form prior to the interview and a debriefing form after the interview. Students were also given twenty dollars in cash for participating. All interviews were audio recorded, transcribed verbatim, and checked for accuracy. In addition, each interviewer kept a detailed research journal with notes following each interview. As outlined by Taylor and Bogdan (1984), the purpose of these research journals was to record an outline of the topics covered during the interview, notes about emerging themes, nonverbal behavior during the interview, and other salient features of the interview—as well as emerging analysis (Emerson, Fretz, and Shaw 2011; Sanjek 1990). These research journals and transcripts were reviewed by the team in weekly meetings throughout the course of the study and formed the bases for our analyses.

3 We surveyed 299 students (131 men and 168 women, mean age = 19.94 years) from three ethnic groups (104 Korean Americans, 102 South Asian Americans, and 93 White Americans) at the University of Illinois. Of the 299 participants, 291 were undergraduate students and eight were graduate students (three Korean Americans, three South Asian Americans, two White Americans). Seventy-three percent of the Korean Americans, 76 percent of the South Asian Americans, and 100 percent of the White Americans were born in the United States. In order to participate, students had to (a) be at least eighteen years of age, (b) have graduated from a Chicago-area high school, (c) identify as Korean, South Asian, or White, and (d) be currently enrolled at the university. They were recruited in one of three ways: through an introductory psychology research subject pool, for which the participants received course credit; through flyers advertising a paid web survey that were distributed at campus libraries, dormitories, ethnic student organization meetings, and Korean language courses; and through snowball sampling, in which survey participants were asked to refer eligible friends and acquaintances. Participants were given two dollars for every person they referred who completed the survey. All participants recruited by the latter two methods were paid ten dollars, either in cash or in gift certificates, for completing the survey. All Korean American subjects were recruited through campus advertising. Of the 102 South Asian Americans, 76 were recruited through flyers and advertisements and 26 were obtained through the referral system. Of the 93 White Americans, 64 were recruited through advertisements and 29 were recruited through the psychology subject pool. In order to minimize potential barriers to participation, the survey portion of the study was conducted online. Potential participants were screened via e-mail or telephone, and those who met the eligibility criteria received an e-mail containing the link and the password to the survey website. An informed consent form was placed on the first page of the survey so participants could choose to either continue or leave the website. The online survey contained several questionnaires that have been determined to have good psychometric properties.

4 To be sure, Chua is neither the first nor the last to draw stark contrasts between parenting philosophies of Chinese and American parents. Psychology research is replete with cross-cultural contrasts between the "East" and the "West." When prompted by interviewers to discuss the differences between Chinese and U.S. parenting (e.g., Cheah, Leung, and Zhou 2013), immigrant Chinese parents in the United States readily generate many contrasts similar to those drawn by Chua.

5 Jeong Eun Rhee (2013) argued that Chua's erasure of race (e.g., her assertion that anyone regardless of ethnic heritage can be a "Chinese mother" if she or he possesses certain values and plans for success) is strategic. Rhee contends that by casting Chinese parenting ("tiger mothering") as a choice, Chua elevates a neoliberal vision in which ethnic and cultural features can be commodified and consumed.

6 Wesley Yang (2011) points out that the autobiographical details Chua shared in the book and in public appearances actually reveal the limitations of "Chinese" parenting. Chua admits that her immigrant parents' regimen had prepared her supremely well for elite education but had left her ill equipped to function competently in the social world for a good portion of her early career. Nonetheless, Chua's "tiger mother" regimen has become a meme for extreme parenting within the American culture of hyperachievement among the affluent elite (and those who aspire to join their ranks).

7 Jenny and her mother (featured in chapter 5) were, in fact, extensively involved in the classical music scene, and Jenny's mother did exact a rigorous music practice regimen for Jenny. Although the Asian American tiger parenting script around classical music education is often perceived as a means to a character- and resume-building end (Wang 2011), Jenny's mother's motivation behind her music parenting strategy proved far more complicated.

8 "Tiger Mother Chua Gets Mixed Reviews in China," *Wall Street Journal*, January 15, 2011, blogs.wsj.com.

9 "Seong-gonghaneun janyeo kiuneun bigyeol han-in jeonmunga jwadam" (Experts Talk about Secrets of Raising a Successful Child), *Korea Times*, December 27, 2005, www.koreatimes.com.

10 "Beojiniateg chamsa jeonmunga teugbyeol jwadam" (Special Talk by Experts on Virginia Tech Tragedy), *Korea Times*, April 20, 2007, www.koreatimes.com.

11 "Habeodeudaesaeng han-in hagbumo sotong-i gajang jung-yo" (Parents of Korean Student at Harvard Says Communication Is Most Important), *Chicago Kyocharo*, June 23, 2011, www.sem.chicagokyocharo.com.

12 The session was taped with permission and transcribed in Korean, and excerpts used here were translated into English by Nancy and the graduate students.

CHAPTER 2. COMMUNITY CONTEXT

1 As of March 2017, Korean American Community Services had merged with the Korean American Resource and Cultural Center, a cultural and advocacy organization, according to Grace Wong, "2 Chicago Korean-American Groups Merge to Become Hana Center," *Chicago Tribune*, March, 3, 2017, www.chicagotribune.com.

2 C. K. Kim et al.'s (2012) research had also shown support for this pattern of less affluent Korean Americans residing in affluent suburbs to gain access to highly regarded public schools.

3 Korean Americans who affiliate with churches tend to be largely Protestant. According to Lee (2005), the 2003 Chicagoland Church Directory listed 217 Protestant and four Catholic churches, although we were not aware of these figures at the time of the survey administration. The fact that our study sampled from all four Catholic churches probably speaks to the strength of the Korean Catholic networks. Jin-Heon, one of our graduate researchers, identified himself as Catholic and contacted his Korean church network, resulting in all four Chicagoland Korean Catholic churches inviting us to their churches to recruit survey participants. Jin-Heon was also invited to conduct participant-observations at multiple youth events (including a weekend retreat, fundraising car washes, Bible studies) at these churches.

4 The correlation coefficients (Pearson's r) shown here are the bivariate (or "zero-order") correlation coefficient between each pair of variables. Correlation coefficients range from zero (no correlation) to one (perfect correlation), with higher numbers indicating larger associations between two variables.

CHAPTER 3. BEN

1 East Creek is a suburban town adjacent to Valley Vista (where the Park family featured in chapter 5 resided). The two towns, along with some unincorporated areas nearby, share school districts for K–8 and the high schools, with most students from East Creek attending Valley Creek East High School and most students from Valley Vista attending Valley Creek West High School.

CHAPTER 4. DOUG AND ESTHER

1 See, for example, John W. Berry, "Immigration, Acculturation, and Adaptation," *Applied Psychology* 46 no. 1 (1997): 5–34.

2 That immigrant Asian American parents direct their children toward prestigious professional careers that require educational credentials has been documented by various scholars (e.g., Sue and Okazaki 1990; Lee and Zhou 2014).

3 This campus church, a pan-Asian but still heavily Korean American one, is quite well known in the Chicagoland Korean American community, with the majority of the congregation consisting of current college students and three quarters being from Chicagoland (Abelmann and Lan 2008).

CHAPTER 5. JENNY

1 We note, however, that Mrs. Park's goal of raising Jenny to become a professional classical musician departed somewhat from the motivations for most other Asian "music moms" studied by Wang in her ethnography of immigrant Korean American and Chinese American mothers of Juilliard precollege music students. Like Mrs. Park, Wang's "music moms" (so called because of their

full engagement and management—tinged with competitiveness—in their children's extracurricular activity, akin to "soccer moms") viewed classical music as a counterforce to the realities of their immigrant lives, rife with language discrimination, downward occupational mobility, and racism. However, unlike Mrs. Park, most immigrant Asian music moms viewed classical music training as an investment in elite education with goals of cultivating cultural capital (e.g., appreciation of classical music) and soft skills (e.g., work ethic, discipline) that would translate into academic success, but not necessarily as a career choice. Mrs. Park, while diligently preparing Jenny for a music career, also believed that the soft skills gained through classical music training would serve Jenny and her other piano students in life regardless of career choice. Wang (2009) also notes the contradictions inherent in racialized discourses, on the one hand about Asians and Asian Americans who are seen as disciplined, hard-working, imitative practitioners of Western classical music, and on the other hand about the "universal" language of music that can transcend race, class, and gender.

2 "Skirt wind" is a Korean expression to point to women's brisk social activities. Brisk movements cause women's skirts (e.g., traditional *hanbok* with a long skirt) to catch the wind like a sail. The expression could connote disapproval of socially active women.

3 As soon as Grace had heard of this past incident (which was over a year after its occurrence), she contacted Sumie, who is a clinical psychologist, and together Grace and Sumie conducted suicide risk assessment with Jenny to ensure that she was not at risk for self-harm.

CHAPTER 7. JUN-HO

1 Our team, of course, had made it clear that their decision whether to volunteer for the study or not had no bearing on their future admission to the University of Illinois.

2 It turned out that South Korean ESA was in its most rapid escalation phase at the time the Hyuns moved from South Korea to the United States.

3 Although we are unsure what Mrs. Hyun may have meant by ESA "ruining their character," studies have indeed documented significant emotional challenges that unaccompanied adolescent Korean ESA students face in the United States (Kim and Okazaki 2014).

4 Although a rumor of an ESA student being killed by her legal guardian sounds far-fetched, it is not an uncommon phenomenon for an unaccompanied Korean ESA student to live with a host family (sometimes the student's relatives or family acquaintances but also sometimes a host who provides room, board, and legal guardianship for a fee). Such living arrangements with a nonrelative guardian can be quite conflictual (e.g., Kang 2015; Kim and Okazaki 2014).

5 This is a common dilemma noted by school administrators (Williams 2015) as well as Korean ESA students themselves (Kim and Okazaki 2014).

6 Korean American college students whom Sumie and Nancy's team had interviewed at the University of Illinois at Urbana-Champaign had also echoed a similar process of coming to appreciate the immigrant parental sacrifices through a Christian lens (Kang et al. 2010).

CONCLUSION

1 Kim 2003.

2 Abelmann and Lie 2009.

3 Kim 1999.

4 "Korean-American Population Data," *Asia Matters for America*, www.asiamatters foramerica.org.

5 See Lo, Abelmann, Kwon, and Okazaki 2015.

6 Okazaki and Kim 2018.

7 See, for example, Kwon's (2014) study of working-class Korean American children of immigrant parents, who, through language brokering for their parents, learn about parents' various financial and legal problems.

8 See, for example, Karen Pyke's (2000) work based on interviews with Chinese American and Vietnamese American adults who regarded White middle-class American families as the "normal" ideal against which they evaluated their own families' perceived failings. More recently, Angie Y. Chung (2016) argued, on the basis of a large number of ninety-minute interviews with second-generation East Asian adults ages twenty-five to thirty-eight (including twenty-one Korean Americans), that adult children of Asian immigrant parents experience and articulate complex and contradictory emotions about having grown up in immigrant households.

REFERENCES

Abelmann, Nancy. 2009. *The Intimate University: Korean American Students and the Problems of Segregation*. Durham, NC: Duke University Press.

Abelmann, Nancy, and Jiyeon Kang. 2014. "Memoir/Manuals of South Korean Pre-college Study Abroad: Defending Mothers and Humanizing Children." *Global Networks* 14(1): 1–22.

Abelmann, Nancy, and Shanshan Lan. 2008. "Christian Universalism and US Multiculturalism: An 'Asian American' Campus Church." *Amerasia Journal* 34(1): 65–84.

Abelmann, Nancy, and John Lie. 2009. *Blue Dreams: Korean Americans and the Los Angeles Riots*. Cambridge, MA: Harvard University Press.

Abelmann, Nancy, Nicole Newendorp, and Sangsook Lee-Chung. 2014. "East Asia's Astronaut and Geese Families: Hong Kong and South Korean Cosmopolitanisms." *Critical Asian Studies* 46(2): 259–86.

Arnett, Jeffrey J. 2000. "Emerging Adulthood: A Theory of Development from the Late Teens through the Twenties." *American Psychologist* 55(5): 469–80.

Berry, John W. 1997. "Immigration, Acculturation, and Adaptation." *Applied Psychology* 46(1): 5–34.

Cheah, Charissa S. L., Christy Y. Y. Leung, and Nan Zhou. 2013. "Understanding 'Tiger Parenting' through the Perceptions of Chinese Immigrant Mothers: Can Chinese and US Parenting Coexist?" *Asian American Journal of Psychology* 4(1): 30–40.

Chua, Amy. 2011. *Battle Hymn of the Tiger Mother*. New York: Penguin Books.

Chun, Hyock, Kwang Chung Kim, and Shin Kim, eds. 2005. *Koreans in the Windy City: 100 Years of Korean Americans in the Chicago Area*. New Haven, CT: East Rock Institute.

Chung, Angie Y. 2016. *Saving Face: The Emotional Costs of the Asian Immigrant Family Myth*. New Brunswick, NJ: Rutgers University Press.

Costigan, Catherine L., and Daphné P. Dokis. 2006. "Relations between Parent–Child Acculturation Differences and Adjustment within Immigrant Chinese Families." *Child Development* 77(5): 1252–67.

Diener, Edward D., Robert A. Emmons, Randy J. Larsen, and Sharon Griffin. 1985. "The Satisfaction with Life Scale." *Journal of Personality Assessment* 49(1): 71–75.

Emerson, Robert M., Rachel I. Fretz, and Linda L. Shaw. 2011. *Writing Ethnographic Fieldnotes*. 2nd ed. Chicago: University of Chicago Press.

Epstein, Nathan B., Lawrence M. Baldwin, and Duane S. Bishop. 1983. "The McMaster Family Assessment Device." *Journal of Marital and Family Therapy* 9(2): 171–80.

Hau, Caroline S. 2015. "Tiger Mother as Ethnopreneur: Amy Chua and the Cultural Politics of Chineseness." *TRaNS: Trans-Regional and -National Studies of Southeast Asia* 3(2): 213–37.

Hurh, Won Moo, and Kwang Chung Kim. 1990. "Religious Participation of Korean Immigrants in the United States." *Journal for the Scientific Study of Religion* 29(1): 19–34.

Hwang, Wei-Chin. 2006. "Acculturative Family Distancing: Theory, Research, and Clinical Practice." *Psychotherapy: Theory, Research, Practice, Training* 43(4): 397–409.

Hwang, Wei-Chin, Jeffrey J. Wood, and Ken Fujimoto. 2010. "Acculturative Family Distancing (AFD) and Depression in Chinese American Families." *Journal of Consulting and Clinical Psychology* 78(5): 655–67.

Jo, Kwang Dong. 2005. "History of Korean Americans in the Chicago Metropolitan Area." In *Koreans in the Windy City: 100 Years of Korean Americans in the Chicago Area*, ed. Hyock Chun, Kwang Chung Kim, and Shin Kim, 13–35. New Haven, CT: East Rock Institute.

Juang, Linda P., and Adriana J. Umaña-Taylor. 2012. "Family Conflict among Chinese- and Mexican-Origin Adolescents and Their Parents in the US: An Introduction." *New Directions for Child and Adolescent Development* 2012(135): 1–12.

Kang, Hyeyoung, Sumie Okazaki, Nancy Abelmann, Chu Kim-Prieto, and Shanshan Lan. 2010. "Redeeming Immigrant Parents: How Korean American Emerging Adults Reinterpret Their Childhood." *Journal of Adolescent Research* 25(3): 441–64.

Kang, Jiyeon, and Nancy Abelmann. 2011. "The Domestication of South Korean Pre-College Study Abroad in the First Decade of the Millennium." *Journal of Korean Studies* 16(1): 89–118.

Kang, Joshua (Namkyu). 2015. "My Life in the States, Alone." In *South Korea's Education Exodus: The Life and Times of Study Abroad*, ed. Adrienne Lo, Nancy Abelmann, Soo Ah Kwon, and Sumie Okazaki, 270–89. Seattle: University of Washington Press.

Kim, Caleb K., Philip Young, P. Hong, David J. Treering, and Kyungsoo Sim. 2012. "The Changing Map of Characteristics and Service Needs among Korean American Immigrants in Chicago: A GIS-Based Exploratory Study." *Journal of Poverty* 16(1): 48–71.

Kim, Claire Jean. 2003. *Bitter Fruit: The Politics of Black-Korean Conflict in New York City*. New Haven, CT: Yale University Press.

Kim, Eunjung. 2011. "Intergenerational Acculturation Conflict and Korean American Parents' Depression Symptoms." *Issues in Mental Health Nursing* 32(11): 687–95.

Kim, Eunjung, and Kevin C. Cain. 2008. "Korean American Adolescent Depression and Parenting." *Journal of Child and Adolescent Psychiatric Nursing* 21(2): 105–15.

Kim, Hyun Joo, and Sumie Okazaki. 2014. "Navigating the Cultural Transition Alone: Psychosocial Adjustment of Korean Early Study Abroad Students." *Cultural Diversity and Ethnic Minority Psychology* 20(2): 244–53.

Kim, Kwang Chung, ed. 1999. *Koreans in the Hood: Conflict with African Americans.* Baltimore, MD: JHU Press.

Kim, Kwang Chung, Shin Kim, and Won Moo Hurh. 1991. "Filial Piety and Intergenerational Relationship in Korean Immigrant Families." *International Journal of Aging and Human Development* 33(3): 233–45.

Kim, Kwang Chung, Siyoung Park, and Jong Nam Choi. 2005. "Demographics and Residential Distribution." In *Koreans in the Windy City: 100 Years of Korean Americans in the Chicago Area,* ed. Hyock Chun, Kwang Chung Kim, and Shin Kim, 37–53. New Haven, CT: East Rock Institute.

Kim, May, and Irene J. K. Park. 2011. "Testing the Moderating Effect of Parent-Adolescent Communication on the Acculturation Gap–Distress Relation in Korean American Families." *Journal of Youth and Adolescence* 40(12): 1661–73.

Kim, Mi Ja. 2005. "Korean Nurses in the History of Immigration." In *Koreans in the Windy City: 100 Years of Korean Americans in the Chicago Area,* ed. Hyock Chun, Kwang Chung Kim, and Shin Kim, 153–64. New Haven, CT: East Rock Institute.

Kwon, Hyeyoung. 2014. "The Hidden Injury of Class in Korean-American Language Brokers' Lives." *Childhood* 21(1): 56–71.

Lau, Anna S., Kristen M. McCabe, May Yeh, Ann F. Garland, Patricia A. Wood, and Richard L. Hough. 2005. "The Acculturation Gap–Distress Hypothesis among High-Risk Mexican American Families." *Journal of Family Psychology* 19(3): 367–75.

Lee, Daniel B. 2005. "Korean Churches in the Chicago Area: Looking at Their Paths for Immigrants' Special Journey." In *Koreans in the Windy City: 100 Years of Korean Americans in the Chicago Area,* ed. Hyock Chun, Kwang Chung Kim, and Shin Kim, 153–64. New Haven, CT: East Rock Institute.

Lee, Jennifer, and Min Zhou. 2014. "The Success Frame and Achievement Paradox: The Costs and Consequences for Asian Americans." *Race and Social Problems* 6(1): 38–55.

Lee, Richard M., Jennifer Choe, Gina Kim, and Vicky Ngo. 2000. "Construction of the Asian American Family Conflicts Scale." *Journal of Counseling Psychology* 47(2): 211–22.

Lew, Jamie. 2006. *Asian Americans in Class: Charting the Achievement Gap among Korean American Youth.* New York: Teachers College Press.

Lim, Soh-Leong, May Yeh, June Liang, Anna S. Lau, and Kristen McCabe. 2008. "Acculturation Gap, Intergenerational Conflict, Parenting Style, and Youth Distress in Immigrant Chinese American Families." *Marriage & Family Review* 45(1): 84–106.

Lo, Adrienne, Nancy Abelmann, Soo Ah Kwon, and Sumie Okazaki, eds. 2015. *South Korea's Education Exodus: The Life and Times of Study Abroad.* Seattle: University of Washington Press.

McAdams, Dan P. 2001. "The Psychology of Life Stories." *Review of General Psychology* 5(2): 100–122.

McAdams, Dan P., Jeffrey Reynolds, Martha Lewis, Allison H. Patten, and Phillip J. Bowman. 2001. "When Bad Things Turn Good and Good Things Turn Bad: Sequences of Redemption and Contamination in Life Narrative and Their Relation to Psychosocial Adaptation in Midlife Adults and in Students." *Personality and Social Psychology Bulletin* 27(4): 474–85.

Miller, Ivan W., Nathan B. Epstein, Duane S. Bishop, and Gabor I. Keitner. 1985. "The McMaster Family Assessment Device: Reliability and Validity." *Journal of Marital and Family Therapy* 11(4): 345–56.

Okazaki, Sumie, and Jeehun Kim. 2018. "Going the Distance: Transnational Educational Migrant Families in Korea." In *Parenting from Afar and the Reconfiguration of the Family across Distance*, ed. Maria Rosario T. de Guzman, Jill Brown, and Carolyn Pope Edwards, 321–38. New York: Oxford University Press.

Park, Jin-Kyu. 2009. "'English Fever' in South Korea: Its History and Symptoms." *English Today* 25(1): 50–57.

Pyke, Karen. 2000. "'The Normal American Family' as an Interpretive Structure of Family Life among Grown Children of Korean and Vietnamese Immigrants." *Journal of Marriage and Family* 62(1): 240–55.

Qin, Desiree Baolian, Tzu-Fen Chang, Eun-Jin Han, and Grace Chee. 2012. "Conflicts and Communication between High-Achieving Chinese American Adolescents and Their Parents." *New Directions for Child and Adolescent Development* 2012(135): 35–57.

Radloff, Lenore Sawyer. 1977. "The CES-D Scale: A Self-Report Depression Scale for Research in the General Population." *Applied Psychological Measurement* 1(3): 385–401.

Raijman, Rebeca, and Marta Tienda. 2003. "Ethnic Foundations of Economic Transactions: Mexican and Korean Immigrant Entrepreneurs in Chicago." *Ethnic & Racial Studies* 26(5): 783–801.

Rhee, Jeong-Eun. 2013. "The Neoliberal Racial Project: The Tiger Mother and Governmentality." *Educational Theory* 63(6): 561–80.

Ryder, Andrew G., Lynn E. Alden, and Delroy L. Paulhus. 2000. "Is Acculturation Unidimensional or Bidimensional? A Head-to-Head Comparison in the Prediction of Personality, Self-Identity, and Adjustment." *Journal of Personality and Social Psychology* 79(1): 49–65.

Sanjek, Roger. 1990. *Fieldnotes: The Makings of Anthropology*. Ithaca, NY: Cornell University Press.

Shim, Doobo, and Joseph Sung-Yul Park. 2008. "The Language Politics of 'English Fever' in South Korea." *Korea Journal* 48(2): 136–59.

Smilkstein, Gabriel, Clark Ashworth, and Dan Montano. 1982. "Validity and Reliability of the Family APGAR as a Test of Family Function." *Journal of Family Practice* 15(2): 303–11.

Sue, Stanley, and Sumie Okazaki. 1990. "Asian-American Educational Achievements: A Phenomenon in Search of an Explanation." *American Psychologist* 45(8): 913–20.

Szapocznik, José, and William M. Kurtines. 1993. "Family Psychology and Cultural Diversity: Opportunities for Theory, Research, and Application." *American Psychologist* 48(4): 400–407.

Taylor, Steven J., and Robert Bogdan. 1984. *Introduction to Qualitative Research: The Search for Meanings.* New York: Wiley.

Telzer, Eva H. 2011. "Expanding the Acculturation Gap–Distress Model: An Integrative Review of Research." *Human Development* 53(6): 313–40.

Waldow, Florian, Keita Takayama, and Youl-Kwan Sung. 2014. "Rethinking the Pattern of External Policy Referencing: Media Discourses over the 'Asian Tigers' PISA Success in Australia, Germany, and South Korea." *Comparative Education* 50(3): 302–21.

Wang, Grace. 2009. "Interlopers in the Realm of High Culture: 'Music Moms' and the Performance of Asian and Asian American Identities." *American Quarterly* 61(4): 881–903.

Wang, Grace. 2011. "On Tiger Mothers and Music Moms." *Amerasia Journal* 37(2): 130–36.

Wang, Yijie, Su Yeong Kim, Edward R. Anderson, Angela Chia-Chen Chen, and Ni Yan. 2012. "Parent–Child Acculturation Discrepancy, Perceived Parental Knowledge, Peer Deviance, and Adolescent Delinquency in Chinese Immigrant Families." *Journal of Youth and Adolescence* 41(7): 907–19.

Waters, Mary C., Van C. Tran, Philip Kasinitz, and John H. Mollenkopf. 2010. "Segmented Assimilation Revisited: Types of Acculturation and Socioeconomic Mobility in Young Adulthood." *Ethnic and Racial Studies* 33(7): 1168–93.

Williams, Rick. 2015. "Coming to Terms with Our 'Asian Invasion': A Practitioner's Perspective on the Korean Education Exodus in a Christian School Setting." In *South Korea's Education Exodus: The Life and Times of Study Abroad*, ed. Adrienne Lo, Nancy Abelmann, Soo Ah Kwon, and Sumie Okazaki, 257–69. Seattle: University of Washington Press.

Yang, Wesley. 2011. "Paper Tigers." *New York Magazine*, May 11.

Ying, Yu-Wen. 2007. "Strengthening Intergenerational/Intercultural Ties in Immigrant Families (SITIF): A Culturally Sensitive Community-Based Intervention with Chinese American Parents." *Journal of Immigrant and Refugee Studies* 5: 67–90.

Ying, Yu-Wen. 2009. "Strengthening Intergenerational/Intercultural Ties in Immigrant Families (SITIF): A Parenting Intervention to Bridge the Chinese American Intergenerational Acculturation Gap." In *Handbook of Mental Health and Acculturation in Asian American Families*, 45–64. New York: Humana Press.

Yoon, In-Jin. 1997. *On My Own: Korean Businesses and Race Relations in America.* Chicago: University of Chicago Press.

Yu, Eui-Young, Peter Choe, and Sang Il Han. 2002. "Korean Population in the United States, 2000." *International Journal* 6(1): 71–107.

Zhou, Min, and Susan Kim. 2006. "Community Forces, Social Capital, and Educational Achievement: The Case of Supplementary Education in the Chinese and Korean Immigrant Communities." *Harvard Educational Review* 76(1): 1–29.

INDEX

acculturation to American culture, 8,
56–57; acculturation gap, 4–5, 10,
56, 221n3; acculturation gap-distress
hypothesis, 7, 57–58, 86, 221n3
American dream, 12, 86–88, 93, 110, 185
Arnett, Jeffrey Jensen, 221n2
Assimilation strategy, 32–33, 85, 87, 95, 113.
See also acculturation to American
culture

Battle Hymn of the Tiger Mother (Chua).
See Chua, Amy; tiger mother
Ben (family ethnography). *See* Koh family
Brian (undergraduate researcher), 158

campus study. *See* data collection and
methodology; University of Illinois at
Urbana-Champaign
Center for Epidemiologic Studies Depression (CES-D) scale, 53, 57–58, 218–220
Chicago Kyocharo, 30. *See also* ethnic
media
Chicagoland, 3–4, 9–10, 14; Korean
Americans in, 21, 38–48, 203;
suburbanization of Korean Americans
in, 40, 42
Chicagoland family survey, 8, 10, 51–58;
parent findings in, 51, 54–55; parent-
teen findings in, 55–58; teen findings
in, 51–55
chogi yuhak. See early study abroad
Christine (family ethnography). *See* Shin
family
Chu (graduate researcher), 4

Chua, Amy, 21–23, 35, 117, 131, 205,
223ch1n4, 223ch1n5, 223ch1n6,
223ch1n8. *See also* tiger mother
Chung family (family ethnography), 11,
60, 86–115, 116–117, 148, 159, 172; career
expectations of, 97, 100, 102–103,
108–112; church and faith of, 88,
98, 102–103, 204; Doug, 92, 104–115,
202, 205; language barriers in, 91;
Esther, 96–103, 205; Mr. Chung, 93–96,
102–103, 114–115, 202; Mrs. Chung,
89–92, 101, 105, 114
Chung, Grace. *See* Grace
colleges admissions, 4, 28–29, 31, 101, 158,
195, 205–206

data collection and methodology, 10, 207,
223n12; of campus survey, 217–219,
222n3; of campus study interviews,
222n2; of ethnography, 3, 4, 59–61,
148, 208–209; mixed-method, 3, 10, 15;
surveys, 3, 36–38, 49, 147–148, 207–208.
See also Chicagoland family survey;
University of Illinois at Urbana-
Champaign
David (campus study case), 13, 17–18,
221n1
Doug (family ethnography). *See* Chung
family

early study abroad (ESA), 21, 23–26, 343,
203–204, 225ch7nn2, 3, 225ch7nn4, 5;
students in Chicagoland, 23, 25–26, 37,
41, 176–179, 203

ABOUT THE AUTHORS

Sumie Okazaki is Professor of Applied Psychology at New York University Steinhardt School of Culture, Education, and Human Development.

Nancy Abelmann was the Harry E. Preble Professor of Anthropology, Asian American Studies, and East Asian Languages and Cultures at the University of Illinois at Urbana-Champaign.